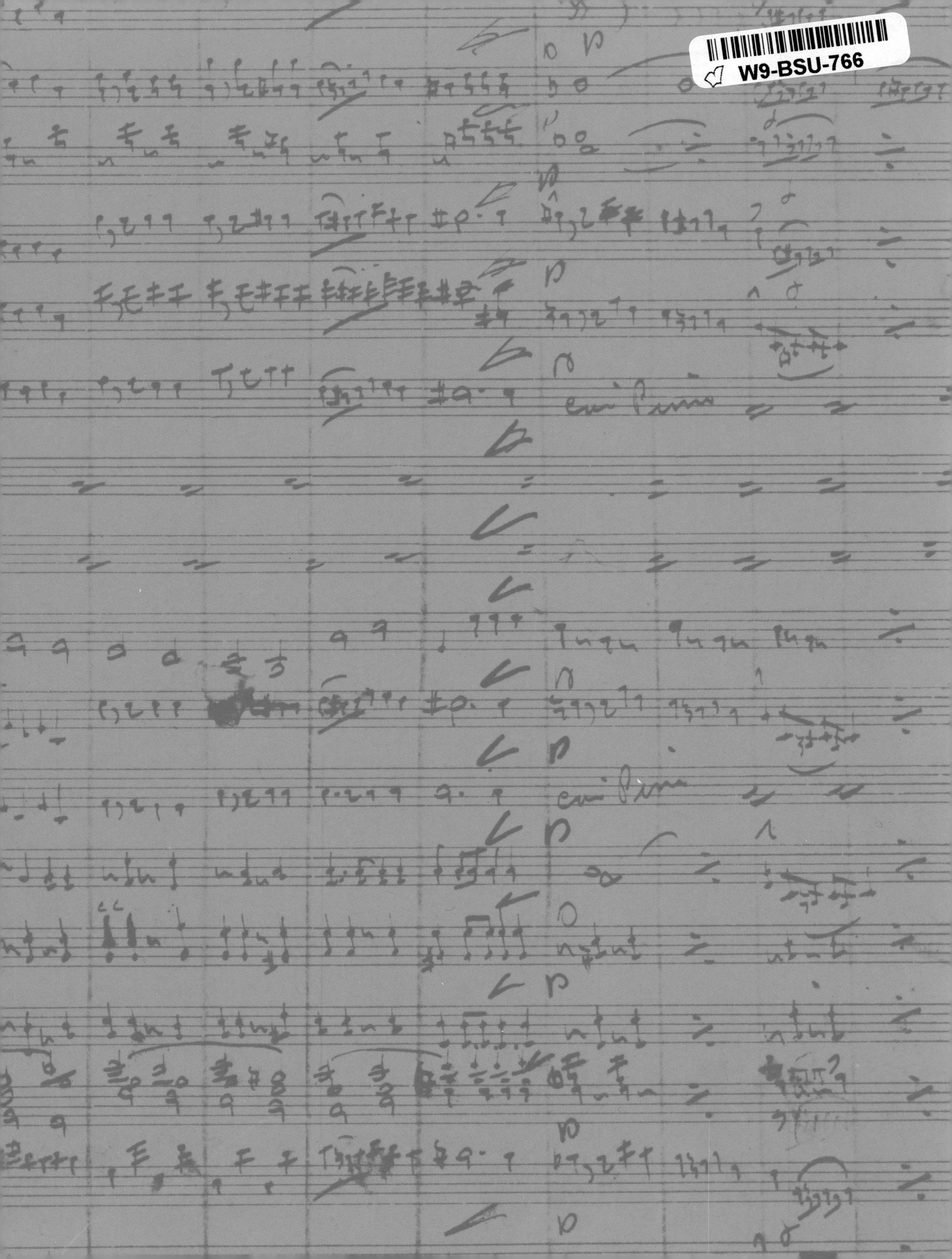

PERSPECTIVES ON JOHN PHILIP SOUSA

John Philip Sousa in his uniform as leader of the U.S. Marine Band. — *U.S. Marine Band.*

PERSPECTIVES ON JOHN PHILIP SOUSA

Edited and with an Introduction by

Jon Newsom

Music Division   Research Services

Library of Congress   Washington   1983

Library of Congress Cataloging in Publication Data

Main entry under title:

Perspectives on John Philip Sousa.

   Contents: Introduction / Jon Newsom—Semper
fidelis / William Schuman—John Philip Sousa and
the culture of reassurance / Neil Harris—[etc.]
   Supt. of Docs. no.: LC 12.2: So8/2
   1. Sousa, John Philip, 1854–1932—Addresses, essays,
lectures. I. Newsom, Jon. II. Library of Congress.
Music Division.
ML410.S688P47 1983   785'.092'4   83–600076
ISBN 0–8444–0425–X

ENDPAPERS: From the first page of the full score of *The
Stars and Stripes Forever*, in Sousa's hand.

iv

Contents

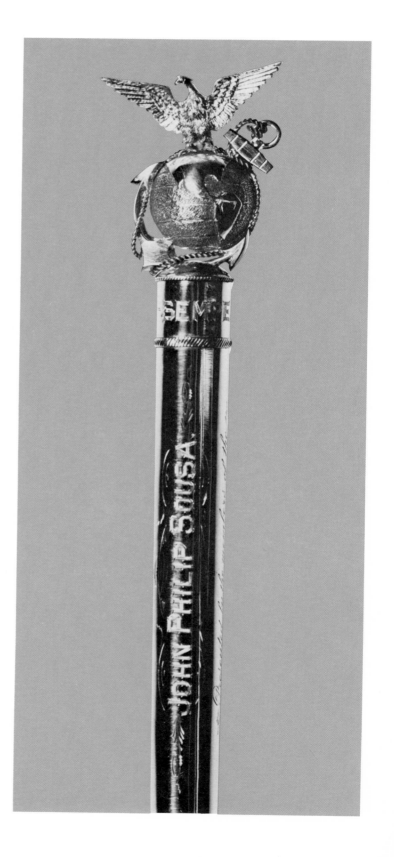

Preface

Three decades ago, the Music Division in the Library of Congress received a major collection of John Philip Sousa manuscripts from his daughters, Helen Sousa Abert and Jane Priscilla Sousa. Their donation, in 1953, of some of their father's most famous works established the Library as an important center for Sousa research. Then, in 1971, John Philip Sousa III, representing the corporation that owns the remaining collection of Sousa's manuscripts, deposited in the Library two trunks and three cartons of papers containing mostly music but also handwritten and typed drafts of his grandfather's autobiography and several of his novels.

The papers constitute a wealth of still untapped information about the "March King"'s composing methods and approach to instrumentation as well as his literary interests and accomplishments. As now organized and indexed, they provide access to materials for performers and scholars interested in the works of a man who was not only a great composer but a national genius who became a cultural statesman of international importance.

It seems fitting that such a collection, housed as it is in the Music Division of the Library of Congress, should occasion the publication by the Library of a book of essays on John Philip Sousa. For, during the past decade, the Music Division has produced lectures, concerts, recordings of nineteenth-century American band music, and a major discography of recordings made by the Sousa Band. Moreover, drawing on its extensive collections of performing and research materials covering the development of the band from the American Revolution to the present, it has preserved and made available on microfilm many of its most significant holdings in these areas. To date, we have filmed more than four thousand works for band from the late eighteenth to the early twentieth centuries. There are virtuoso pieces for keyed bugles and ophicleides from the 1840s, historic brass band pieces from the Civil War, elegant arrangements of operatic classics, brilliant marches for Barnum and Bailey and other circuses, and amusing novelties for slide trombone. The titles of topical and occasional works are a study in themselves: *President Cleveland's Wedding* (by. T. B. Boyer), *Yellowstone Trail* (by K. L. King), and *Battleship California* (by H. J. Crosby) are but three marches bearing straightforward titles, while *Kraper's Peculiar* (by C. Barnhouse), *Itsgud* (by C. Carleton), and *Blunderbuss* (by L. P. Laurendeau) are more whimsical and obscure in origin.

Sousa's own titles for his marches and other pieces clearly reflect the people, institutions, places, events, and matters of popular interest at the time they were written. Yet, while a handful of the thousands of marches composed before and during Sousa's era are still played, the number of Sousa's marches that are remembered today for their intrinsic musical worth is so much greater that he truly merits our attention as a composer of the first rank. However, his stature as a composer should not eclipse the historically important role he played as a vitally influential figure in the culture of his time.

Because the Sousa Band appealed to the eye as well as the ear, we have included contemporary photographs, both formal and informal, in concert and on the road, in a photo essay which we have amplified with pictures of various documents that illuminate the story of Sousa's success. In addition to drawing on our own collections of manuscript and printed music, programs, and periodicals, we have been fortunate in having access to the collections of the United States Marine Band Library, the Rare Book and Manuscripts Division of the New York Public Library, and the family photograph albums in the possession of John Philip Sousa III, for which we are most grateful. It is hoped that these pictorial materials, together with the essays collected in this volume, will stimulate interest in the further study of the man and his era.

Introduction

by Jon Newsom

The first major event in John Philip Sousa's professional life occurred in 1868, when his father decided to enlist him—at the age of thirteen—in the United States Marine Band. There he learned the indispensable craft of musical leadership. The second major event was Sousa's decision to leave the band in 1892 to form his own musical organization. In so doing, he cut loose not only from the particular conventions of the military band but from all the existing conventions of the entertainment business.

It is difficult today to appreciate how utterly unconventional the Sousa band, that all-American institution, was in its conception and realization. After all, the marches themselves, which are what we remember, are not so unusual. For all their brilliance and originality, they are very much a part of musical tradition. But the real difficulty lies in the fact that the band's unconventionality was born not of rebellious eccentricity or the wildly innovative spirit that commands attention for the sake of mere novelty but of the very opposite—the desire to reconcile disparate but deeply rooted values. As a performer, Sousa was able to combine art and business, highbrow and lowbrow, upper-class and middle-class, even, to some extent, feminine and masculine values, in a synthesis of which music was a vehicle made articulate not by qualities of the art alone but by all the carefully contrived trappings of its presentation. These ranged from the uniforms the bandsmen wore—and over which Sousa exerted as much control as he did over his own dress and manners—to every institutional and technological entity and device that was available and could serve as a means to his ends, from fairgrounds and resorts to the steam locomotive. Sousa pursued his career shrewdly and with the intensity of a man running for public office, though in Sousa's case the office had to be invented, its existence justified by the need its inventor perceived in the public to whom he appealed.

Sousa's puzzling aversion to the phonograph, and later to the radio, can be understood in the light of the probability that notwithstanding their obvious commercial merits, he saw nothing in them useful to his own enterprise. If this was indeed his privately held view, history has justified him in that respect, for the phenomenon of the Sousa band was clearly a creation of and for its time, and could not have been captured for replay by any means then, or now, available. Not only would its charisma elude the recording medium; it was not made to be apprehended by a timeless or universal audience. Its sensational effect depended on a temporal sensibility. The wonder is that, closely associated as his marches were with the aesthetic of their day, so many of them have continued to find a lively place in our own very different times.

As the word *perspectives* in our title is intended to convey, the purpose of this collection of essays on John Philip Sousa is not to provide a definitive study of that cultural hero so aptly called "an American phenomenon" in the subtitle of Paul Bierley's Sousa biography. Rather, we wished to gather some perspectives on the man as an important figure in our nation's social as well as musical development. Therefore, the authors we invited to contribute their thoughts include men and women with diverse careers in music, history, business, and journalism.

From William Schuman's appreciation of Sousa's compositional genius to John Philip Sousa III's personal observations in which, among other things, he argues persuasively that his legendary grandfather actually existed, we have a number of essays any one of which could be the starting point for a new volume. Each author complements the others' views by focusing on a particular aspect of Sousa's accomplishments. If any single theme emerges, it is that both as a brilliant practical musician and showman in his own time and as a composer for all time he achieved success by no accident but by the methodical application of his many talents.

Of course, influential as Sousa was in his own era, he could not have planned the particular challenge and potential of the fast-changing world into which he was born. These he must have observed from an early age, for the story of his success is the story of how well he took advantage of the resources of an America that, during the 1890s when he was at the very height of his own career, was to reach an apex of gregarious self-confidence and optimism. Yet, as Neil Harris reminds us, that age—an "American Renaissance" in art and architecture—was not without its anxieties.

During Sousa's formative years class distinction had begun to exert a divisive effect on what kind of music could properly be heard where and by whom. Two editorial comments by the eminent Boston music journalist, John Sullivan Dwight, published in his *Journal* in 1852 and 1869 respectively, reflect a change in the relative social integration that one might expect to find at public concerts before and after the Civil War. "When shall we have music for the *People*?" asks Dwight in 1852. "Music that all who will may hear, without money and without price; free to all ears, as the sparkling fountain on the [Boston] Common is, to all eyes." Thus he begins a campaign to improve musical taste.

At that time, cultural events were promoted with far less concern for the social prestige their attendance bestowed upon the attendee than some years after the war when, on the same subject but with a far more patronizing air, Dwight writes: "It is easy to sneer at popular music, and to exalt the education of the ear to be derived from listening to classical or intricate compositions. But while the common people are the listeners to the concerts on the Common, and the class who patronize the great organ, the opera and the oratorio are away at Swampscott and Mount Washington, the preferences of the popular heart have a right to be consulted."

While Dwight implies a continuing social mixture on the Boston Common, he also refers to places where only the "class who patronize" may hear music. By the 1880s, with the organization of permanent city orchestras, even people with a taste for art music were excluded from orchestral concerts as they were becoming exclusive affairs at which price of admission and codes of dress effectively screened the class of patrons.

These developments had the effect—so clearly expressed by Dwight—of creating a polarity between what was considered vulgar popular music and a relatively more cultivated and socially acceptable music for the affluent and genteel. It is important to note that the distinction was hardly based on the objective discrimination of a musically educated elite, although by the last half of the nineteenth century we did not lack the competence to make judgments of artistic merit. Our lingering sense of cultural inferiority was, until recently, a persistent barrier to our full acceptance and support of native talent and genius.

Besides the class issue, there was the matter of sex and sexism. The growing pre-dominance of women in the highly organized world of art music, in its administration as well as its patronage, caused many American men who might, in some other respects, have happily emulated the fashionable customs of dress and behavior of their European counterparts to resist involvement in so-called serious music, except as reluctant tagalongs at the concerts their ladies attended. Eventually, this male role in musical life was regularly satirized, most memorably in the comic strip "Bringing Up Father."

Into a world of such prejudices and anxieties, Sousa entered not merely with the confidence that he could cope, but with an uncanny self-assurance that enabled him to convince a vast and heterogeneous audience by no means sure of their own tastes that what he offered was what they wanted, and that it was good. His personal integrity would not permit him to offer less than the best, and that quality of integrity was projected, no doubt, in his person as well as in his many published statements and interviews. Perhaps one of his most valuable insights in the matter of cultural salesmanship—one might better call it statesmanship—was his sense that his audiences did not want to be educated or be made to feel inferior. He maintained that they wanted to be entertained, and he expressed this clearly in his autobiography, *Marching Along*. After a stimulating conversation with the prominent founder and conductor of the Chicago Symphony Orchestra, Theodore Thomas, Sousa returned for the evening to his hotel room and mused on the essential difference between Thomas, with his organized but traditional orchestra, and himself, with his equally well-organized but unprecedented ensemble of wind instruments. Thomas, Sousa concluded, believed he was educating his audience while he, Sousa, hoped he was entertaining his.

Regarding the question of Sousa's dependence in his achievement on the help of his first manager, David Blakely, the reader has two essays from which to draw conclusions or on which to base further study. Neil Harris, writing on Sousa and "the culture of reassurance," has relied largely on the more than eighty Sousa band press books in the United States Marine Corps Museum in Washington. Margaret L. Brown, in her study of the David Blakely papers at the New York Public Library, offers a different perspective, that of the manager who, all would concede, played a major role at the critical time of Sousa's transition from military service to the world of practical show business.

Concerning Sousa's musical influences, innovations, and composing methods, we have three essays. Pauline Norton discusses the march tradition to which Sousa was heir; Frederick Fennell presents an experienced conductor's view of the most important marches; and James R. Smart examines the evidence of Sousa's composing method applied to what is probably his greatest piece, *The Stars and Stripes Forever*.

And, if the reader has not already done so—or even if he has—he is invited to look at the illustration section with the accompanying captions. We hope that these will provide some sense of the time, place, and style that were the milieu in which Sousa worked and thrived and to which he made his own unique contribution.

JON NEWSOM
Assistant Chief
Music Division

The Stars and Stripes forever
March

Semper Fidelis

by William Schuman

We live in a time when the granting of honors has so proliferated that almost weekly, it seems, there is some widely publicized prize letting. We move easily from our Oscars to our Tonys to our Emmys to our Grammys and to a growing number of specialized halls of fame located in various parts of the country. We have halls of fame for sports, baseball, of course, being the most famous, but there is also one for basketball; there is also one for football. And, in music, we have one for Country Music, for Cowboy Music, for Tin Pan Alley composers, and there is one now under way for Rhythm and Blues.

If the value of prizes has been diminished by their numbers and, in some instances, by their self-serving caste, the Hall of Fame for Great Americans stands apart.* It remains a signal honor. It is a classic, old and revered, untainted by commercialism, and with a selection process which, in itself, is a model of enlightened democratic functioning. An extraordinary body of outstanding citizens lends its accumulated wisdom in dedicated deliberation tempered by the qualitative distillation of time. No prospective honoree for the Hall of Fame can be considered until at least twenty-five years after death. And, there is the additional collective voice of the hundreds of individuals and organizations who sponsor particular candidates with such fervor that the electors are virtually inundated with supporting documentation.

How happy Sousa would be to know that his enshrinement in the Hall of Fame for Great Americans was so effectively espoused by the prestigious American Bandmasters Association.

Some months before I received the invitation to come here today I had begun writing the introductory chapter to a book on American music. The subject, therefore, of the American character as expressed in music has been very much on my mind and, as a natural consequence, so has Sousa. I mentioned Sousa in my introductory chapter because when one thinks of American music, he immediately comes to mind. One of the exciting aspects of this celebration is the recognition of an American composer who, in his specialized sphere, is so widely accepted as the quintessence of the American spirit in music.

The marches of Sousa are as thoroughly American as the waltzes of Strauss are thoroughly Viennese. The thought of asking whether Sousa's marches are American would never occur to us. Even to articulate such an inquiry about Sousa's music would be foolish, gratuitous and, I suppose, even un-American. But, the more generally considered question of Americanism in music is not so easily answered as might seem possible at first.

When a piece of music draws the comment, "Only an American could have composed that," the meaning is far from precise. What is "American" in American music is only peripherally (if at all) measurable by the criteria of scholarly investigation. Americanisms have more to do with feelings, and these feelings spring from a complex of factors, largely, I would think, from emotional recollection. The qualities that make music identifiably American are to a large degree, if not basically, in the ear of the beholder. When enough beholders perceive the product to be indigenous, then so it becomes. A body of recognizable characteristics has emerged through the collective experience of listeners over a long period of time and we call the result American. However, since listeners are as varied in their sophistication as the extraordinary range of American music itself, the inexact nature of these characteristics becomes the more apparent, especially when you attempt to pinpoint or define.

What really are the characteristics that we like to think of as American? Is American music as American as, say, the music of Spain is

*This address was presented on the occasion of the enshrinement of John Philip Sousa into the Hall of Fame for Great Americans at the John F. Kennedy Center for the Performing Arts in Washington, D.C., on August 23, 1976. Copyright © William Schuman 1983.

Spanish, of Russia, Russian, of France, French, and so on down the line? The answer is yes. A great deal of music has been produced by now in our country which unquestionably exudes the pulse and flavor of the land and of its people—a feeling of national spirit. Sousa is obviously one American composer who has made such a contribution and it is a special joy not only to be inducting another composer into the Hall of Fame, but one who is so American. Now, clearly, music that we recognize as American is not better or worse for that fact. We are not talking about a qualitative distinction, but, rather, a distinction that is extramusical. When a composer creates music which evokes a sense of shared national identification, an extra element has been added to purely musical values. As I was thinking about Sousa and American music, my thoughts naturally went to the other two composers who were previously elected to the Hall of Fame, Stephen Foster and Edward MacDowell.

Parenthetically, let me say that at this point in the preparation of these remarks I sought the advice of an authority on Sousa, namely, Howard Shanet, distinguished author and musician and Chairman of the Music Department at Columbia University. I am delighted to be able to incorporate some of Shanet's observations in this address.

As noted, until today there have been only two other composers in the Hall of Fame, Stephen Foster and Edward MacDowell, and certainly they represent almost opposite ends of the spectrum of American music. There is Stephen Foster, largely self-taught, the creator of "Old Folks at Home," "Jeanie with the Light Brown Hair," "Oh, Susanna!," "My Old Kentucky Home," "Old Black Joe," and "Beautiful Dreamer," songs whose simple but spirited tunes, perfectly wedded to the natural word rhythms of American English, have become part of the folk heritage of our nation. Foster, then, was clearly not just born an American composer, but an American American composer.

Edward MacDowell, on the other hand, was a cultivated musician—the pupil in piano and composition of some of the greatest names of his day in the European concert world—a composer of grand sonatas and concertos, of symphonic poems and orchestral suites, and the first professor of music at Columbia University. MacDowell, for all the remarkable achievements that are undeniably his, is certainly not an American American composer. John Philip Sousa, who today becomes the third American composer to be inducted into the Hall of Fame, combines some of the best qualities of both of his predecessors.

Like Foster, he knew how to find that simple directness that reached the average man as well as the sophisticated listener and that made his marches as much a part of our popular heritage as the songs of Foster. When a military band anywhere in the world swings into *The Stars and Stripes Forever*, or the *El Capitan* march, or *The Washington Post*, or *Thunderer*, or *Semper Fidelis*, what pair of feet can keep still? Yet, at the same time Sousa, like MacDowell, was a thoroughly schooled musician; he had studied the violin as well as a number of wind instruments from boyhood, and he was a skilled conductor and a brilliant master of instrumentation, inventive in his melodies, his harmonies, and his rhythms.

Nor were Sousa's artistic and intellectual achievements limited to his marches. Tonight's program gives us a glimpse of the variety of his creations. Just before the intermission you heard selections from his comic opera, *The Free Lance*, but by his own count Sousa wrote no fewer than ten comic operas, several of which vied in popularity with the Gilbert and Sullivan operas at the turn of the century, not only in America but also in Canada, Germany, and England, where they toured. It has always seemed to me that if he had had a librettist who could have compared in any way with the brilliant W. S. Gilbert, his light operas might very well still be in the popular repertory. But Sousa also wrote suites for orchestra and band (*Looking Upward* was played earlier this evening). He wrote a symphonic poem, two overtures (one of which you heard tonight), a cantata and a Te Deum. He wrote more than fifty songs and a large number of waltzes, fantasies, caprices, and other such pieces, a few of which have been performed tonight. He compiled for the U. S. Navy a valuable collection of "National Patriotic and Typical Airs of All Lands." He wrote an instruction book for the trumpet and drum, and a "Book of Airs" for the violin. What is more, he was a gifted writer of words as well as of music, the author of a fascinating autobiography entitled *Marching Along* and—very few people are aware of this—of three novels! (It seems fitting that one of Sousa's novels, called *The Fifth String*, is now being used as the libretto for an avante-garde opera by a young American composer.) What a man!

In thinking of the quality of Sousa's music it is too easy simply to conclude that it is all lightweight stuff because of its enormous popularity. He bears more than a superficial relationship to Sir Arthur Sullivan. Both were the composers of enormously successful scores and both were classically trained musicians. I can recall many, many years ago, when I was a young professor, giving a course on how to listen to music. For a whole year my students were trained in the art of virtuoso listening. I remember the final examination; the students had no idea of what work I would be asking them to analyze. They were astonished when, after a full year devoted to the great symphonic masterpieces, the examination consisted of a request to analyze the *El Capitan* march of Sousa. For, within this single composition, one finds all the attributes, the niceties of form, and all the other qualities that are expected of high level music making. Therefore, I, for one, do not accept any judgment which says, "Well, yes, Sousa was a superb composer of marches." Sousa was a superb composer, period.

After all, the essence of any artist's creative success is his ability to be convincing in the area of the art that he has carved out for himself. For example, we are lucky that Chopin decided that his métier was really the piano rather than the orchestra; that Brahms had the good sense to know that opera was not for him. Part of the gift of being a creative artist is knowing the realm in which you can best function. And, Sousa is a prime example of one who knew precisely what his principal métier was.

It has been suggested by some that the peculiarly American qualities of at least some of Sousa's music came from his subject matter, that is, the titles, such as *The Stars and Stripes Forever* and *Jazz America* or *Over the Footlights of New York*. It is perfectly true that titles often can be quite misleading. One of the famous examples in the history of music is that Robert Schumann, functioning as a great critic, listened to one of Mendelssohn's symphonies, the *Italian* Symphony, and he remarked, after hearing it, that it was so Italian that one really did not even have to visit that blessed country, one got the feeling right through the music. There is only one problem with that. The symphony of Mendelssohn that he was listening to was not the *Italian* Symphony, but the *Scotch* Symphony. So, of course, titles can mislead. But, I like to think, and I do think that Sousa's Americanisms were much more genuine than those simply evoked by some of his indigenous titles.

It seems to me that the Americanisms of Sousa have basically to do with his free-wheeling artistic spirit. In 1940, only eight years after Sousa's death, the late Ashley Pettis, then head of the famous Composers' Forum-Laboratory of the WPA in New York, tried to characterize American music in the following words, which really seem to be a description of Sousa's style:

There are in American music clear characteristics, the same as the characteristics of the American people—a certain snappiness, a certain clear-cut quality of speed and the direct grappling with any problem, with every fact of life, a peculiar sense of humor, a certain dash, vivacity and verve, a certain snap, something which is carefree—perhaps I should say a certain gay and attractive showmanship. Such music is American, just as Mark Twain and Walt Whitman are American. In its broad, epic qualities, all of this is characteristic of the best in American music.

In 1928, when Sousa looked back over his life as he finished writing his autobiography, he offered a veteran's advice to young American composers:

Be yourself and never an imitator. Do not be obscure, and do not be a materialist. . . . Remember always that the composer's pen is still mightier than the bow of the violinist; in you lie all the possibilities of the *creation* of beauty. . . . The rest of the world has had a long start, but the American composer with his heritage of creative genius from a race which has produced thirteen out of twenty of the great inventions of the past three centuries, is well qualified to catch up! We require time, but (to employ the American vernacular) "we'll get there!"

When Sousa said that "the composer's pen is still mightier than the bow of the violinist," he was in no way attempting to denigrate the performing artist. In fact, were Sousa alive today, he would, of course, take enormous pride in the fact that American performing artists are in demand the world over and our professional music education has reached such a high point of development that serious students now come here to study from the old centers of learning in Europe, as well as virtually everywhere else in the world. No, Sousa is reminding us of something else.

Performance and education alone, however excellent, do not by themselves make the culture of a country. It is the creative artists that give a country its distinctive stamp. In music, we have developed our own composers who certainly stand on a level with those of any other country in the world. How pleased Sousa would have been to witness what has taken place in America, especially the remarkable array of native music that was performed during our Bicentennial year.

But to apply Sousa's phrase to himself, he "got there." And he got there by taking his own advice as a composer. For, as you listen to the last work on this program, Sousa's most famous march, *The Stars and Stripes Forever,* you will hear how he really was himself and the natural originality which, without any seemingly conscious effort, rejected obscurity in favor of directness. Does there exist a more brilliant example of what Ashley Pettis meant when he spoke of Americanism in terms of dash, vivacity, verve, humor, snap, and a gay and attractive showmanship?

This is indeed a wonderful day for our American music.

Advance work for Sousa's first tour, when he was still with the U.S. Marine Band, seems to have been trying, as this note to his manager, David Blakely indicates. Advance men were to assure that all advertising for the band had been effectively arranged for in each city it was to tour. This report states that "the Marine Band did not take with the public so well *on advance work,* as [Patrick] Gilmore or [Eduard] Strauss." But, it continues, "the Band is making a *Grand Record* and everybody more than pleased."

Regarding a proposed second tour, it warns that "there must be *far different & better routing.*" In her essay, Margaret L. Brown describes the difficulties of promoting the Marine Band's first tour.

Blakely Papers, New York Public Library.

Mr Blakely — I find the Marine Band did
not take with the public so well on advance
work, as Gilmore or Strauss — and you
will pardon me for saying it, but it is dam
hard work to boom or work up the Marine
Band — & to take them out on this first tour
& come in even (saying nothing about any
profit is a Miracle — and the advance work
has been the Star, not the Band (to draw)
But the Band are makeing a Grand Record and
everybody more than pleased, hence good
profit can be made on another tour but
there must be far different & better routing —

Yours Sousa

John Philip Sousa and the Culture of Reassurance

by Neil Harris

John Philip Sousa and his America seemed made for each other. Their love affair, particularly during the Indian summer years preceding World War I, was neither coy nor covert, but entered into demonstratively and exuberantly by both sides. To later generations, caught up in waves of nostalgia and curious about a national mixture of assertion and self-confidence that seems impossible to recapture, Sousa continues to epitomize a whole way of life. His image evokes strutting drum majors, band concerts on soft summer nights, strolling couples, playing children, tranquil and reassuring evocations of a time of well-ordered pleasures. The marches remain a major national treasure, disciplined statements of national exuberance as unmistakeably American as the Strauss waltz is Viennese.[1] Sousa has become, in short, a perfect textbook tag, a cigar-box label guaranteed to produce the proper associations. He is as useful an historical resource as, in his own day, he was a national possession whose presence immediately produced attention, respect, and patronage.

The creation of this spectacular success story, undarkened by all but the smallest cloud, poses problems for subsequent biographers. There seem to be no hidden corners in Sousa's life, no buried secrets, no squalid episodes to shock admirers or provoke defenders. In countless interviews, in articles and columns, in autobiography and public statements he acknowledged his ambition and his success openly; he refused to be intimidated by either. His political opinions resembled those held by most of his countrymen, nor was he swayed by particular emotion for any special cause or social reform. He was what he appeared to be: a hard-working, prolific, and energetic musical genius who marketed his special talents effectively (and profitably) for more than forty years. His compositions stir us, as they moved his contemporaries, for understandable reasons. His conducting technique, while not uncon-troversial, employed established conventions. Examining the Sousa image then, seems doomed to footnoting the obvious generalizations: the story is too clear and uncomplicated to repay lengthy investigation.

But there may be some reasons for exploring Sousa more carefully; they lie in the very intensity and longevity of his success. The Sousa career was a managed one, created to stimulate and satisfy consumer interest and oriented to market-place approval. Skillful publicists fashioned the Sousa image, appealing to the mass market created by modern journalism. Musical history contains many instances of masters writing on demand for fame or income. The impressario-performer, brought to prosperity by clever promotional techniques, was well established long before Sousa's birth. But rarely before had a composer-conductor so clearly identified himself with the cultural needs and public taste of his day. Seldom had an artist more easily made his peace with the commercial ethos surrounding him, or become so unambiguous a symbol of community ambition. And, in America at least, never had anyone achieved this for so long a period of time, basically unshaken in prestige by otherwise comprehensive changes.

American monarchs, royalty in a republican society, tend to reign in performing arenas—acting, sports, and music. The March King was, in his own way, as popular a figure as the Sultan of Swat. The fact that Sousa determined to document this role, in the eighty-five volumes of newspaper extracts which inform this essay, indicates a concern with reputation and a willingness to keep his clipping-service busy recording it.[2] Sousa sensed, along with his audiences, that he had assumed a set of crucial cultural roles—pedagogic, patriotic, and paternal. His band and his music were unrivalled because they captured in sound the values official spokesmen celebrated verbally. Sousa's success built upon a formula. The repeated conventions of a Sousa march, or a Sousa band performance, along with their timely adjustments to meet important events, were not entirely original. But the close fit they achieved, and never lost, owed much to Sousa's public personality.

In a country where artistic talent had generally been segregated from the active, practical skills of business and the professions, Sousa brought them together. During his lifetime the world of the performer became a highly specialized one, demanding the talents of managers, press agents, programmers, tour managers, theatre owners, and advance men. Sousa was a careful student of managerial skills; by his later years he had become a master strategist. The sense he had of American musical culture and his functions within it, the response of critics and audiences to his marches and audiences, both say something about the way this culture functioned. Sousa was an authentic cultural hero. His work reassured his countrymen about the essential benevolence of their national task, their political beliefs, and the vitality of their creative life. Courting the great middle classes who were his sponsors, Sousa realized that his strength lay in the close connections forged between performance and social confidence in Victorian America. Both the image and the image making deserve some further attention.

Just as Edison did not invent electricity, Sousa did not invent the band. Two generations of Americans had been enjoying band music by the 1860s, the decade during which young John Philip grew up in Washington. As historians of American music have shown, there were several traditions to choose among.[3] During the 1840s and 50s small groups of brass and reed instrumentalists performed assorted airs, waltzes, schottisches, two steps, ballads, and polkas for enthusiastic if informal audiences. This repertoire, popular and unself-conscious, was obviously not competing with the more complex compositions published in contemporary Europe which were rapidly assuming classic status. There were, in any event, few American ensembles capable of performing major symphonic works before the Civil War, although several orchestras had been organized.

But the popular bands shared attention with another variant, the military band, normally created by militia groups to provide music for social festivities and training exercises. The relationship between the wind band and the military band was centuries old by this time in Europe, and in one or another form it had existed in America since the eighteenth century. However, the absence of a standing army (or indeed of almost any type of uniformed service) and the unwillingness of public authorities to pay for such luxuries meant that support of military band music depended on the ambitions and self-respect of individual regiments, or occasionally on townships with a tradition of sustaining a musical organization. On the eve of the Civil War there were several reasonably accomplished such bands, the best of them being the group led by a young Irish-born musician who had emigrated after serving in the British Army in Canada, Patrick Sarsfield Gilmore.[4]

The bands, military and civil, were numerous and popular, but hardly dominated American musical life in the ante-bellum period. The paying public divided into two parts: first, a select group of subscribers to opera or symphony concerts, confined to the large cities and ritualistically maintaining a tradition of middle-class patronage modelled on Europe's.[5] The other sector, more heterogeneous and spasmodic, flocked to great discoveries and performing celebrities, also European imports, like Jenny Lind, Alboni, and the bandmaster Jullien.[6] These performers were the sensations of their age, centerpieces of elaborate and faddish worship, but their vogue usually ebbed in a short time and they returned home. So loose and ill-defined was national musical life that immigrant groups,

Germans in particular, found it necessary to establish their own musical organizations, singing clubs, tournaments, festivals, and music halls. German orchestras, choral societies, Saengerfest, Harmonieverein, Saengerbund, developed in cities like Cleveland, Cincinnati, Pittsburgh, Chicago, and St. Louis, but this active approach to performing was more an ethnic possession than an American characteristic.[7] With a small elite supporting the opera and symphony, a larger group dogging the footsteps of imported celebrities, and a set of people who simply enjoyed informal ensembles playing tunes of the day, the American public was served on the whole by small, badly equipped and poorly trained bands, the largest of which had no more than fifteen or twenty members. And, according to touring artists and native critics, it was an audience prepared to accept poor musicianship and naive programming in return for a little showmanship and diversion.[8]

Before the Civil War no great conductor had emerged in America, at least no one whose name alone could attract crowds. It was not very different in Europe. Historians argue that it was only in the 1840s and 50s, with Musard in Paris, Jullien in England, and Strauss in Vienna, that the first celebrity conductors appeared, "able to draw audiences to the concerts. . . . quite independently of any other attractions that were offered or of any other influences that were in operation."[9] And these three conductors featured dance music. Soloists and composers remained the dominant draw.

But the American band received a boost in popularity from the Civil War. Especially active in the early days of recruiting rallies and mass enlistment, military bands to accompany the troops were created in such numbers that Congress passed bills limiting their growth and forcing some reduction. Bands had traditional roles in warfare: the drum and bugle corps met important signalling needs, organizing the training camps and punctuating daily activities with their dis-

tinctive calls. In battle they relayed commands and, on occasion, bolstered morale; on the march they provided indispensable accompaniment and relief from the prevailing monotony. Above all the war evoked a spirit of patriotism which vented itself in patriotic music, rousing martial tunes superbly suited to the military band along with mournful ballads which they could also perform.[10]

This growth of military ceremonial and patriotic sentiment provided a new base for American instrumentalists; while many new bands did not survive the war a taste for band music did. And a few conductors, notably Patrick Gilmore, developed enthusiastic followings. Gilmore became involved with several extravaganzas bringing him further publicity, his concerts in occupied New Orleans and two massive Peace Jubilees in Boston being the most memorable. By the late 1870s he had settled down to a career of national tours and extended stays at important resorts and major municipal expositions. His dynamic personality and vivaciousness on the platform, along with the professionalism and discipline of his bandsmen, made him a significant American ensemblist for almost twenty years. Gilmore supplied a diet of popular marches, operatic medleys, patriotic airs, and favorite songs of the day; he claimed few educational objectives, and was not noted for any off-stage antics.[11]

His one rival for American affections, however, had a very different set of goals. Theodore Thomas was six years younger than Gilmore and like him had been born abroad, at Esens, the son of a musician. He studied the violin, and for a time served in Jullien's orchestra while the French showman was touring America. After stints in the Philharmonic Society of New York and more touring, he began his conducting career at the Academy of Music, launching his own orchestra (1864-65) at Irving Hall in New York. Thomas competed with the New York Philharmonic and introduced serious symphonic music to audiences that still preferred waltzes, 13 galops, and popular medleys. Thomas played almost everywhere: in Central Park, for a series of summer night concerts; at music festivals; at fairs and expositions; and in concert halls, lecture rooms, and auditoriums all over the United States. After holding a succession of major conducting posts and teaching positions, by the 1890s Thomas finally arrived at a secure professional home in Chicago with the Symphony Orchestra that he founded, but his career had been filled with frustrations, bitter defeats, and financial hardships. Acknowledged almost universally as the major figure in serious American performance, he suffered the fate of a pioneer, struggling simultaneously to instruct, entertain, and refine audiences; attempting to instill a sense of concentration, discipline, and decorum while he introduced Americans to a range of contemporary music. Befriended and idolized by many of the country's major political, literary, and artistic figures, Thomas was identified with the self-conscious didacticism and moralism that dominated American high culture during the late nineteenth century.[13]

Between the world of Gilmore and the world of Thomas there appeared to stretch an impassable gulf—on the one side the high-spirited, unpretentious Irish bandmaster, with few illusions about the ennobling impact of his performance, and on the other the serious-minded, disciplined German conductor, intent upon transforming American musical taste and musicianship. It was into this gap that Sousa would move, subject to the criticism of partisans in both camps, the popular and the serious, attacked either for trying to highbrow public taste, subjecting it to implausible and unsuccessful manipulation, or for pandering to public sentiment by filling his programs with light, unseemly musical ditties. Sousa, in fact, served a large middle-class audience which was growing progressively more knowledgeable and even experimental about its music, but which continued to enjoy popular works that made few demands on patience or understanding. Expectations about levels of musicianship rose through the 1870s and 80s, fed by an increasing frequency of musical performance, wider travel, urbanization, tours of foreign bands, and the American love for festivals—industrial, patriotic, and civic—which, as in Victorian Britain, supported professional musicianship. A prospering middle class, enjoying the pleasures of summer vacations and savoring the advantages of musical educations for their children, could be expected to attend concerts more regularly.

Prescient promoters (and musicians also) sensed in the 1880s that profits and fame awaited those who could satisfy this new market. This required, on the one hand, new levels of quality and technique, and on the other, music that did not unduly challenge public tastes. David Blakely, Sousa's future manager, experienced in the arts of promotion and printing, was one of those who realized what the audience wanted. In the early 1890s, as rumors began to circulate that Blakely would enter the market with a band of his own, backed by the fabulous wealth of a Chicago syndicate, musicians begged for his attention. From Elgin, Illinois, in the fall of 1891, the musical director of the Elgin Military Band asked Blakely, as "the most successful manager of the present time," to take over the administration of his outfit and create a permanent Chicago band.[13] That same year, as hints of Patrick Gilmore's impending retirement began to spread, Jules Levy shot off an importunate series of letters to Blakely, pleading with him to "take my fortune in your hands. . . . There must be a great Band in America," Levy argued; he could be its bandmaster. "I will bind myself to you, I will follow your advice in all things," he swore.[14] But Blakely had already begun his association with Sousa, managing a tour of the Marine Band in 1891, as he would again in 1892. He sensed that it was Sousa, not Levy, Liberati, or F. N. Innes, who would take over Gilmore's title as America's most popular musical figure.

14

The first tours, certainly, were not easy ones. Sousa had already achieved some reputation as a composer of marches and he had transformed the Marine Band from a lackluster and little known ensemble to a popular and well-supported group, at least in Washington, presiding over a broad range of official ceremonies. Indeed, Sousa's increasing dissatisfaction with the restrictions of governmental employment, and the publicity given his move to private management, mirrored the growing presence of a federal bureaucracy in the 1880s and 90s. Sousa had to press to get permission for his Marine Band to tour under Blakely's management; general competition between military and civilian bands was a source of bitterness, not only in America but in Germany and Great Britain as well.[15] Military musicians, underpaid but also underworked, grabbed concert jobs at rates lower than those demanded by civilian bandsmen. In St. Louis, in the 1880s, five private bands were driven out of business when the cavalry department's recruiting band transferred there from Carlisle, Pennsylvania.[16] Although Sousa got the pay for Marine bandsmen raised in 1891, there was no question that military musicians suffered from official niggardliness. Sousa's departure from government symbolized the attractions of private capital, "Chicago gold," according to the New York *Evening Journal*, the same gold that allowed William Rainey Harper to raid the faculties of Europe and America for his new University of Chicago. "The East is becoming more and more disgusted every day with Chicago's way of doing things."[17]

Dreams of wealth appealed to Sousa; Blakely increased his income several-fold, and sales of his marches swelled agreeably. But Sousa was also attracted by the idea of creating a new kind of musical organization, one that would compete artistically with the greatest European bands, like the Garde Républicaine, but would also, with a newly arranged instrumentation, present a novel repertoire to popular audiences. In later years

Sousa was asked why (as a former violinist) he did not become an orchestra conductor. His response was that the orchestra represented too confining a tradition. With no wish to perform "ponderous symphonies" or "massive preludes," and believing that "entertainment is of more real value to the world than technical education in musical appreciation," Sousa sought an alternative. The cabaret orchestra, one possibility, was too limited and the military band "too vague in its instrumentation." But "a new combination, unhampered by tradition, which could get at the hearts of the people was my desideratum." If his autobiographical reflections are to be believed, Sousa sought an original, innovative approach to performance and programming, and a special place for himself and his musical organization in the public heart. "I wanted to avoid those musical combinations governed by certain laws as enduring as those of the Medes and the Persians, and institute one which I felt would cater to the many rather than the few."[18] Innovation and popularity, these two goals would dominate his activities.

Sousa's talents obviously impressed Blakely, despite the problems that his advance men were having publicizing the Marine Band's two early tours. J. H. Laine, one of them, wrote to Blakely from Indianapolis in 1891 that "the Marine Band did not take with the public so well in *advance work* as Gilmore or Strauss," and found it "dam [sic] hard work to boom or work up" the group.[19] The second tour, with better routing, tripled the profits, and Blakely's five-year contract practically guaranteed him a financial windfall. With his pick of potential attractions, the business manager determined that it was Sousa who had the brightest future.

Some of this appeal was highly personal. In the late nineteenth century the musical world contained more than its share of temperamental personalities, alternating bouts of romantic self-celebration with periods of guilt and depression. Many performers, moreover, had few attractions or accomplishments beyond their musical skills. Sousa, with only a limited formal education, somehow managed to acquire a certain polish and a set of broader interests, which he tied to a clearly stable and rather optimistic temperament. In mid-1892, when Blakely was still trying to put together a syndicate by selling shares, he wrote to a prospective purchaser, Hobart Weed of Buffalo, that Sousa would soon be appearing there. Invite Sousa to your club, he urged Weed; here was a "thoroughly polished gentleman, a magnificent musician, a remarkable composer, and a devilish good fellow generally," who would cause his host no blushes.[20] Sousa's carriage and self-discipline, combined with his gift for self-command, would make him a good gamble for the ambitious businessman.

There remained, to be sure, the unknown quality of his public charm. When Sousa began, the band field was dominated by the vigorous presence of Patrick Gilmore, now in his sixties and possibly on the eve of retirement, but certainly the most popular conductor ever to perform in America. Sousa would have to communicate some special excitement to be fully successful. J. H. Johnston, manager of the Pittsburgh Exposition, a lucrative engagement for a touring band, protested Blakely's demand for a $3,100-a-week contract. This was higher than he had paid Gilmore, and "it was Gilmore's strong personality that carried the day" rather than *"his Band."* Pittsburgh, with broad exposure to a number of musical organizations, might be difficult. "Of Sousa's *personal characteristics* I know absolutely nothing," Johnston wrote, but "everything depends upon the *personal magnetism* of the leader. . . . *he has to prove his worth in this respect.*"[21]

The test would be met by Sousa's assembling a band to rival the best competition, and by Blakely's arranging for maximum possible exposure and publicity. About the first, the *Musical Courier* was not optimistic. Reacting, in July 1892, to the announcement that Sousa's new band would perform at the dedication of Chicago's Columbian Exposition in October under the contract arranged by Blakely, the *Courier* described this New Marine Band as "a travesty," a "blaring, glaring noise producer, and its success, wherever it had any, was due to the lack of discernment on the part of the public." Exaggerating the Marine Band's faults, probably under the influence of rival bandmasters, the *Courier* argued "a brass band is not created by special design; it is a matter of evolution, even if all the material is acceptable. It takes a long time to make a brass band a musical organization. Mr. Sousa may be a genius, but thus far he has not demonstrated it."[22]

Sousa set about with characteristic energy to gather his musicians. Letters of application poured in, most from candidates expecting Chicago to be the new permanent home of the organization. Some players listed their varying engagements on their stationery, summoning up the fairs, resorts, and settings that Sousa would dominate in coming years: the Manhattan Beach Hotel; the Congress Hall at Cape May; the St. Louis, Kansas City, and Pittsburgh Expositions. Blakely's management record, Sousa's fame as composer, legends of the limitless wealth of the Chicago backers, and the assistance of friendly instrument makers permitted Sousa to get his pick of fine musicians. Several were willing to leave well-established posts, because of the new group's promise.

Sousa was further aided by the death of two principal rivals, within months of his signing the contract. In September 1892 Patrick Gilmore, visiting St. Louis to fulfill an engagement for the city's annual exposition, suddenly died. And in early 1893 the leader of New York's famous Seventh Regiment Band, Carlo Alberto Cappa, a noted innovator himself, also died unexpectedly.[23] Sousa was suddenly the major figure of the band world, able to draw on members of these older organizations.

The weeks of drill and rehearsal that preceded the band's premiere in the fall of 1892 were accompanied by careful planning on its manager's part as well. Besides Patrick Gilmore, no bandmaster had led an independent (and profitable) band, at least not for more than a year or two. Some thought the new venture was impossible. There had been earlier failures. The most notable was that of Frederick N. Innes, who abandoned his Great Band, after just a couple of years, for the security of regimental sponsorship. But Innes did not have the services of an expert manager like Blakely. "I think I know exactly what to do to make the people feel, when one of my organizations comes to their city, that they simply must hear it; they cannot afford to remain away," Blakely told a potential backer in 1892.[24] Publicity, publicity, and more publicity got Sousa before the public eye; interviews, photographs, magazine articles, planted newspaper stories, all helped. "There isn't a book or stationery store that has not one or more of Mr. Sousa's pictures in his show window," Emily Howard wrote Blakely from St. Louis in October 1893, "and the handsome white uniform on the handsome brunette man shows off in great shape. There is always a crowd around these windows!"[25] Sousa was entertained "royally" by local figures in these first trips, again establishing the personal contacts that helped produce favorable newspaper reviews and crowded audiences.

But there were many uncertainties. Profits at first were slim. Despite Blakely's conviction that his new contract was a "valuable plum," Sousa remained an unknown quantity as a star. Inevitably he was compared with Gilmore, and in some cases found wanting. Thus the Hartford *Times* in 1893 praised Sousa's performance but found the band still far "from that notable unity and solidarity of retention, and that wonderful success in expression and beauty of shading which made Gilmore's band . . . famous."[26] During the same tour the Lowell *Journal* lamented that Sousa did not possess "the personal presence and ability of the matchless Bandmaster," Patrick Gilmore.[27] The New York *World* complained that the reeds were rough and the brass blared. However intelligent and agreeable, Sousa lacked "the indescribable gift of personal magnetism. . . of placing himself en rapport with his auditors."[28] Some quarreled with the name—Sousa's New Marine Band—or took issue with the number of encores.[29] And audiences were smaller than expected.

Still, critics agreed, it was an impressive achievement. In a matter of weeks Sousa had trained an ensemble to produce sounds that more experienced bands had not achieved in years of practice. There was "a neatness of attack, a certainty and precision" more characteristic of string organizations, said the Chicago *Record*, calling this "the best military band in the nation."[30] The Hartford *Times*, despite its qualifications, dubbed it "the foremost military band in the world."[31] Sousa's recruiting ability, according to the Philadelphia *Times*, was as impressive as his musicianship; now that he could select his own musicians, he surpassed all he had done before.[32]

Despite newspaper references to a military band, this seemed a novel organization, "a compromise between an orchestra and a field band. There is not the loud twanging that has made the indoor playing of the old organization objectionable."[33] The much larger proportion of reeds, part of Sousa's plan for creating a new ensemble, permitted a wider repertoire. "In making reeds do the concert work of strings and yet retain the effectiveness and beauty of the orchestral score," the Kansas City *Star* explained, "Mr. Sousa has undertaken a big work."[34] So respectful grew the Boston *Herald* that it was drawn to a local comparison. Sousa's Band and the Boston Symphony were created by similar methods, "ample financial means" placed "at the disposal of a thoroughly competent musician." But Sousa's outfit demanded a special classification. It was basically "a military orchestra, that is, a body of the usual instruments included in the makeup of a military band but capable of producing the effects commonly confined to the players of a concert orchestra."[35] The brass sections, noted another newspaper, were subordinated but not put out of hearing. Just as the beer in a shandy-gaff cut the acerbity of the ginger ale and the ale sweetened the bitterness of the beer, "so here the reeds temper the blare of the brass, and the brass spices the reeds."[36] In an era when the New York *Times* could argue that American brass bands were Bedlam and Pandemonium combined, and suggest arranging bandstands on a pivot at seaside hotels "so that when the terrible creature within begins to lash himself into fury" the stage be turned to the sea "and the horrid voice of the monster poured out upon the illimitable ocean," this was high praise.[37] Here was a new sound developed by a "man of brains," and audiences were impressed.

During the first year or two of touring, observers raised themes which would continue to surface as responses to Sousa during the next three decades. One of them concerned his physical skill as a leader. Orchestral tone depended not only on practice, but on Sousa's capacity to direct it during performance. The "simple lash of his eye, the motion of his little finger," wrote an awed critic in the Worcester *Telegram*, "were sufficient to control the melodious noise of the hushed harmony of one of the finest bodies of instruments in the world."[38] Sousa "woos the harmony out of the men with the air of a master," a Midwestern newspaper agreed.[39] He had "such perfect control over his magnificent organization," the Williamsport *News* reported, "that every effect was brought out without any apparent effort."[40] "No conductor ever seen in Corning had his men under better or more complete control," ran another conclusion, a compliment whose sincerity compensated for its rather limited sphere of comparison.[41]

The conductor's magical control

excited considerable comment during the late nineteenth-century performances.[42] Sousa's concert band was not huge by orchestral standards—containing nearly sixty men during a normal concert—but Americans were accustomed to the sloppy, ragged playing of much smaller amateur groups. And they were caught up by the subservience of this musical mammoth to the baton's movements. The posture and bearing of the conductor were important parts of any effective concert and the carefully groomed Sousa, clad in tight-fitting uniform and spotless white gloves, acted out the maestro for his audiences. Compared to the great and furious movements favored by some older leaders, his conducting style, at first, seemed modest and restrained. Sousa offered an intriguing but well-controlled set of motions, meticulously analyzed by music critics and journalists at a level of detail that reveals the importance of the concert's visual features.

The Saginaw *Globe*, for one, was impressed by the economy of his gestures. Holding his men "as under a spell," every baton motion brought a response. "Unlike the great Gilmore, Sousa does not make himself conspicuous by his vigorous work, but is very quiet and unassuming. Yet the result is the same."[43] The Brooklyn *Daily Eagle*, writing in the summer of 1893, shortly after David Blakely had invited several hundred connoisseurs to watch Sousa perform, apparently agreed. Gilmore, of blessed memory, the *Eagle* wrote, was a passionate, spectacular conductor who employed energy and "snap" to intensify effects. "Gilmore wore the awful front of angry Mars when he worked up a crescendo. He rode the harmonious storm as furiously as the wild huntsman rides his phantom steed, dominating it and spurring it on to the climax." Organizing a diminuendo Gilmore was a different person, "smiling above his men like the white winged cherub of peace."[44] The terrible warrior could suddenly become an angel of light.

Sousa was something else. Appar-

18

ently not a creature of moods he was "a small man with a natty figure and a black beard. He is the quietest conductor ever seen in these parts. He is not at all spectacular."[45] But if the fire did not get into the conductor, it got into the music. And audience responses grew stronger. The Duluth *Herald* labelled Sousa "an ideal leader. He is not overly demonstrative and no violence characterizes his movements, but every motion is graceful and expresses exactly what the music conveys. A deaf person might almost watch Sousa and understand the music."[46] The Syracuse *Standard* described him as "the very personification of masculine grace," the Lewiston *Journal* applauded this "masterly yet modest way" of conducting, a baton with "magic in it," vigorous yet with a "refined musicianly manner," and to the Duluth *Herald* Sousa's directions were so graceful that he seemed to be "waltzing with the music."[47] A Syracuse critic applauded Sousa's avoidance of whole arm movements, and his apparent reluctance even to use half arm gestures. He possessed, instead, "a wrist made flexible by long practice with the violin bow and it is with graceful wrist movements that he does most of his directing. He adds force to any passage by movements of the body and the waist. His feet are seldom moved."[48]

The combination of discipline and languor—in the same paragraph the Buffalo *Enquirer* invoked gestures from a "lady-like shrug" to "the vigorous action of a baseball pitcher"—was new and exciting.[49] It was an arresting synthesis of military precision and balletic grace. While one critic could liken Sousa's conducting to "the sheer delight of a little girl playing mother with her dolls," another described him as "a consummate general . . . alert, active, watches every man."[50] Sousa's vigor, his energy, his masculine appeal rescued him from charges of affectation and effeminacy, charges which some American musical artists faced at the turn of the century.[51] Sousa's visual impact was as powerful in its own way as the arrangements his band played.

Yet his methods did arouse controversy. Debate mounted in subsequent years, when Sousa's conducting gestures grew more animated and more sweeping, but even in the first stage a few dissenters grumbled. A Buffalo newspaper found Sousa to be "almost as much of a poseur as Nikitsch of the Boston Symphony Orchestra." Some of his attitudes "were 'very fetching.' "[52] But clear admiration formed the consensus, approval for the precise, nonmelodramatic motions exerted by the band conductor. The military metaphors embedded in the descriptions reflected contemporary respect for organization. The 1890s, the decade of Sousa's commercial debut as his own bandmaster, hosted a series of organizational expansions—in commerce, education, transport, and manufacturing—and the management of complex human enterprises like world's fairs and international trusts. Historians have suggested the many influences exerted by these revolutions in scale, and the evolution of the new bureaucracies.[53] Master executives, bringing comprehensive order from this potential chaos, were heroes of the age. Industrial magnates, railroad masters, department store owners, and financial wizards had as counterparts the new executives of performance culture, from baseball managers and football coaches to circus owners and theatrical agents. Sousa's tours were as intricately managed as his musicians were drilled. But the bandmaster had a special capacity for symbolizing the control, the disciplining of powerful forces. This small man could, with one baton movement, draw forth enormous sound; or as quickly, with a single gesture command silence. Sousa's popularity reflected his ability to synthesize powerful archetypes of his day—artist and general, bureaucrat and athlete, pedagogue and matinee idol—but at its heart lay this sense of total control. He was trying, he told a reporter a decade later, to make his musicians and himself into "a one-man band. Only, instead of having actual metallic wires to work the instruments, I strike after magnetic ones. 19

I have to work so that I feel every one of my fifty-eight musicians is linked up with me by a cable of magnetism. Every man must be as intent upon and as sensitive to every movement of my baton, or my fingers, as I am myself."[54]

But the control itself required amplification. Like other contemporary business masters, Sousa readily accepted the customer's presence. He admitted the need for pleasing his audience, which meant salesmanship and advertising. Showmanship, he commented later in his autobiography, was effective "in every walk of life. Men may object to being called showmen, but the history of mankind is a record of continual showmanship from the very beginning. The Queen of Sheba's appearance before Solomon was showmanship of the cleverest sort." And so, Sousa added (this in the late 1920s), was Henry Ford's sense of drama in introducing the new Model A.[55]

Sousa's interest in pleasing his audience showed up in many ways besides his dramatically designed gestures and military posture. His composing and his programming bore evidence of his search for popularity. In his first few seasons, for example, he developed a series of musical narrations, easy to follow and based upon contemporary interests. His suite, *The Chariot Race*, exploited the popularity of Lew Wallace's *Ben Hur*. A New Britain newspaper commented that what Wallace had done in words—painting the Roman scene—"Sousa has done in music and with greater effect."[56] *The Chariot Race* introduced "as realistic effects in music as ever did M. Zola bring into literature," the Middlesex *Times* argued. "The tap of the horse's hoofs, the rattle of harness, the clash of the chariot wheels, the snap of whips. . . . This was not exactly music," the newspaper admitted, "but it was fun."[57] And so was *In a Clock Store*, a descriptive piece by another composer, in which an apprentice wound up a series of ticking and striking clocks, producing a series of noises appropriate to alarms, cuckoos, and chimes. Sousa's *Last Days of Pompeii* drew on

Bulwer-Lytton's novel, and the program notes included lengthy quotations. Indeed, these descriptive numbers were all accompanied by extended program comments enabling the audience to follow the narrative. During the nineties Sousa also featured other descriptive pieces like *Sheridan's Ride*, humoresques like *The Band Came Back*, in which the musicians entered, individually or in groups, playing their instruments, *Good-Bye*, and a whole series of variations on popular tunes of the day, snatches from musical comedies, or, in later years, movie music.

The inclusion of these numbers and of popular songs like *Daddy Wouldn't Buy Me a Bow-Wow* (often, to be sure, as encores) led to considerable debate from the outset about Sousa's programming philosophy and his impact upon national musical taste. For decades reviewers in major American journals like *Harper's*, the *Century*, the *Atlantic Monthly*, and *Lippincott's*, had been anxiously examining American taste for signs of increasing refinement. Among all the arts, musical judgment appeared to show the most progress. A public was now apparently prepared to accept serious music on its own merits, with enthusiasm and discrimination. In the seventies and eighties particularly, many critics argued that Americans made more demanding listeners than Europeans, able to distinguish good from mediocre performers, and capable of absorbing complex and difficult music.[58]

Nonetheless, there were frequent admissions that this sensibility was still confined to a fairly small portion of the national audience. And by the nineties, there was less confidence in its continuing growth. It was up to conductors and managers to reach out and educate a broader mass, encouraging them to support the orchestras, opera companies, chamber music groups, and composers that a great civilization should possess. According to theorists of genteel improvement, serious-minded musicians had an obligation to raise the level of their audiences' musical desires, to instruct as well as to entertain. Certainly Theodore Thomas, in his tireless crusades to popularize European symphonic music, accepted such a role. Indeed he pursued it with such energy and single-mindedness that there were occasional complaints about his didacticism. Critics and musical educators argued furiously, of course, about the means of improvement. Some insisted that people who listened to music, any music, however common or popular, would gradually seek a higher standard. Others urged, from the outset, that trivial and trashy tunes be barred from performance in favor of higher standards. Pedagogues and promoters divided.

It was into this climate of anxiety about public taste, hope for improvement and concern with contemporary programming, that Sousa introduced his touring band. Bands had, traditionally, belonged to a lower part of the musical hierarchy than serious soloists, orchestras, chamber groups, and choral societies. They were identified with a more limited repertoire and with a performance style that exaggerated the vulgar, favoring flashy overtures, blaring marches, sentimental ballads, and incongruous pastiches. Even Patrick Gilmore disdained portions of the band repertoire. He upbraided David Blakely for trying to get him to perform a "false" and "inartistic . . . circus of war songs" in 1891. "I have fired the public beast through *cannon* and *anvil*," Gilmore admitted, "but I gave them great music *withal*. I would not touch the *War Song Panorama* for any amount of gold."[59]

Nonetheless, despite this protest Gilmore was widely identified with a relaxed and tolerant approach to programming. Gilmore's fame, the New York *World* explained, "was not based upon the satisfaction he gave our intellect; it rested upon the gratification he furnished to our senses. He played the simple melodies of our homes, and the tears filled our eyes." Gilmore knew public sentiment; he combined it with his own magnetism to fill men with "good nature"

and make them "more contented, more cheerful and happier."[60] Gilmore, wrote the Kansas City *Journal*, "was more a caterer than a teacher," although he may well have been justified by the primitive level of national taste that existed when he began his conducting career.[61]

Sousa was harder to analyze. Articulate and aggressive about marketing his musical philosophy, certainly much more vocal and self-conscious than Gilmore had been, he gave concerts which appeared to be too heterogeneous and even volatile in quality for critics to take any clear line upon them. From the start he seemed more serious than previous band conductors, in part because of his heavier reliance upon winds and his concern with arranging more accurate and evocative transcriptions of orchestral compositions. Where Gilmore had sown, ran the refrain, Sousa would reap, appealing to and sustaining a more serious level of musical knowledge. This band leader "is not catering to popular taste," insisted the Elmira *Star* in early 1893. "He prefers a better quality of music than brass bands usually play or brass band audiences care to hear."[62] The playing of Grieg's *Peer Gynt* Suite, of Wagner's *Lohengrin*, of Schubert, Rossini, and Tschaikowsky revealed sophistication and skill. Even in lighter portions of the program, the Kansas City *Journal* wrote, there was a "dignity of treatment" which removed it from vulgarity.[63]

But most early comments about Sousa focused on his programming breadth and his playing of popular music. They did so, approvingly or disapprovingly, pondering the point of organizing a band so skillful and disciplined in order to play this more common range of tunes. Those who accepted Sousa's tributes to mass taste as a basis for programming agreed with him that there was nothing wrong with popularity. And a band was no fit interpreter of serious music anyway, some of them continued. "Mr. Sousa's excellent sense is shown in bowing to the popular will and giving the people what they want and what they pay for," a New York newspaper commented. Sousa had been advised to depart from the Gilmore tradition and emphasize classical music more, the paper admitted, but he realized his audiences did not come to be educated but to be entertained.[64]

The Chicago *Herald* agreed. Applauding Sousa's enormously popular performances at the Columbian Exposition, it attacked the Fair's musical directorate (including Theodore Thomas), who sought a means of "educating" the public. Many people, the *Herald* argued, found it "almost a punishment to hear classical music, while all their senses rejoice at listening to a simple and familiar melody."[65] Sousa's open air concerts, on the Grand Plaza of the fairgrounds, were an unexpected 1893 sensation and helped establish his early reputation.

But some reviewers were appalled by the heavy proportion of popular tunes and dismayed by the missed opportunities. The Duluth *Daily Commonwealth* detected a disproportion of "coconut dance and clog dance and Salvation Army parody" in Sousa's program, even while admitting that the audience seemed to love it. The "thousand people who heard with delight the overture to the Flying Dutchman and the Hungarian Rhapsodie" departed feeling "partly degraded" by this cheaper music. "A conductor should try to give his audience as much music as they can hold, and a Duluth audience has a better capacity than Mr. Sousa supposed."[66]

Other newspapers, reflecting the ambitions of the musically literate, voiced similar concerns. The Springfield *Republican* praised the fine musicianship, but regretted to see "such superb material wasted upon such empty and meaningless music." Nonetheless, it accepted the fact that "people who attend band concerts do not go to hear Beethoven."[67] In the end the journalists were realistic. Their complaints were temperate, and several, like the *Evening Wisconsin* in Milwaukee, advised Sousa to stay within his orbit and not get too fancy or "usurp the field of the symphony orchestra."[68] It is very doubtful, the Syracuse *Standard* concluded, "if anybody cares to have strings emulated by brass." The "brass band will never be the equal of the string band for concert work any more than the orchestra will ever rival the brass band in the martial music of the street parade."[69]

Sousa himself explained his philosophy of programming in a series of interviews, beginning during his first tours. He disliked making hard and fast distinctions between educating and entertaining the public, although he attacked those who insisted that reliance upon strictly classical repertoires was the only way to proceed. While popular taste was improving—"I believe a programme composed entirely of so-called popular music would now be as dismal a failure as one wholly made up of classical pieces"—he insisted it was foolish "to try to play above the heads of one's listeners. The audience at big out-door concerts is composed largely of the masses. . . . They don't care for what some folks are pleased to call classical music. . . . I have always believed in playing airs that I found everybody likes."[70]

In any event, Sousa went on, the term classical was used too arbitrarily. Any tune was classical, he insisted, that had "achieved a lasting popularity and become a standard. 'The Swanee River' I call classic." If critics were patient they would find public appreciation of "high class" music increasing, particularly if it was "mixed judiciously with favorite tunes and dealt out in small doses." Finally, Sousa suggested that performance style itself could aid public refinement. When he played "Molly and I and the Baby," a popular tune that some found particularly offensive when it was juxtaposed with Wagner or Grieg, instead of presenting Molly as "a frowzy-headed girl," he dressed her up "in a clean white frock" and had her "washing up the baby."[71] Sanitized, the music was entertaining *and* refining.

22

The burden on the band conductor was heavy, because most observers agreed that band music, by reason of its popularity, was the music of the people. It could "be made a stepping stone to something higher." Sousa's own special mix was a strategy for such advancement. His secret, according to the Chicago *Herald* in 1892, was a "tacit promise" to his audience that if they were patient through the serious numbers, they would get the "sweetmeats that are presented as encores. . . . Just as in the circus the buffoonery of the clown amuses as much as the daring feats of the acrobat, so here also the musical joke is appreciated not less than the serious composition."[72] Sousa himself, in an interview the following year, argued that through "some mysterious mesmeric process which is beyond my power of analysis" he could tell when the audience was with him. If interest lagged in a certain number, his next selection would "be something totally at variance with the one that preceded it."[73] Writing his autobiography he tried to provide a long pedigree for his mix and match procedure. In the theater, he argued, it was not unusual to see comic scenes following immediately upon tragic ones. Shakespeare was noted for such contrasts. And in romantic drama laughter frequently followed tears. "So it is that I have no hesitation in combining in my programme tinkling comedy with symphonic tragedy or rhythmic march with classic tone-picture."[74]

One device Sousa employed to introduce these lighter notes (and his own marches) excited special attention. Although they would occasionally be scheduled as part of the program, his vast repertoire of popular numbers entered the concert hall through unannounced encores. But the encores became so invariable a part of his presentation that they soon were expected. Indeed they often made up more than half of the actual performance. Using the encore in this fashion served several needs. For one, it involved the audience more actively in the creation of the concert. Sousa, keenly interested in listener reaction, enjoyed widening the area of participation. One of the reasons for his brilliant success at Chicago's Columbian Exposition was having the audience sing along. According to Sousa it was the vocal director of the Exposition who made the actual suggestion. Sousa invited the audience to join in, and thousands sang while he played old favorites and hymns, giving the open-air performance the mixed flavor of a patriotic ritual, a concert, and a church meeting.[75]

The encore also became an instrument for shifting some responsibility onto the audience. In return for its enthusiasm would come a display of generosity on the part of the band and its conductor. Reviewers continually thanked Sousa for his encores, for gratifying the audience's wishes, despite the fact that the encores were planned and without them the performance would have been very short indeed. Some critics still objected that the encores shifted the balance too heavily in favor of merely popular and transient tunes. But they permitted Sousa to play his own marches without having to fill the printed program with his own name.

Sousa's authority and popularity then, rested on a set of accomplishments which were almost fully mature by the time he finished his first season with his own band: a reputation for training musicians and selecting soloists to achieve harmonic precision and tonal balance; a capacity, semimilitary, semimagical, to coax delicate and disciplined performances from his men; a genius for gentlemanly celebrity; a dramatic yet restrained platform manner; an articulate philosophy of musical composition and performance which supported the varied programming plans; and a set of devices, most notably the encore, for encouraging audience enthusiasm and allowing an immediate response to public preferences.

In addition to all this there was one final aspect to Sousa's career which brought him the personal power required by a great conductor.

And that was his own massive contribution to musical composition, most particularly the Sousa marches that had begun to appear with regularity in the 1880s and continued to augment the American band repertoire for the next four decades. The marches were liquid bliss to expectant Americans, who were hoping for a native composer with an international reputation. Critics made extensive and repeated attempts to analyze the basis of their appeal, their capture of something incarnate in the national life. Almost from the first Sousa's marches were seized upon as quintessentially American in their bounce, their liveliness, their jaunty discipline. But the structure of the Sousa march and the mystery embedded in its evocation of national character are less relevant here than the authority they transferred to the conductor. Sousa's fame came through creation rather than performance. Even without the thousands who watched and listened to him, he had become a celebrity by the mid-nineties. Composition brought the Sousa on the podium an additional source of magnetic appeal, a hint of personal genius which demanded audience attention. It was rare to see a genius in action, and a genius who so actively eschewed the affectations of the artist. Wearing "long hair, goggles, an air of mystery and . . . always smelling of Dutch cheese," Sousa told an interviewer for the New York *Advertiser* in August 1893, did not necessarily mean talent.[76] He contentedly obeyed the obvious conventions. Exuding a common-sense patriotism, Sousa differed from most of his audience only by his grander style of life, the material emblem of growing wealth. In place of his meager governmental salary, the rewards of private industry brought the musician the luster of financial success. By 1894 or 1895 he stood alone, setting the standard at which others aimed.

Many aspects of the Sousa legend,

then, were firmly in place by the end of one or two years of independent touring. The search for Gilmore's successor was a short one; the gamble of establishing the new band seemed in hindsight nothing short of a sure thing. The nineties would be rich in band performance: Victor Herbert, Frederick Innes, Giuseppe Creatore, Thomas Brooke, Alessandro Liberati, Patrick Conway, and others provided stern competition. Some of Sousa's own instrumentalists would soon leave to found their own bands. Several of these leaders were brilliant musicians, a few were capable composers, and their tours often earned heady tributes from newspaper reviewers.[77] But it proved impossible to pass Sousa once he had hit his stride with the public. By the late nineties his energies overflowed into many aspects of creation and production, from musical comedy and light opera companies to writing fiction. "If there is any limit to Sousa's success as leader and composer," the *Musical Courier* wrote in 1896, it was not yet apparent. For four years he had continually been touring and giving concerts; "his face is probably more familiar to the people of the United States than that of any other public man in the country."[78] "Sousa earns over $100,000 a year!" exclaimed H. M. Bosworth in the San Francisco *Examiner*. "What fact can instance more emphatically the elevation of musical art in popular estimation?"[79] He received more money than the president of the United States. That same year, in 1899, the Wilkes-Barre *Daily News* argued that "we can now look upon a tradition of Sousa compositions and Sousa concerts. . . . There's hardly a way now of comparing Sousa's Band, except with itself."[80] Sousa "is omnipresent," the Dayton *News* enthused. "In the military camp, in the crowded streets of the city . . . in the ball room, in the concert hall, at the seaside and on the mountains, go where you may, you hear Sousa, always Sousa. . . . It is Sousa in the band, Sousa in the orchestra, Sousa in the phonograph, Sousa in the hand organ, Sousa in the music box, Sousa everywhere," the man "not of the day, or of the hour, but of the time."[81]

Sousa furthered his reputation by extending the techniques he developed during his first tours. He was continually posing for newspaper photographers, interviewed on his love for horses, his bicycle riding, or his trap shooting, invited to judge contests and to offer opinions on the major controversies of the day. New York newspapers showed photographs of the conductor taking boxing lessons at Manhattan Beach. "Here, then, you see bared before the camera the muscular right arm that has wielded the baton to the delight of millions, the sturdy fist that wrote 'El Capitan.'" "Within a few years of hard training," his teacher, Jock Cooper, manager of the Manhattan Beach Race Track insisted, "Mr. Sousa could easily develop into a world beater."[82] His reading habits provoked observation; so did his views on cultural patronage, foreign music, national character, and international relations. Those who know Sousa only from his conducting podium, one critic wrote in 1901, "know only half the man. The Sousa of keen insight, the Sousa of discriminating fancy, the student of musical tradition and of musical development; the man of affairs able to take up any of the questions of the day and dissect them; able to take his side of an argument and hold his own; the man of refinement and toleration, the patriotic American, the husband and father," here was the Sousa who was always "an inspiration to meet. . . . His intellectuality glimmers from as many sides as the facets of a diamond."[83]

The reputation was abetted, moreover, by a squad of press agents, who fed descriptions of the musical master to a squad of hungry journalists. Year after year the same anecdotes, the same descriptive phrases, the same metaphors appeared among the dozens of reviews Sousa received in an average week. The concerts were often covered by reporters better equipped to analyze a baseball game. They were grateful for the publicity suggesting just which musical virtues to emphasize, which conducting skills to ferret out. Old interviews were unearthed. Stories about couples filing for divorce because of a spouse's passion for Sousa music surfaced in time to catch local interest.[84] Successful formulas were forged in the publicity campaign no less than in the concert programs.

But Sousa's own beliefs and public pronouncements also helped. They were such as to please middle-class Americans, conservative in their political orientation, fiercely patriotic when cultural comparisons were made, supportive of home, family, and active citizenship. Invited by American Commissioner-General Ferdinand Peck of Chicago to be the official American Band at the Paris 1900 Fair, Sousa undertook his first European tour. He seized the occasion to write articles condemning the effect of state subsidies on art. National theatres, orchestras, bands, and conservatories were destructive. "An artistic organization that is fostered by State aid is like a hardy plant brought up in a hot-house. It may keep on living, and that's all you can say about it." Sousa's conviction that real art needed no public support suited domestic suspicions of public expenditures for culture. "If a musician, a writer, or a painter, has anything in him," Sousa wrote in his autobiography, "he will dig it out of himself, if the State will only let him starve long enough."[85]

Such sentiments did not, of course, please all Americans. But when one wrote to a European newspaper, complaining about Sousa's super-patriotism, and his attack on official subsidies, Sousa went even further. America, he insisted, had invariably improved upon European ideas. Europe presented the "tallow candle, but like grateful children we sent in return the electric light; Europe gave us the primitive hand-power printing press of Gutenberg and in our simple-hearted way we showed her the Goss perfecting press. . . . Europe put the bare needle in our fingers and we reciprocate with the modern sewing

25

machine." "My sin," Sousa concluded, if it was a sin, "lies in my not accepting everything in Europe, including the people, customs and arts, as superior to what we have at home. Gentle stranger," he begged his critic, "do not decry the McCormick reaper because they use a sickle in the grain fields of Europe . . . do not decry a Hudson River steamer because it would not have room to turn in the Seine! Be big-hearted; be without prejudice; see good in all things, even if they are American."[86]

Such spread-eagle boasting was normally the realm of the politician. When a certified artist took it up, a musician and composer with an international reputation, there was bound to be approving editorial comment. Sousa's cultural nationalism fit a long-established groove, its origins going back to the early nineteenth century. His sink-or-swim philosophy of musical survival fit easily, as well, into a vulgarized Spencerianism, which frowned upon special favors shown any group of people, artists or not.

Sousa's published fiction carried forward, less effectively perhaps, a set of views quite consonant with orthodox Republicanism. In *Pipetown Sandy*, a novel he published in 1905, Sousa created a highly sentimental and melodramatic story based upon his boyhood memories of Washington. Reviewers of the book were not uniformly impressed. "It would be very disconcerting to the rank and file if clever people could do everything well," the Buffalo *News* admitted, before going on to characterize the book as "altogether harmless" and "without much claim to distinction."[87] The New York *Evening Sun* found it "childlike and harmless and altogether pointless," while the Denver *Republican* placed it back "with the old style of Sunday school library book of the ever triumphant poor boy who saves the sister of his rich young patron. . . . it is of the good old time of our fathers' boyhood, when wrong stalks openly through boys' books to be mocked by virtue equally openly tagged and classified and not to be confounded." It was "Back to the music rack, Sousa."[88]

But *Pipetown Sandy* not only permitted Sousa to express his love for exercise, shooting, and fishing, his affection for funny stories, and his delight in comic lyrics. It allowed him to exalt clean-living American virtues and to condemn complaining radicals who did not fit easily into American life. The chief villain, Dennis Foley, was "a self-elected Ishmaelite, his hand against every man and every man's hand against him. He was of the lowest stratum of that peripatetic community that sprang into existence after the Civil War, now known as 'tramps.' In the case of some of these aimless wanderers there may have been extenuating circumstances, for perhaps, through no fault of their own, they found themselves out of tune with the new conditions. But Foley was a vagabond, bummer, and thief from choice."[89] And he was an army deserter as well.

Too embarrassing to be taken seriously, the book suggested the sincerity of Sousa's own prejudices and the simplicity of his political views. His beliefs were a disarming reflection of what most in his middle-class audiences believed also. "Bohemianism has ruined more great minds then any one other thing in the world," he told the Oakland *Enquirer* in 1899. "The greatest thing and the most beautiful thing about this great American nation is its home life. . . . The whole language of the Frenchman does not contain the word 'home' in its meaning to us. . . . Get the American home life into your music and into the life of the musicians, and we will have the greatest musical community, in God's good time, that the world has ever known."[90]

In later years, also, Sousa identified more fully with the American businessman. His organizational gifts were evident from the start but some obstacles stunted his claims for commercial genius. In 1897, during the legal disputes that followed upon David Blakely's death, newspapermen stared at the earlier contracts in disbelief. "It looks as if Sousa had practically given the Blakely people something like an independent fortune," the Wilkes-Barre *Evening Leader* commented, "and as if his leg has been pulled to the stretching point." Why had Sousa made such a contract, giving away 80 percent of the profits and 50 percent of the march royalties? "There is hardly a record of such a gigantic swindle." The only easy answer was that "Sousa, like many another genius, hasn't got the band business head that looks out for his own interest," and so had permitted himself to be robbed by his ingenious manager.[91]

Of course this image of a bumbling businessman may have been spread by Sousa and his agents, to appear more favorably amidst the suits and counter-suits that developed when Mrs. Blakely sought to impose the contract's terms and Sousa refused. But after the flurry had died down, Sousa devoted himself more emphatically to a business philosophy. "The organizing and maintaining of a superior band I regard in the light of a calm, calculative, business proposition," he wrote in the *Criterion* during 1900; the task was as practical as the selection of a bank teller. "As the head of a counting-house exercises powers of selection in gathering about him a staff as nearly perfect as possible, so is the bandmaster untiring in his search for the best available talent. . . . the principle of the survival of the fittest is strong."[92] Sousa's use of commercial similes, his friendship with entrepreneurs, his insistence upon established business practices, testified to his confidence in the marketplace.

His autobiographical reflections also emphasized a firm and practical approach to problem solving, particularly when dealing with dishonest, incompetent, or unrealistic promoters. During a 1911 tour of South Africa he was startled by the naivete of the arrangements. The Sousa Band was to give its concert in a public park "with no way of controlling the ingress or egress of the audience. That honest-hearted South African representative believed that the dear public would hunt up the ticketseller, buy tickets and wait in line to pass the proper entrance," even though no fence surrounded the park. Sousa immediately engaged the only hall in town, and filled it with an audience of 1,100. Thousands who had come to hear the band were disappointed. "But, since our expenses were $2,500 a day on the tour and we were certainly not touring for our health, we felt no compunction."[93]

Indeed, Sousa confessed that no less an authority than the great Theodore Thomas had warned him to be careful about business matters. "Managers will stick close when you are making money," Thomas supposedly told him, "but they'll desert you without a qualm when the first squall blows up." Sousa distinguished himself from his great hero by his more diplomatic and prudent response to the opinions of others. While he admitted many parallels between Thomas and himself, Sousa felt less "given to irrevocable dicta. I would listen to advice, and if I knew it was no good, would quietly say, 'I'll think that over,' leaving the other fellow with no ammunition to discuss the matter further." Despite some unparalleled gifts, Thomas was "primarily an educator."[94] Tenacious of purpose, he lost his sense of proportion and came into occasional but sharp conflict with the public, who resented being told what they were meant to admire. Sousa's style better suited a country coming to value the power of salesmanship, and the stern but self-restrained consistency of a successful business leader.

Sousa's assurances that American politics, values, and social habits were fundamentally healthy and not at all antagonistic to the arts gained in persuasiveness when he extended his foreign tours after 1900, and achieved, in effect, a conquest of European audiences. The *Musical Courier*, the premier professional periodical of the day, excitedly reprinted newspaper reports from the ancient cities of the Old World, attesting to his extraordinary popularity. Fannie Edgar Thomas sent back a description of the Paris Fair Concerts in

1900 which was a veritable paean to Sousa's Americanism and his spirit of system. Even the very preparations stood out. When the trunks full of chairs and stands and platforms arrived on the scene in a cart, "instead of a regiment of useless and snarly old people surrounding" it, screaming themselves "hoarse and wearing themselves out in gesticulation, one very quiet young man in uniform was there . . . and without seeming to speak a word had the trunks unloaded and placed beside the place in a few seconds." French observers, according to Fannie Thomas, were amazed at the speed and silence with which a few Americans arranged the chairs and stands. The flag bearers "bore the pride of youth and health, and fearlessness of carrying the big flag of a big nation," and then came the bandsmen well groomed, well dressed, "straight, healthy, happy, clean and polished looking. . . . Without being rigidly disciplined, they have the impression of uniformity of movement. Without special grace, they were also without awkwardness." Most of the men, Fannie Thomas admitted, were in fact foreigners, German-born, but apparently that did not dampen their American appearance of sensible, well-organized, good humor. And finally there appeared the "quick, neat, fresh" and "radiant" Sousa himself, handsome and even exotic looking, his uniform "the perfection of fit and finish," who proceeded, on schedule, to dazzle his vast audience.[95]

The European triumphs underscored what many Americans already believed and what Sousa told them tirelessly: that human beings were, fundamentally, everywhere the same, and responsive to beauty, good will, and disciplined effort. He played his music for the people, not attempting to "stuff things down their throats, or rather into their ears," according to Fannie Thomas, but simply to please. "He chooses his music pure and simple because it is always and everywhere and with all people—attractive."[96] This confidence in popular taste was the cultural counterpart of an age-old commitment to the spread of democratic values, and the conviction that in time all people would agree on the nature of government and social order, an agreement that Americans felt they had worked out in final form in the late eighteenth century. Political developments in the early nineteenth century challenged Enlightenment optimism about the diffusion of democracy, but this cultural universalism was in some ways a legacy of the older hopes. And no American before Sousa had so successfully translated this impulse into a palpable reality.

Just as his world tours demonstrated the organic connections binding peoples everywhere together, Sousa's domestic appeal built upon the appearance of unity. Sousa "is peerless because he plays the music of the people," wrote one newspaper;[97] all classes enjoy his music, wrote another. His audience, "so diversified in its parts, yet brought together as one in enthusiasm," formed his proudest laurels.[98] American cities actively supported or sought sponsorship for municipal band concerts as a social therapy; increasing social tension which accompanied industrial growth, the more violent confrontations between labor and capital in the last years of the century, underscored the value of communal occasions to demonstrate the placid good will of the majority. Reviewing the history of music in Baltimore, one chronicler gauged the importance city fathers attached to band music from the "alertness" with which they "produced the cash whenever the musicians balked."[99] City after city featured summer meccas in electric parks, some developed by streetcar companies. And resorts existed just outside the city limits, to which local and imported bands repaired with regularity. Estimates ran that there were an many as 10,000 bands in America, amateur and professional, by the century's end; supplementing them were touring Canadian Kilties, British Grenadiers, German, Hungarian, Filipino, Mexican, Italian, Russian, and Irish groups. The band concert became, as it were, a ritual testifying to the unspoiled benevolence of national life, free of charge in the new park bandshells, or modestly priced accompaniments to fairs, industrial expositions, and summer hotels. A good band frequently made the difference between financial profit and disaster for promoters. Sousa's broad appeal made him a particularly attractive feature for periods of several weeks at major expositions and vacation spots. Although Sousa refused to play for dancing, he happily appeared at trade fairs or the newly popular food fairs, providing background music for the exchange of commercial and consumer information.

Sousa's ability to create what amounted to aural icons for the era's patriotism and commercialism, his capacity to fuse the popular with the classical and to reassure his vast, middle-class audiences that they deserved respect for their aspirations as well as their achievements, was paralleled in the 1890s by the growth of a sophisticated graphic art in the service of American advertising. Two of the men most closely connected with Sousa's management were themselves deeply into the mysteries of printing publicity. David Blakely's interests included ownership of a large printing company specializing in advertising. And Everett Reynolds, a director of the Long Island Railroad, who took over management of the Manhattan Beach Hotel after Austin Corbin's death and managed tours for Sousa and De Wolf Hopper, was also president of the Metropolitan Printing Company and helped amalgamate theatrical poster companies under the title of the Consolidated Lithograph Company.[100]

Thus Blakely and Reynolds were adept at distributing the new, colorful, technically advanced advertising which helped in the 1890s to support a revolution in American graphic design. The same decade that Sousa launched his band saw the rise of a generation of American poster artists—Will Bradley, Edward Penfield, Will Carqueville, Ethel Reed, Frank Hazenplug, and J. J. Gould among them. Contributing to the "poster craze" of the nineties, this new corps of commercial artists represented an impulse not so very different from Sousa's—the attempt to synthesize popularity with sophistication and create a novel medium for public communication. The broad, flat strokes many poster designers relied upon, their references, sometimes ironic, to the artistic traditions of the higher arts, their semihumorous and usually benevolent treatment of their fellow Americans—on bicycles, on streetcars, reading magazines, strolling through city crowds, on holiday, at work in the office—flattered and amused simultaneously. Like Sousa, the images many of the poster artists created rested on exaggeration and burlesque.[101] Sousa's fiery marches, after all, were enjoyed by audiences seated pacifically in bandshells or auditoriums, while his popular musical comedies were set in exotic, even fantastic surroundings. Both the new illustrators of the nineties and Sousa exploited mass production, knowing their creations would be available in thousands and even tens of thousands of copies. And they relied upon the newest technologies, often adding technical innovations of their own.

Sousa, however, offered one dissent here, producing a rare moment out of step with his public. Infuriated by the popularity of the phonograph he coined the term "canned music" to express his dissatisfaction. More specifically he was incensed by the failure of the recording companies to pay composers royalties on their music. This seemed like simple theft, and he was an active force in the creation of ASCAP to protect and define the rights of creators.[102]

But Sousa's dislike of the phonograph was greater than simply economic. He realized that it threatened the monopoly of the performance as a musical medium. His own concerts were visual displays as well as musical renditions; the uniforms, the movements, the bearing of conductor and musicians added decisively to the impressiveness of the music. Sousa's is

29

a pantomimic art, a Philadelphia paper commented. "At one of his concerts it is not alone the ear that is pleased and charmed, it is the eye also that is captivated and satisfied."[103] The New Haven *Leader* in 1899 used the phrase "see the original" in urging audiences to attend the concerts. "One does see Sousa's music; you see it grow under the magic of his baton, every note brought to life at its command as a picture grows under the artist's brush."[104] Sousa, wrote H. M. Bosworth in the San Francisco *Examiner*, was not so much a metronome as an expression. "What the physical illustration by face, attitude and gesture is to the spoken words of an orator the graceful attitude and gestures of Sousa are to the combined musical utterances of his executants."[105] They helped the audience enjoy the music. "Is there not possibly some occult power, some hypnotic spell, existent in that peerless back?" asked the Chicago *Tribune*. "And that matchless left hand, immaculate in purest white—what mystic magic lies concealed within it that it thus should set a-sway humanity's inmost being?"[106] If Sousa were placed behind a screen or made in some way invisible, the newspaper mused, the music could not possibly be as impressive. Sousa knew, then, that recorded he would lose much of his power, and it was as a performer that he received his fullest satisfactions.

Nonetheless, newspapers and magazines repudiated his assault on the phonograph. It was bound to improve public taste in the long run. "John Philip Sousa overindulges in mince pie, his dreams are filled with contorted talking machines and 'canned music' assumes the aspect of an ogre." "Sousa should be the last one to complain of mechanical music, however applied," another critic objected.[107] For once the bandmaster had miscalculated.

But with this exception, Sousa managed to affirm the taste and judgment of his audiences. "All the way through a Sousa program you can see the old flag waving, hear the clothes flapping on the line in the back yard, and smell the pork and beans cooking in the kitchen;" these homely metaphors were offered by the Topeka *Daily Capital* in 1902. "The principal soloist was born in St. Joseph, Mo., and the average man can pronounce the names of the members of the organization as they appear on the hotel register." There was admittedly, here and there a suggestion of "Die Wacht am Rhein" and a whiff of macaroni. "But Sousa's band is for Tom Jones and John Smith and their families."[108] The Springfield *Republican*, in 1897, acclaimed Sousa's sway. "It seems as if he always gives just the thing that the audience is in the mood for . . . the delight he gives people is rather more unrestrained and unaffected than one ordinarily notes in audiences. Sousa and his hearers are thoroughly *en rapport*."[109]

So powerful was the conductor's presence by the late nineties that sermons were preached and poems written as testaments to his power of inspiration. In May 1898, a Baptist minister used a Sousa concert as his text in a sermon that newspapers happily reprinted, "Spiritual Suggestions from Sousa." The conductor was transformed into a symbol of purity and leadership, a bringer of order from chaos. And his musicians represented the discipline of a well-run church, obedient and responsive. "The performers were content to play the score as it was given to them. They did not rewrite, compose a new one, or strike out in a few new lines. . . . If only the church and its preachers could be content with the faith once delivered to the saints." Each man played his own part, without worrying whether another's was better. There was variety to the music Sousa scheduled, a reminder that "in salvation's song something can be found fitted for every feeling, taste, aptitude." And the leader, controlling his men with "no contortion, no violent motion, no mighty sweep of his arm" recalled Christ's presence, quiet and continuing, even without obvious miracles or transfigurations.[110]

The conservative implications of a

Sousa performance were complemented by its patriotism. The Sousa Band received many of its most tumultuous ovations during the war fever of the 1890s. "If the present Administration ever takes action against persons who arouse public patriotism," one newspaperman wrote, "John Philip Sousa should be selected as the first victim to be punished."[111] Sousa insisted upon playing the "Star Spangled Banner" at his concerts, producing frenzied reactions among normally staid listeners. Some of the excitement was caused by the stirring themes of Sousa's new march, perhaps his most enduring one, *The Stars and Stripes Forever*. If war came Sousa deserved government employment, argued one reporter. "One blast upon his bugle-horn would be worth 10,000 men."[112] Adapting himself to the bombastic rhetoric, Sousa created a new piece, *The Trooping of the Colors*, grouping the flags of friendly foreign powers to the tunes of their anthems, and swaddling it all in patriotic melodies. The Chicago *Times-Herald*, a frequent critic of Sousa, was repelled by the promotional rhetoric of his management and worried about its injudicious advertisement of patriotism. It was a wonder that "the stars on the flag have not been transformed into boxes of soap, bicycles, and the photographs of political candidates," while the employment of patriotism as "a marketable ware is certainly not commendable, especially at the present time when cool-headed judgment is the better part of valor."[113]

Sousa himself was no master prognosticator—"There will be no war with Spain," he told reporters after the Maine explosion—and his jingoism continued to meet opposition. The *Mirror* found his *Stars and Stripes* meretricious. "It is riotous and stormy, but it does not represent the deeper emotions of patriotism which one finds in 'My Country, 'tis of Thee.' There is no trace of solemnity or of reverence." Its chief quality, as in the rest of Sousa's music, was a "tonic flashiness," appropriate for a piece that was "loud and vulgar. Its effects are crude. . . . It is good music for the crowd . . . but . . . its educative tendencies are directly opposite to those which true lovers of music would like to see encouraged."[114]

But then Sousa's cultivation of mass emotion during the war was simply one example of a larger stance that irritated cultural conservatives. "Mr. Sousa aims only at popularity," the Chicago *Times-Herald* warned.[115] The Washington *Post* and the Syracuse *Standard* isolated Sousa's descriptive music as particularly unfortunate panderings to modern taste. It was, they insisted, impossible and implausible to use music to describe horse races, thunderstorms, or picnics; even Wagner, "the greatest of all the masters of harmony and musical effort" would not attempt such absurdities without the aid of "a mise en scene which helped materially to tell the story."[116] Sousa continued to be fond of visual effects to emphasize a composition's argument, but this violated the integrity of the musical form. In March 1901, the Chicago *Post*, whose critic felt that Sousa had received far too little criticism for his own good, printed several hostile evaluations of the Sousa "fad." One of them found the interest in his performances "less musical than pathological," feeding the nervous excitement and noise of modern life. The band's discipline had all the precision "of a Turkish rug made in New Jersey," and stood on a par with "the quick, ordered tumult of a business lunch. As is Grand Rapids to furniture, so is Sousa to music. He represents the complete negation of dignity, leisure, feeling, temperament." Looking over a Sousa program was to enter "the bargain counter of a department store."[117]

The debate, once again, was an old one. Sousa had managed to identify his band and his music with fundamentally popular forces. Meliorists, insisting that the artist's task was to reveal and then refine the discordant aspects of contemporary civilization, found Sousa's popularity disturbing. He was not fulfilling a critical role, the function of a serious performer. He mixed vaudeville airs with serious music, pandering to crowd emotions rather than warring upon them in the interest of a higher cause. He accepted his audience's values; he did not try to remold them.

And yet, he was a serious composer and an accomplished musician; he had to be taken seriously, for there was no denying his native powers. The problem was that he employed them in the interest of entertainment, grafting on to the formal setting of a concert selections more properly hummed in a burlesque house or community sing. Sousa caused further stir by his vigorous adoption of ragtime, and his incorporation of ragtime arrangements into many of his concerts. Ragtime, he argued, was "an established feature of American music. It will never die any more than Faust and the great operas will die."[118] Suspicious of the claim, and outraged by the comparison, critics took issue. To treat ragtime as a distinctive national contribution was to demean the achievement of serious composers like Edward MacDowell and George Chadwick, who had been working for years to develop a national school. Sousa was charged with self-interest, because the "ragtime encore" had become so regular a part of his performance. So closely had Sousa "identified himself with ragtime," the St. Paul *Globe* wrote in 1903, that "were the syncopated music to lose in popularity, perhaps the conductor would lose, also."[119]

But the defenders again were numerous. "An element of the public goes to hear music when Sousa plays that would not otherwise go to a concert—no, not for Weingartner, not for Mottl, nor for Richter," the Rochester *Post-Express* argued. Sousa delighted crowds with showman tricks, bringing instrumentalists up to the front of his band and marching them back after their spectacular solos were finished. But in return for this histrionic appeal the "non-musical public allows itself to be lured into hearing music which it would vote a bore, if anybody else played it. Such is the magic of personality."[120] And when Sousa

tried to become too highbrow, to create programs that featured orchestral music transcribed for the concert band, he was condemned by other critics for being overly ambitious and failing to recognize his natural level and his audience's taste. Thus there was no absolutely safe harbor for the bandmaster.

The continuing popularity of his organization and his drawing power rested on his ability to walk the line between mass idolatry and critical rejection. The athletic matinee idol of the nineties was succeeded by a somewhat more restrained conductor, less given, apparently, to mannerisms, graver, more dignified.[121] But Sousa had also gained immensely through the associations and world fame he had acquired. Seeing the conductor, American audiences beheld a world traveler, a celebrity whose decorations testified to the respect of foreign potentates.[122] He had been called by command performance to play before the king of England, and every detail of this royal honor was devoured by newspaper readers, anxious to catch a bit of the reflected glory. His marches had joined the repertoires of bands in Manila, Constantinople, Berlin, and Paris. One visiting Englishman confessed that he did not realize that the Washington *Post* was a newspaper as well as a musical composition.[123] Sousa was linked to a great cosmopolitan world, proof that American genius could win laurels on the concert stage as American athletes were winning medals at the newly organized Olympic Games. He was conqueror, athlete, businessman, and sportsman, as well as genius.

The Sousa Phenomenon inevitably also became an anniversary event. Just as the programs tended to repeat their formulas from year to year—the mixture of operatic medleys, popular tunes, classical excerpts and Sousa marches serving his Band as it would most of his competition—so the Sousa visits became devices to measure the passing years and the changing seasons. The annual stays at the Manhattan Beach, or the

Willow Grove concerts near Philadelphia, were symbols of continuity in a civilization where so much else was changing. There was a certain irony in this, for Sousa's Band and its style were labelled, at various times in the nineties, a fad, a passing fancy which could be outgrown like so many other crazes. And Sousa did try to capture contemporary songs and events. Yet his band performances became a symbol of stability, of constancy, of predictability. As his conducting career became longer, observers loved to chart subtle differences in his appearance and technique—the figure growing stockier, the hair grayer, the gestures more languid and restrained—reluctant tributes to approaching age, or, in the case of the conducting techniques, signs of a new maturity and ever-increasing mastery. The nostalgic aspects of the Sousa cult developed, in fact, within only a decade or so of the Band's actual premiere, so strong was the need for recurrence and so few the major entertainers with such staying power. Sousa continued to pour out marches and musical compositions right up through the year of his death, although his most popular compositions had been published, for the most part, by 1910. However, his gift for catching the public temper during moments of crisis remained, and the Sousa Band acted almost like an official representative for national spirit.

Into the teens and twenties Sousa remained an imposing figure. After American entry into World War I he assumed the task of training a band for the Great Lakes Naval Station, and his Jackies, as they were called, appeared at the band rallies which were a crucial part of the ongoing propaganda effort, along with movie stars, opera singers, and political personalities. Sousa no longer stood unrivalled as a stimulant to crowd emotion. Tin Pan Alley, through Irving Berlin and George M. Cohan, produced a series of songs that came to symbolize the American military commitment. But Sousa's *U.S. Field Artillery March*, based on a song written by an army lieutenant, sold hundreds of thousands of records, and became as indelibly associated with the Army as *Semper Fidelis*, written almost thirty years earlier, came to symbolize the Marines.

Some of Sousa's patriotic gestures were, of course, less successful. Sharing the fierce revulsion to things German, Sousa announced a substitute for the German wedding marches that traditionally had accompanied American couples on their stroll down the aisle. After enormous publicity the *American Wedding March* appeared in 1918, but it failed to create a place for itself and like Sousa's fierce rejection of German music, proved a transitory event.[124] The Oklahoma City *Oklahoman* pointed out that assigning Sousa to rewrite Mendelssohn and Wagner was "about as apposite as would be that of Bud Fischer to do a Mona Lisa."[125] Sousa's patriotism had become shrill, in keeping with the national mood.[126] And given his earlier popularization of German music, and the large number of German musicians in his organization, his exaggerated rhetoric about the war may have expressed a desire for expiation.

While he remained a figure of influence then, Sousa's most important years were probably the first two decades with his Band, before live performance was challenged so successfully by the new electronic media; and before he was challenged, as well, by the steady growth of the two cultures he had attempted to straddle. Motion pictures, jazz, radio, comics, dance bands, automobiles, all represented forces paying little heed to many older cultural verities that Sousa, despite his quest for popularity, believed in. And on the other end of the creative spectrum, American poets, painters, museums, orchestras, were now engaged in an international dialogue, achieving levels of performance, exhibition, and execution of serious art that were available in the America of the 1890s to only a few.

Sousa was in fact unhappy with the trends of modern music. Like the other arts, by 1910 it had borne aggressive rebellion against formal conventions. To Sousa music meant melody, rhythm, good humor, and sentiment. Like the older academic painters, angered and bewildered by the apparent defiance of craftsmanlike canons, he refused to accept the new trends. "The real development of music," he told a Spokane reporter in 1915, "will come no more through the efforts of the modern French school or strivings of Schoenberg and his class, than the real development of painting has come through futurists, cubists and all the other 'ists' of art." All of them, composers and painters alike, were "seeking a short and easy road to Mount Olympus, and it does not exist." The *Musical Courier*, reprinting the interview, vigorously agreed. "Tunes—real tunes, good honest tunes—that is what the public demands, and with absolute right."[127] Honest labor, evident in the score, without flimflam or cute tricks, not the lazy deceptions of the new Bohemians.[128]

Ironically, in view of the earlier fears of vulgarization, Sousa became an ideal to some conservative critics. Sousa's marches, wrote D. C. Parker in the *Musical Courier*, several years later, were a corrective "to all the vague syncopisings and sophisticated hesitations of the extreme anemic aesthetes. They said 'Yes' to life with unmistakable emphasis." Some had labelled Sousa's music "vulgar," but it was not; vulgarity "consists in a discrepancy between a thing and its surroundings, and if anything is comfortably at home in the world of 1917 it is Sousa's music. By the cynic, popularity has been called an insult." But it was no insult to label Sousa's music popular. Instead it gave "documentary evidence of important phases of the modern world."[129]

In concentrating upon the issue of popularity, Parker focused upon a key aspect of Sousa's achievement. The composer-conductor created a repertoire and performance style to integrate broad portions of the population and various ranges of musical experience. The hodgepodge of numbers that made up his program, from the comic to the solemn and the serious to the trite, were meant to demonstrate that audiences otherwise separated into the baseball park, the opera house, the vaudeville show and the movie palace, could here share a common ground. The symphonic band, with its expanded repertoire, claimed special national status because of its more inclusive capabilities. Sousa found popularity worth aiming at, and made it a test for his own programs. As music "is universal," he told an Australian newspaperman in 1911, "it becomes necessary to heed the wishes of the masses if one hopes to succeed."[130]

Sousa's identification of entertainment with education mirrored a larger cultural conviction that artistic progress occurred by exposing any taste, however primitive, to art. Refinement grew from familiarity. In this view there were no fundamental antagonisms cleaving the popular from the classic. Sousa's cultural meliorism, his conviction that one great audience could subsume most contemporary contrasts, mirrored the middle-class view of social consensus. The reassurance he offered, verbal and musical, expressed his personal conviction rather than a manipulated posture designed to win applause.

But the America that was growing older along with Sousa was also becoming more specialized, subdividing into cultural subgroups whose age, education, or needs for diversion determined their recreational patterns. The concert band's audience, at the turn of the century, included thousands of amateur musicians serving in municipal, lodge, ethnic, corporate, and veterans' bands scattered across the country. Small, amateur, often casually trained and led, these bands had little in common with the size and splendor of the Sousa establishment. But in dozens of small towns to which orchestras and professional opera troupes never found their ways, bandsmen and their families felt a kinship with Sousa, and his band represented for them the acme of polished performance.

After World War I, however, bands developed other associations. The expansion of America's educational system, in particular the growth of the public high school, produced a new set of adolescent rituals and a series of institutions designed to occupy and socialize teenagers.[131] That range of extra-curricular activities which now form the staple of the high school experience— debate clubs, athletic teams, fraternities and sororities, student newspapers, drama societies, and school bands—soon developed. Many were modelled on their collegiate counterparts, but the much larger number of high schools meant that imitation would parody rather than replicate the originals.

In the 1920s then, on both a collegiate and a high school level, music instruction and performance multiplied, school systems began to purchase instruments and costumes, to hold competitions and public concerts. Although orchestras were included in this expansion, it was the school band that became the most visible and most glamorous symbol of national attachment to musical training. The band appealed on the grounds of its athleticism and marching, the colorful uniforms, the somewhat repetitive character of its repertoire, its patriotic associations, and the fact that its audiences, expecting a good deal of noise, were not particularly upset by any failure to achieve total precision, or by a loss of subtlety in rendering its boisterous music.

Increasingly it was this kind of band, playing in holiday parades, at pep rallies and football games, at picnics and political meetings that came to represent the Sousa tradition. University bands—and others—gave formal concerts, and creative bandmasters like Edwin Franko Goldman attempted to expand the repertoire of original compositions and special transcriptions. Several composers volunteered with interesting new pieces. But to a larger extent than its serious leaders wished, the band became identified with a youth and school culture. This represented considerable shrinking of the popularizing, integrating role that Sousa hoped for when he first organized his own organization.

Sousa died on the eve of an artistic movement which sought to reassociate indigenous cultural motifs with the institutions of high culture. There had been many preparations and intimations during the 1920s, but in the thirties composers, print-makers, painters, sculptors, and craftsmen, along with literary critics, historians, and anthropologists turned back into American history for folk motifs, mythic heroes, icons, and rituals which formed the usable past that could anchor a drifting society. In the W.P.A. Murals, the Index of American Design, the Farm Security Administration photographers, the folk music project of Alan Lomax, and the music of Randall Thompson, Roy Harris and Aaron Copland, one finds efforts to reattach the popular to the classic, to legitimize the vernacular and acknowledge the staying power of ordinary experience. Like Sousa, many of these artists and composers employed a light touch, occasionally indulging their sense of humor. But unlike him, they were both more self-conscious and more critical in their deployment of native materials, exploiting them frequently in the interest of reform. They held contemporary life up to other standards, contrasting the doubts of their day with the expansive force of another.

Sousa's was not a critical philosophy. He projected a supportive vision of national destiny that mingled folksiness, martial arts, gallantry, and commerce. To extract simply the marching tunes from his rich contemporary reputation is to lessen his impact and to dilute his goals. He took himself seriously (and so others took him) as a bridge between cultural communities. And as an instrument to lessen the forbidding awe felt for creative genius. The Sousa performance did more than merely display his marches to advantage. It was an occasion on which to reassure and conciliate an ambitious if unsophisticated public. We no longer have the 35 performances; we do have the marches. If the legacy is reduced, it is no less real.

Notes

1. Comparisons between Sousa and Strauss have been numerous, both in the nineteenth and the twentieth centuries. See Wilfrid Mellers, *Music in a New Found Land* (London, 1964), p. 257; Paul E. Bierley, *John Philip Sousa: American Phenomenon* (New York, 1973), p. 5. Bierley's book is the most detailed study of Sousa's career. Sousa received the title of "March King" because a British author argued that if Johann Strauss, Jr., could be called the "Waltz King," Sousa deserved this new title (Bierley, *American Phenomenon*, p. 50).

2. As the notes will make clear, most of the citations for this essay are based on the Sousa Band press books, more than eighty volumes of clippings covering the Sousa Band between 1892 and 1931. The volumes are on deposit in the U.S. Marine Corps Museum in Washington, where I inspected them. Microfiche copies have been made, however, and I worked from these. I determined, therefore, to cite the sources according to the microfiche cards. These are numbered. The first number represents the series, usually coinciding with a date or season, and moving in roughly chronological order; the second number corresponds to the card number within the series. Each microfiche card is so identified. Although many of the clippings are identified, so far as date and newspaper are concerned, others are not. I will cite the newspaper and date when available, along with the fiche card; when I have not been able to identify the newspaper or date, I will merely cite the card, although the date (and often the place of publication) can usually be approximated. The citation for the scrapbook collection will be JPS.

3. For background on the nineteenth-century American band I have relied upon Jon Newsom, "The American Brass Band Movement," *Quarterly Journal of the Library of Congress* 36 (Spring, 1979): pp. 114-39; Richard Franko Goldman, "Band Music in America," Paul Henry Lang, ed., *One Hundred Years of Music in America* (New York, 1961), pp. 128-39; Alberta Powell Graham, *Great Bands of America* (Toronto, New York, Edinburgh, n.d.); and a series of articles in the *Journal of Band Research*. For interesting comparative material see E. D. Mackerness, *A Social History of English Music* (London, Toronto, 1964), chaps. iv-v; and Ronald Pearsall, *Edwardian Popular Music* (Rutherford, N.J., 1975), chap. 8. Kenneth Young, *Music's Great Days in the Spas and Watering-Places* (London, 1968), contains fascinating material on another aspect of popular musical performance, again for Great Britain.

4. Matwood Darlington, *Irish Orpheus: The Life of Patrick S. Gilmore Bandmaster Extraordinary* (Philadelphia, 1950) covers Gilmore's impressive career.

5. The early pages of John H. Mueller, *The American Symphony Orchestra: A Social History of Musical Taste* (Bloomington, Ind., 1951); and Philip Hart, *Orpheus in the New World* (New York, 1973), contain some background on American symphonies. John Erskine, *The Philharmonic Symphony Society of New York, First Hundred Years* (New York, 1943); Edward Henry Krehbiel, *Philharmonic Society of New York* (New York, 1892); Max Maratzek, *Revelations of an Opera Manager in 19th Century America* (New York, 1968) also contain relevant information. For comparison see William Weber, *Music and the Middle Class: The Social Structure of Concert Life in London, Paris and Vienna* (New York, 1975).

6. There is an enormous literature on many of these celebrities, the Jenny Lind bibliography alone being quite extensive. Milton Goldin, *The Music Merchants* (New York, 1969) contains sketches of some of the famous touring artists. Ivor Guest, *Fanny Elssler* (Middletown, Conn., 1970); Gladys Denny Shultz, *Jenny Lind: The Swedish Nightingale* (Philadelphia and New York, 1962); Adam Carse, *The Life of Jullien: Adventurer, Showman-Conductor . . .* (Cambridge, 1951), are among other useful texts here.

7. The immense German contribution to American musical life is recorded in a series of local studies like Bayrd Still, *Milwaukee: The History of a City* (Madison, 1948); F. Karl Grossman, *A History of Music in Cleveland* (Cleveland, 1972), among many others. Louis Moreau Gottschalk, *Notes of a Pianist* (Philadelphia, 1881), remarked in 1863 that a volunteer military band was assembled in Williamsport, Pennsylvania on the major square. Is "it necessary for me to say that it is composed of Germans (all the musicians in the United States are Germans)?", p. 202.

8. Gottschalk was one of those offering severe comments about American audience taste. See Gottschalk, *Notes of a Pianist*, p. 17.

9. Carse, *Life of Jullien*, p. 11.

10. See Jack Felts, "Some Aspects of the Rise and Development of the Wind Band during the Civil War," *Journal of Band Research* III (Spring, 1967): 29-33; William Carter White, *A History of Military Music in America* (New York, 1944; Westport, Conn., 1975). Another important study, published after this essay was written, is Kenneth E. Olson, *Music and Musket: Bands and Bandsmen of the American Civil War* (Westport, Conn., 1981).

11. Gilmore did attempt to persuade Congress to adopt his new National Anthem, "Columbia," which he first presented Christmas Day, 1879, and whose words, he claimed, were dictated by an angel. However, it was his performing, rather than his composing or philosophizing, that earned him his popularity. See Darlington, *Irish Orpheus*, passim.

12. Thomas's career is examined in Ronald L. Davis, *A History of Music and American Life*, vol. II, *The Gilded Years, 1865-1920* (Huntington, New York, 1980), chap. I; and Rose Fay Thomas, *Memoirs of Theodore Thomas* (New York, 1911). Theodore Thomas, *A Musical Autobiography* (Chicago, 1905), 2 vols., George P. Upton, ed., remains a major source, and so does Charles Edward Russell, *The American Orchestra and Theodore Thomas* (Garden City, 1927).

13. J. Hecker to David Blakely, Elgin, September 26, 1891, Blakely Papers (hereafter BP), Band Correspondence, New York Public Library.

14. Jules Levy to Blakely, New York, May 8, 1891; Jules Levy to Blakely, Weehauken Heights, N.J., August 13, 1891; and Jules Levy to Blakely, Weehauken Heights, August 26, 1891, BP, Band Correspondence.

15. This subject is treated extensively in Martin J. Newhouse, "Artists, Artisans, or Workers? Orchestral Musicians in the German Empire" (Ph. D. diss., Columbia University, 1979); and Abram Loft, "Musicians' Guild and Union: A Consideration of the Evolution of Protective Organizations Among Musicians" (Ph. D. diss., Columbia University, 1950), chap. V.

16. Loft, "Musicians' Guild and Union," pp. 314-15.

17. New York *Evening Journal*, June 11, 1892, JPS 938-6.

18. John Philip Sousa, *Marching Along* (Boston, 1928), pp. 274-75.

19. J. H. Laine to Blakely, Indianapolis, April 13, 1891, BP, Band Correspondence.

20. Blakely to Hobart Weed, New York, June 23, 1892, BP, Band Correspondence.

21. J. H. Johnston to Blakely, Pittsburgh, January 5, 1893, BP, Band Correspondence.

22. *Musical Courier*, July 27, 1892, p. 13. By October 8, p. 15, the *Courier* was congratulating Sousa and looked ahead to a bright future. By February 1893 (Gilmore and Cappa were now dead), the *Courier* was calling him the most conspicuous figure in the band world. *Musical Courier*,

February 2, 1893, p. 23.

23. Cappa had begun a series of Saturday and Sunday concerts in Central Park Mall, performing Mendelssohn, Beethoven, Wagner, Schubert, Bizet, Verdi, Gounod, etc. Born in Sardinia, Cappa enlisted in the U.S. Navy in the 1850s; went with Grafulla, another famous conductor, to the 7th Regiment Band when Grafulla became its leader, and conducted the 7th Regiment Band himself for twelve years.

24. Blakely to Elias Lyman, New York, June 18, 1892, BP, Band Correspondence. In the letter Blakely reviewed the profits he had made from the tours of the Gilmore Band, the Strauss Orchestra, two small tours by Theodore Thomas, and two tours by the U.S. Marine Band, led by Sousa. Between 1886 and 1892, Blakely told Lyman, he had made some $234,228 in profits.

25. Emily Howard to Blakely, St. Louis, October 1, 1893, BP, Band Correspondence.

26. Hartford *Times*, JPS 937-2.

27. Lowell *Journal*, JPS 937-2.

28. New York *World*, July 9, 1892, JPS 938-4. The *World* called Sousa's personality "intelligent and agreeable but severe and scholarly." However, it admitted there was great promise. The Wilkes-Barre *Record* was another newspaper arguing that "Sousa is not as magnetic as Gilmore," although it too appreciated his skillful training of the ensemble. JPS 937-3.

29. Both the Chicago *Inter-Ocean* and the Chicago *Times* were among those suggesting a name change. The Chicago *Times*, in a generally favorable review, wrote "The Marine Band of Washington has been so long famous that it would have been in better taste to have chosen an original name for the new organization. The encores were altogether too numerous and made the performance tiresome toward the end." JPS 937-2.

30. Chicago *Record*, JPS 937-2.

31. Hartford *Times*, JPS 937-2. The newspaper's comment here came in the context of describing the backing of "Chicago capital and all that money could do."

32. Philadelphia *Times*, JPS 937-2. The newspaper was commenting on an 1892 concert in Philadelphia's Academy of Music.

33. Philadelphia *Enquirer*, JPS 937-2. This newspaper, among many others, was still referring, in 1892 and 1893, to the inadequate salaries the government paid its musical artists.

34. Kansas City *Journal*, May 15, 1893, JPS 938-3. The Kansas City *Times*, May 15, 1893, JPS 938-3, complained about the small crowds coming to hear the Sousa Band on a Sunday, and also complimented Sousa for leading "the greatest military band in the country."

35. Boston *Herald*, JPS 937-2. "It will no longer be necessary to hold up the playing of the famous Garde Republicaine band of Paris as a standard of excellence."

36. Wilkes-Barre *Truth*, JPS 937-3.

37. "Coney Island," New York *Times*, July 18, 1880, p. 6. For some reason, during the summer of 1880 the *Times* was engaged in a campaign against brass bands, whose popularity it blamed on the Civil War's demoralization, long years of depression and poverty which had led many to "drown their miseries in brass" and the pernicious influence of bandmasters like Jules Levy. See "The Brass Instrument Habit," New York *Times*, July 28, 1880, p. 4; and "The American Brass Band," New York *Times*, August 25, 1880, p. 4.

38. Worcester *Telegram*, JPS 937-3.

39. This was a newspaper in Rockford, Illinois. JPS 937-2. The comment was made in 1892, while Sousa was making his first tour and expected to settle in Chicago.

40. Williamsport *News*, JPS 937-1.

41. Corning *Morning-Democrat*, JPS 937-1. In a similar genre, the Altoona *Tribune* observed of the Sousa Marine Band, "its superior has never been heard in Altoona." JPS 937-2.

42. One fascinating commentary on this was William F. Apthorp, "Orchestral Conducting and Conductors," *Scribner's Magazine* XVII (March, 1895): 384-92. The orchestra "has been converted into a great, composite musical instrument on which the conductor actually *plays*," and a generation of conducting virtuosi have sprung up, "exercising the same fascination over the great crowd of music-lovers that other virtuosi have, time out of mind." p. 387.

43. Saginaw *Globe*, JPS 937-1.

44. Brooklyn *Daily Eagle*, July 13, 1893, JPS 938-4.

45. Ibid., JPS 938-4.

46. Duluth *Herald*, May 20, 1893, JPS 938-3.

47. Syracuse *Standard*, May 9, 1893, JPS 938-2; Lewiston *Journal*, JPS 937-3; Duluth *Herald*, May 20, 1893, JPS 938-3.

48. Syracuse *Standard*, JPS 937-3. The *Standard* believed that Sousa was at heart "a leader of strings and his ideal in brass band music is not blare and a great volume of sound but true harmony. He is the Theodore Thomas of band leaders." This was said during the first tour of the independent band, 1892-93.

49. Buffalo *Enquirer*, May 10, 1893, JPS 938-2.

50. Syracuse *Standard*, May 9, 1893, JPS 938-2; a Rockford newspaper in 1892, JPS 937-2. Countless reviewers likened Sousa to a general, emphasizing his qualities of leadership. "To be able to command men is a gift possessed by comparatively few, and the great general is no more difficult to discover then the great conductor. . . . Not the least enjoyable thing about a Sousa band concert is the masterly control of the leader over the human instrumentality before him." Detroit *Tribune*, April 6, 1899, JPS 944-23.

51. For more on this subject see "Music and Manliness," *The Nation* LXXV (July 24, 1902): p. 66, which refers mainly to the English situation; and Edith Brower, "Is the Musical Idea Masculine?" *Atlantic Monthly* LXXIII (March, 1894): 332-39. "In the practical business world generally music has not been reckoned one of the manly arts," Edith Brower wrote, p. 333, but at the same time the vast majority of composers had been men.

52. An unidentified Buffalo newspaper in the summer of 1893, commenting on a Sousa concert at the Buffalo Music Hall, JPS 938-5.

53. A considerable literature has been devoted to this theme. See, among others, Robert H. Wiebe, *The Search for Order, 1877-1920* (New York, 1967); Burton Bledstein, *The Culture of Professionalism* (New York, 1976); Samuel Haber, *Efficiency and Uplift: Scientific Management in the Progressive Era, 1890-1920* (Chicago and London, 1964); Jerry Israel, ed., *Building the Organizational Society* (New York, 1972).

54. *Musical Courier*, February 8, 1905, p. 23. This was a reprint of an interview Sousa gave to the London *Daily Express*. In it, Sousa went on, "I know precisely what every one of my musicians is doing every second or fraction of a second that I am conducting. I know this because every single member of my band is doing exactly what I make him do."

55. Sousa, *Marching Along*, p. 153. There were limits, of course, to Sousa's showmanship. For a contemporary bandmaster, John S. Duss, who built his career primarily on showmanship and the work of a clever publicity agent, R. E. Johnston, see Richard D. Wetzel, *Frontier Musicians on the Connoquenessing, Wabash, and Ohio: A History of the Music and Musicians of George Rapp's Harmony Society (1805-1906)* (Athens, Ohio, 1976), chap. 6.

56. Unidentified New Britain newspapers, 1892, JPS 937-3.

57. Middlesex *Times*, 1892, JPS 937-2.

58. For an extended discussion of these issues see Joseph A. Mussulman, *Music in the Cultured Generation: A Social History of Music in America, 1870-1900* (Evanston, Ill., 1971). See also Arnold T. Schwab, *James Gibbons Huneker: Critics of the Seven Arts* (Stanford, 1963), for the development of a new kind of musical criticism and musical philosophy in America.

59. Gilmore to Blakely, St. Louis, October 18, 1891, BP, Band Correspondence.

60. New York *World*, July 9, 1893, JPS 938-4.

61. Kansas City *Journal*, May 15, 1893, JPS 938-3.

62. Elmira *Star*, undated, but during the first touring season, JPS 937-1.

63. Kansas City *Journal*, May 15, 1893, JPS 938-3.

64. Unidentified New York newspaper, July, 1893, JPS 938-5. Sousa was playing at the time at the Manhattan Beach Hotel which was not, this newspaper continued, "a conservatory of music where taste is to be cultivated and people to be educated, but a pleasure resort where they come to be entertained."

65. Chicago *Herald*, June 28, 1893, JPS 938-4.

66. Duluth *Daily Commonwealth*, May 20, 1893, JPS 938-3. The St. Paul *Pioneer Press*, May 21st, also found the program weak in places, arguing that Sousa's Salute of the Nations to the Columbian Exposition "is of the claptrap variety, and did not succeed in evoking much enthusiasm." JPS 938-3.

67. Springfield *Republican*, undated, but during the first touring season, JPS 937-3.

68. *Evening Wisconsin*, May 22, 1893, JPS 938-4.

69. Syracuse *Standard*, May 9, 1893, JPS 938-2. The brass band's function, the newspaper concluded, "is to play what Gilmore always called 'masculine music.'" And the Buffalo *Enquirer*, May 10, 1893, agreed that the band should play more military numbers and not try to imitate orchestral sounds. JPS 938-2.

70. Sousa interview in New York *World*, August 6, 1893, JPS 938-6. In this interview Sousa used medical analogies, arguing that the result is "being reached by homeopathic doses, so to speak; the allopathic treatment would not do at all in this case."

71. Sousa in Chicago *Herald*, June 27, 1893, JPS 938-4.

72. Chicago *Herald*, undated, during the first touring season, JPS 937-2. The *Herald* hoped that Sousa would bear in mind "that upon him, in a measure, devolves the responsibility of educating the taste of the people so that they may eventually learn to appreciate the higher forms of orchestral music. For band music always appeals to the masses and can thus be made a stepping stone to something higher."

73. Sousa in New York *Advertiser*, August 27, 1893, JPS 938-6. Here again, Sousa used the analogy of a skilled physician, saying he covered his pills with sugar.

74. Sousa, *Marching Along*, p. 275.

75. Ibid., p. 133.

76. Sousa in New York *Advertiser*, August 27, 1893, JPS 938-6. "The people who frequent my concerts are the strong and healthy," Sousa told an interviewer. "I mean the healthy both of mind and body. These people like virile music. Longhaired men and shorthaired women you never see in my audience. And I don't want them." Houston *Post*, May 17, 1903, JPS 951-11. This interview was given in Paris.

77. For more on Sousa's rivals in the late nineteenth century see H. W. Schwartz, *Bands of America* (Garden City, 1957). Schwartz treats Gilmore extensively, and devotes space to Liberati, Innes, Brooke, Creatore, Conway, Pryor, and Kryl.

78. *Musical Courier*, May 20, 1896, p. 23. In reprinting an article by W. S. B. Mathews, two years earlier, the *Courier* wrote, "The Sousa Band stands alone. It is at the head as much as the Boston Orchestra under Gericke was alone, or the Chicago Exposition Orchestra under Thomas was alone. Nothing has been heard better. . . . That is the beauty of Sousa. You can take culture from him without fatigue." *Musical Courier*, February 28, 1894, p. 21. And the same journal noted, in 1897, "Probably were men empowered and determined to plan an individual to fill the present position of John Philip Sousa invention would fall short in the detail of equipment which the brilliant leader so lavishly enjoys." *Musical Courier*, April 21, 1897, p. 26.

79. J. M. Bosworth, "Musical Comment," San Francisco *Examiner*, March 12, 1899, JPS 945-8.

80. Wilkes-Barre *Daily News*, April 19, 1899, JPS 944-18. "Gilmore's, Victor Herbert's," they are either past or "they never get close enough to the American people to make a comparison direct enough, generally speaking."

81. Dayton *News*, September 29, 1899, JPS 945-7.

82. New York *World*, August 18, 1899, JPS 945-3.

83. Wilkes-Barre *Sunday News*, no date indicated but probably April 1901, JPS 948-10. The article was an attack on critics who were hard on Sousa.

84. See, for example, the story in an 1898 New York newspaper about a local Richmond Hill lawyer, Darmstadt, who blackened his wife Martha's eye because she continually whistled the "Liberty Bell" march. He hit her and made slighting remarks about Sousa. Their case went to court. JPS 942-19. The Rochester *Democrat Chronicle*, November 17, 1897, reported that a Mr. Godfrey Warburton of Tenafly, New Jersey, smote his wife in the eye because she kept whistling Sousa's "Liberty Bell." Curiously, Mmes. Darmstadt and Warburton whistled the march continuously for the same period of time, four days and four nights. The Sousa press agents had a stock of phrases, anecdotes, and observations, which they presented to the local press.

85. Sousa, *Marching Along*, pp. 187-88.

86. Ibid., p. 196.

87. Buffalo *News*, September 17, 1905, JPS 1018-2.

88. New York *Evening Sun*, September 2, 1905; and Denver *Republican*, September 11, 1905, JPS 1018-2. The Cleveland *Plain Dealer* noted, "One would as soon expect a Sunday school library story from D'Annunzio or a ragtime from Puccini as a novel by Sousa," objecting that the story was too ordinary. September 14, 1905, JPS 1018-2. Another Sousa novel, *The Fifth String*, received somewhat better reviews, but got its share of spoofs.

89. John Philip Sousa, *Pipetown Sandy* (Indianapolis, 1905), p. 253.

90. Oakland *Enquirer*, March 18, 1899, JPS 944-14. And newspapers echoed this thought. Sousa "has none of the musical crankiness, none of the intolerance and rabid jealousy that are quite too familiar," a Wilkes-Barre newspaper wrote in 1905. "He does not affect 'airs' or wear his hair in such a shape as to decorate his coat collar. He is a manly, healthful, wholesome American, loaded with genius. . . . Work is his delight." JPS 953-10.

91. Wilkes-Barre *Evening Leader*, April 9, 1897, JPS 942-1.

92. John Philip Sousa, "The Business of the Bandmaster," *Criterion*, August, 1905, JPS 946-6. In the article Sousa insisted: "After twenty years of organization and hard training, entailing the personal examination of more than fifty thousand musicians and the training of perhaps five thousand of them, I have no hesitation in affirming that I have approached the ideal standard."

93. Sousa, *Marching Along*, p. 266.

94. Ibid., pp. 131-32.

95. Fannie Edgar Thomas, "John Philip Sousa in Paris," *Musical Courier*, June 13, 1900, p. 16.

96. Ibid., p. 17. The European triumphs added immeasurably to Sousa's reputation. In December 1901, after Sousa had been decorated by King Edward, the Brooklyn *Eagle* wrote, "The fact that Sousa and his band played for the birthday celebration of Queen Alexandra . . . will give to his concerns an enhanced value in the eyes of the multitude when he comes back to Manhattan Beach." JPS 948-40. Or the Hutchinson *Daily News*, November 17, 1904, "Sousa and his band have come and gone and the only American bandsman who has been able to make kings and queens tremble at will has made Hutchinson another visit." JPS 951-31.

97. Unidentified Duluth newspaper, 1897, JPS 942-2.

98. Kansas City newspaper in 1897, commenting on a concert at the Auditorium, JPS 942-3.

99. Lubov Keefer, *Baltimore's Music: The Haven of the American Composer* (Baltimore, 1962), p. 272. Note the Atlanta *Journal*, April 7, 1899, quoting one local figure that Atlanta must have band music in her parks. "Band music refines the people, it charms them . . . it whiles away the dull hours. It keeps people out of idleness." JPS 944-14. For more on music in the parks see Galen Cranz, *The Politics of Park Design: A History of Urban Parks in America* (Cambridge, Mass., 1982), pp. 10, 13, 258.

100. Everett Reynolds died in December 1905, and obituaries can be found in JPS 953-7. Reynolds's brother, Melville C. Reynolds, was business manager for the actress, Helen Modjeska. And see the obituary for David Blakely, *Inland Printer* XVIII (December, 1896), p. 321.

101. For more on the poster movement two contemporary works, Charles K. Bolton, *The Reign of the Poster* (Boston, 1895), and Charles Matlack Price, *Posters: A Critical Study of the Development of Poster Design in Continental Europe, England and America* (New York, 1913), are helpful, as are two later books, Victor Margolin, *American Poster Renaissance. The Great Age of Poster Design, 1890-1900* (New York, 1975); and Patricia Hills, *Turn-of-the-Century America* (New York, 1977). See also *Broadway Quarterly*, May 1901, JPS 948-7, for an interesting juxtaposition of Sousa's band and the magazine revolution.

102. JPS 953-11 contains many details on Sousa's statements. For a brief discussion of his attitudes see James R. Smart, *The Sousa Band: A Discography* (Washington, 1970), pp. 2-5. Sousa's hostility was extensive. He suggested that sales of musical instruments would lessen and that the vocal chords might become useless. "Wherever there is a phonograph the musical instrument is displaced. The time is coming when no one will be ready to submit himself to the ennobling discipline of learning music, whether instrumental or vocal. Everyone will have their ready made or ready pirated music in their cupboards." Sousa in New York *Morning Telegraph*, June 12, 1906, JPS 953-11. This was a period when canning was becoming an effective (and negative) metaphor. In 1906 "The Can Age" ran as an editorial in a New York periodical, treating illustrated books, slot machines, motion pictures, and simplified spelling. "If we can just crowd everything we want into a can and walk away with the original package, we are perfectly happy." JPS 153-14. And see "Canned Speeches," *Nation* LXXXVI (January 16, 1908): 53-54, an editorial commenting on a new book *Ready-Made Speeches*. Sousa's most complete statement on the subject was "The Menace of Mechanical Music," *Appleton's Magazine* VIII (September, 1906): 278-84. There were strong replies to this in *Appleton's* VIII (November, 1906): 638-40. For Sousa's extensive written work see Paul E. Bierley, *John Philip Sousa: A Descriptive Catalogue of His Works* (Urbana, Chicago, London, 1973), pp. 150-69. In his articles Sousa wrote on everything from baseball and horses to trap shooting, patriotism and, of course, music.

103. Unidentified Philadelphia newspaper, in early 1899, JPS 944-3. The Philadelphia *Inquirer*, January 15, 1899, conducted an imaginary dialogue between Sousa's body and the band, JPS 944-3.

104. New Haven *Leader*, May 8, 1899, JPS 944-20. "The conviction always presents itself afresh that if he laid down that stick the music would stop. Either he illustrates the music, or the music illustrates Sousa, one hardly knows which. When this original conductor turns his head on one side and gently trills the air with the left hand it really seems as though the sound was made by the motion."

105. H. M. Bosworth, "Musical Comment," San Francisco *Examiner*, March 12, 1899, JPS 945-8. "Call this del Sarte or what you will, I call it genius. . . . Whatever he 'conducts' his gestures convey to the audience the proper acceptance of the musical intention."

106. Chicago *Tribune*, September 19, 1903, JPS 951-20. See also Portland (Me.) *Advertiser*, April 1904, "Sousa's band couldn't be what it is without Mr. Sousa's curving figure, the graceful swing of his arms, his delightful nonchalance." JPS 951-27. There are hundreds of comments, scattered through the reviews, on Sousa's postures, gestures, mannerisms;

vaudeville artists made their living imitating Sousa, notably Walter Jones. The Burlington *Hawkeye*, February 15, 1898, wrote "Half the expressiveness of the Italian tongue, if one may venture an Irish bull, is in the gesticulation of the hands, and Sousa employs his after a very fascinating fashion." JPS 942-5.

107. Both quotations from unidentified newspapers, JPS 953-13. The Joplin *Globe*, September 18, 1906, insisted that mechanical music was "merely the instrument of awakening—just as great musicians have in childhood been roused to an ecstasy of delight and aspiration by the music of a humble street band." JPS 953-13.

108. Topeka *Daily Capital*, November 8, 1902, JPS 951-5. Some of the language employed by newspapers objecting to foreign bandsmen was nasty. A Newton, Kansas, newspaper wrote, November 17, 1904, that Sousa's Band contained only a "small number of foreigners of swarthy countenance, as was the case with Banda Rossa . . . most of them smoked cigars and not the nasty little cigarettes the foreign bandsmen seem to take to." JPS 951-31. The Bloomington *Pantagraph*, August 4, 1906, warned that the importation of Italian musicians threatened the existence of local musical organizations, and quoted a bandsman who prophesied that the local band would soon be a "crew of dark-skinned men from the country made famous as the home of Rome." JPS 953-13.

109. Springfield (Ohio) *Republican*, January 29, 1897, JPS 942-2.

110. Rev. M. F. Johnson, "Spiritual Suggestions from Sousa." A Sermon Preached in the Central Baptist Church, May 16, 1898, JPS 942-11. For an example of the Sousa-inspired poetry see "How John Philip Sousa Impressed the Gallery," originally in the Detroit *Journal*, reprinted by the Toledo *Blade*, July 16, 1899, JPS 944-23; and "Uncle Silas Hears Sousa's Band Play," Kalamazoo *Morning Gazette-News*, March 23, 1901, JPS 948-8. An example of the latter:

So I went down to the opery house an' got a fust class seat—
There wuz music in the atmosphere an' music in my feet,
An' when the band come on the stage an' Sousy, too, no doubt,
I jined the folks around me an' jest stamped for all git out.

I had that happy feeling' that I feel onct long ago,
Being' when I got religion over at East Alamo,
When Elder Higgins come to me an' prayed, he did, that night,
An' we kneeled around the altar an' I saw I "saw the light."

111. Unidentified newspaper, JPS 942-26.

112. Unidentified newspaper, JPS 942-26. There was considerable surprise expressed by journalists at the enthusiasm of audiences at these concerts. The "conservative people of Pittsfield involuntarily rose to their feet and waved hats and handkerchiefs in a perfect furore of patriotic enthusiasm," while the band performed the "Star-Spangled Banner." The same thing happened at New Haven in the spring of 1898. In late March, 5,000 at the Metropolitan Opera House rose to their feet during the "Star-Spangled Banner." "It was as if a current of electricity had passed from stage through stalls, boxes and galleries to the very roof of the auditorium. Everyone jumped to his feet. Hats were waved and handkerchiefs fluttered." JPS 942-26.

113. Chicago *Times-Herald*, April 20, 1898, JPS 942-28.

114. New York *Mirror*, September 15, 1898, JPS 943-2.

115. Chicago *Times-Herald*, May 1, 1898, JPS 942-28. "Slam-bang eccentricities in band play may tickle for a time, but one cannot live perpetually on red pepper and musical fireworks."

116. The Syracuse *Standard*, August 18, 1899, in an editorial, "Brass Bands and King Sousa," quoted the Washington *Post* and added its own comments. JPS 945-5.

117. Chicago *Post*, March 16, 1901, JPS 948-10. "Anything so trivial as a Sousa concert ought not to be considered seriously," the newspaper began, acknowledging, however, that Sousa took himself so seriously that he forced some kind of rigorous response. See also Frederick Stevenson of the Los

Angeles *Examiner*, October 26, 1907, who called Sousa the "Harriman of the Music World," one who knew advertising better than music. His band was fine, but played too much trash, Stevenson argued. JPS 953-21.

118. The Sousa interview which incorporated this remark was made in September 1903. It attracted widespread comment. See JPS 951-23. For more on the complex relationships among Sousa, ragtime, and jazz, see Edward A. Berlin, *Ragtime: A Musical and Cultural History* (Berkeley, Los Angeles, London, 1980), and William J. Schafer, *Brass Bands and New Orleans Jazz* (Baton Rouge and London, 1977).

119. St. Paul *Globe*, September 1903, JPS 951-23.

120. Rochester *Post-Express*, April 3, 1906, JPS 956-1. The following day the Geneva *Times*, April 4, 1906, condemned Sousa for playing common music like "Everybody Works But Father." It "seemed a prostitution and profanation of the art of music. This abominable song is such in itself. . . . But still greater was the disgrace that the people actually liked it." JPS 956-1.

121. "For Sousa has lost his gestures, his poses, his delsarte. No longer in great circles does his baton scrape the proscenium arch. The baseball swat and the ping pong volley are things of Sousa's past." San Francisco *Examiner*, October 17, 1904, JPS 951-30. "He is a subdued Sousa compared to what he used to be. Not that he was ever a contortionist. . . . He does not hump; he undulates." Irish *Independent*, February 16, 1911, JPS 966-5. "Perhaps the Sousa nonchalance is a bit accentuated; certain it is that he presents a more passive figure before his instrumental cohorts than of yore." Riverside *Press*, November 1, 1904, JPS 951-30.

122. "A band that has won such laurels in every great city of the world, and among foreigners jealous of and prejudiced against everything American, is something that does not come to Bakersfield every year." Bakersfield *Californian*, November 3, 1904, JPS 951-30.

123. "The Washington Post," New York *Times*, November 2, 1907, p. 8. The visitor was Arthur Walkeley, a drama critic for the London *Times*.

124. See New York *Herald*, June 29, 1918, JPS 979-2.

125. Oklahoma City *Oklahoman*, June 29, 1918, JPS 979-5.

126. Sousa indulged in attacks on various aspects of German culture during the war. At Willow Grove he announced, in the summer of 1918, "The greatest ambition of my life is to lead my band down the Wilhelmstrasse in Berlin playing 'The Star-Spangled Banner' for the delectation of the Hohenzollerns—or what is left of them." Philadelphia *Record*, August 19, 1918, JPS 979-5. On another occasion he declared, "The pro-German in America is the lowest, most sneaking, most cowardly thing on earth—he is even worse than a German in the German army, and that's about the limit of condemnation." Baltimore *News*, October 2, 1918, JPS 979-9. It should be pointed out that these remarks were not much different from many uttered by American cultural leaders at the same time; Sousa, once more, was quite representative.

127. *Musical Courier*, August 19, 1915, p. 22. Sousa was speaking to a reporter on the Spokane *Chronicle*.

128. And honest tunes provided another margin of safety in the postwar world. "If every Bolshevik were made to attend a week's course of concerts played by this famous band, the chances are that at the end of the week he would have caught the contagion and become a loyal citizen of these United States. You cannot think mean thoughts when you hear good music, and you cannot see Red Russia when you hear the 'Stars and Stripes Forever' or 'Who's Who in Navy Blue.' " Portsmouth (NH) *Times*, August 13, 1920, JPS 983-1.

129. D. C. Parker, "Sousa, Philosopher," *Musical Courier*, August 16, 1917, p. 32.

130. Sousa's interview with the Adelaide *Advertiser* was reprinted in the *Musical Courier*, September 9, 1911, p. 31.

131. For more on high school music programs, see Edward Bailey Birge, *History of Public School Music in the United States*, new ed. (Philadelphia, 1928, 1937).

Promotional copy for the Sousa Band. After his success with touring the U.S. Marine Band in 1891, under the management of David Blakely, Sousa retired from the Marines and started his own band, still under contract with Blakely. These testimonials were printed in advertising booklets published and distributed by Blakely.
Blakely Papers, New York Public Library. ▷

WHAT SOUSA'S BAND IS.

It is the Band of Manhattan Beach.

It is the Band of the St. Louis Exposition.

It is the Band of the May and June Concerts of the Madison Square Garden.

It was the great Band of the World's Fair.

It is the great Band of the California Mid-Winter Exposition.

It is the great Band of America and of the World.

Its leader is the magnetic John Philip Sousa, who made the fame of the U. S. Marine Band world-wide.

As a Bandmaster and as a Band composer he stands alone.

His "Washington Post March" has sold by the million.

His "High School Cadets" is a close second in the race.

His "Beau Ideal" is having a simply phenomenal sale.

His new "Liberty Bell," "Manhattan Beach," and "The Directorate" are already in enormous demand.

Hence, and rightfully, is Sousa proclaimed the "March King," and his band without an existing rival.

WHAT PROFESSIONAL MEN AND GREAT MUSICIANS SAY.

"Let me bear cordial testimony to the perfection of Sousa's Band, and his masterly leadership of it."—DUDLEY BUCK, the distinguished composer.

"Sousa's concerts constitute the best performances of any band I have ever heard."—ALEX. LAMBERT, the eminent Pianist, and Director New York College of Music.

"Sousa's Band stands alone, just as the Boston Symphony or the Thomas Orchestra stands alone."—W. S. B. MATHEWS, the distinguished Chicago Musical Editor, Author and Critic.

"The performances of Sousa's Band are a revelation and delight."—HOMER N. BARTLETT, the eminent Pianist and Composer.

"It is a revelation in military music "—NAHAN FRANKO, the well-known New York Violin Virtuoso.

"It is without doubt the best military and concert band in the country."—WARREN DAVENPORT, Musical Editor *Boston Traveller.*

"I consider Sousa to-day the greatest bandmaster living."—Major J. B. POND, the great Lecture Manager.

"I have heard many bands in my time, but never such a one as Sousa's."—DEWOLF HOPPER.

"It gave the best concert I ever heard "—BARNABEE, of the Bostonians.

"The band is a marvel. Its pianissimos are as soft and melodious as the spinning tones of the human voice."—LUISI CAPPIANI, the eminent vocal teacher.

"It is to-day the finest organization of the kind in America." J. THOMAS BALDWIN, Leader Boston Cadet Band.

Nineteenth-Century American March Music and John Philip Sousa

by Pauline Norton

Historical hindsight has established the march form developed by John Philip Sousa as the standard for march composition of the twentieth century. From the perspective of the nineteenth century, however, John Philip Sousa appears at the end of a rich and varied tradition represented by that century's American march music. The conception of the march as a single, rigid musical form did not exist within that tradition. Rather than the march, there existed "music for marching," which included a variety of multistrained forms composed with a strong, steady beat for the purpose of regulating even and uniform stepping. As John W. Moore neatly put it in 1852, the march "is usually quick for ordinary marching, and slow for grand occasions, but no general rules can be laid down for its composition."[1]

The march experienced immense popularity throughout the nineteenth century, the idea of the march—its forward processional movement, and mechanical regularity and uniformity—expressing one of the most basic and pervasive ordering principles of that time. The march served as music for the parade and military band, ballroom, musical theater, parlor, concert hall, and circus. In the very broadest sense, the march in the nineteenth century can be interpreted as a generic term that included all music with a strong, duple beat and multistrained form that could accompany marching. In this way it is possible to understand why nineteenth-century writers sometimes classified galops, polkas, polonaises—even waltzes—as marches. That lack of precise definition imported to march music a fluidity, malleability, and viability that made march music adaptable to the many needs and purposes of nineteenth-century composers.[2]

Nineteenth-century march composition demonstrates three distinct styles, roughly corresponding to the beginning, middle, and end of the century. The "grand march style," with its ceremonial fanfare melodies, slow tempos, dense

Grand March Style - Governor Tomkins New Grand March by James Hewitt (1808-10)

Quickstep Style - Livingston Guards Quick Step by Claudio S. Grafulla (1838-45)

March Style - Brooke's Triumphant March by Raphael Fassett (1894)

43

chordal texture, and heavily accented rhythms dominated the early years of the century; the "quickstep style," with its quick tempos, light swinging rhythms, and lyrical or lilting melodies, was predominant in midcentury; and the more dramatic chordal character, yet rhythmically independent bassline and singable melody of the "march style" emerged in the late nineteenth century. None of these styles, from an historical perspective, has greater significance than the others. Each emerged in response to the conditions and circumstances which characterized the period of its popularity. The quickstep was essentially a new musical form at the opening of the nineteenth century, having emerged from the musical accompaniment of the cadenced step in eighteenth-century military tactics. With its emphasis on tuneful rhythmic melody, and light drum bass accompaniment, the quickstep provided the most significant influence on the nature and structure of nineteenth-century march composition.[3] In the early nineteenth century, the grand march style was the older and more developed musical style, having served the dual role of musical standard for the seventeenth- and eighteenth-century noble-military class and accompaniment for the processional—both in the context of social and theatrical dance as well as outdoor and indoor ceremonial occasions. While the style of the grand march had less influence on the composition of American march music, the ceremonial associations and function of the grand march as dance and parade music remained an integral part of the American march tradition throughout the nineteenth century.

The synthesis of the march style found in Sousa's marches emerges in the 1890s. The preceding decades of the 1870s and 1880s, however, represent the richest and most varied period of nineteenth-century march composition. Musical features which were to characterize the march style had begun to emerge and appeared in march music together with the characteristics of the earlier march styles. David Wallace Reeves, who composed at this time what some consider to be the finest examples of the street march,[4] established the countermelody as an important feature of march composition, an initial step in freeing the bass from its traditional role of accompaniment for the melody. An operatic lyricism, the jiglike character of minstrel tunes, dance rhythms—particularly those of the polka, galop, and waltz—the virtuosic melodies that featured the lead cornet of the brass band, and the bravura style of the parlor piano march had all characterized march music of the midnineteenth century, and all still appeared in march music composed in these two decades. Marches were generally composed in da capo form, which permitted the constant repetition demanded of dance and parade music. Several features not found in earlier march music began to appear regularly: introductions, generally four bars; the march trio form, the trio functioning as a contrasting strain of a softer and more lyrical quality; and a two- or four-bar interlude preceding the trio. The "break" strain of the twentieth-century march was not a regular feature of the nineteenth-century march.

Standardization, however, seemed a remote concept when compared to the compositional practices affecting march music in the 1870s and 1880s. The arrangement of already existing melodies rather than the composition of new melodies was still common practice, while the improvisatory nature of performance practices, both for parades and in the dance hall, created a far different effect for the march than the one notated in published form. Yet the influence of economic and social factors, that of Germanic music culture being one of the most important, had begun to effect major changes in the approach to march composition. The latter included, most significantly, the concept of music professionalism, the emphasis on original composition, the celebration of the individual composer, and the importance granted harmony as opposed to melody.[5]

The declining popularity of the street band and the simultaneous increase in the popularity of the concert band provided two other factors influencing these changes. Economic conditions played a major role in the declining popularity of the street band, as demonstrated by the growth of musicians' unions in the 1880s. The desire to improve musical performance in America was undeniably an important factor in their formation. Their avowed purpose to improve the quality of band musicians resulted in a policy of screening and examining members before granting them union membership. But the unions also sought to improve the economic status of bandsmen by demanding higher wages:[6]

> Previous to the formation of musical unions music was in a very demoralized state, particularly to those who by education were compelled to practice it for their living, and very bad for those who were compelled to hear it . . . The leader collects the stipend, his orchestra made up of his pupils and ambitious amateurs, who were glad to give their services to see the play and to pride themselves as being members of an orchestra. The leader pockets the lion's share of cash and not infrequently keeps it all. This applies to military bands, etc.
>
> The union prevents all this; every member before being voted for must pass an examination proving himself qualified to become a member.[7]

The movement to improve the quality of the bands, however, had far-reaching consequences for the band world, for it eventually helped to put street bands, both professional and amateur, out of business. When the efforts of the musicians' unions won increased wages for bandsmen, organizations which had traditionally hired street bands sought ways in which to reduce their expenses. In the *Musicial Courier* (1880), Claudio S. Grafulla, leader of the well-known Seventh Regiment Band, claimed that as a means of cutting costs, the directors of the Pier at Coney Island demanded that he reduce the size of his band.[8] A month later, the *Courier* reported that the Musical Union (Musical Mutual Protective Union of New York City) had raised musicians' wages to twenty-eight dollars per week, an action which prompted the rumor that Patrick Gilmore had gone to Europe to hire foreign musicians who would work for lower wages.[9] While Gilmore denied the rumor, organizations did in fact turn to the employment of foreign musicians as a means of reducing costs.

While the professional street band was established in the 1890s, it was not destined for long existence. Whatever the reasons—high wages, the economic depression of the early 1890s—professional bandsmen of the 1890s had difficulty finding jobs.[10] Only the big, successful, profit-making business bands, like those of John Philip Sousa, Frederick Innes, and Giuseppe Creatore, were surviving. The point is an important one, for these bands were concert bands, not marching bands, and as the declining popularity of the street band was accompanied by a loss of interest in the street march, so the growing success of the concert band was accompanied by the growing popularity of the concert march.

The emergence of the concert band began about midcentury, stimulated by the American visit of Antoine Jullien in the early 1850s. The initial development of the concert band is generally attributed to Patrick Gilmore, although it was under the leadership of John Philip Sousa at the end of the nineteenth century and in the early twentieth that the concert band is thought to have experienced its most successful period.[11]

In 1887, the *Metronome* noted the influence of concert performance on march composition: "Few leaders seem to realize the fact that the best march for concert purposes is not, as a rule, the best for street use."[12] In 1896, the journal published a series of articles on the composition of march and dance music which revealed both the growing importance of the concert march as well as an increased "formalism"—the idea of prescribed rules—in march composition. The form prescribed for march writing in this series emphasized the features of the late nineteenth-century march, including most noticeably distinct march and trio sections, and a specified length (number of measures) for both the individual strains and the entire composition. The *Metronome* included the concert march as a march type, and recommended to march composers that they use the marches of European composers as models for the composition of concert marches, particularly the "works of Schubert, Mendelssohn, Wagner, and other composers." Mendelssohn's celebrated *Wedding March* and Wagner's *Tannhauser* march were cited "as examples worthy of special study."[13]

Sousa's marches had become enormously popular by the time of the publication of the *Metronome* article. While the compositional style that Sousa developed appears to represent a formula, Sousa does not appear to have consciously and deliberately attempted to create such a formula, nor to have turned to foreign music traditions as models for his own marches. Sousa seems to have approached march writing in the way Americans had approached it throughout the century—in response to the particular functions required for the music and by using as models the marches of other American composers immediately at hand. His particular talent and abilities created a style that responded better than that of any other march composer to the events, needs, and purposes of the late nineteenth century.

In contrast to the traditional march, Sousa used the through-composed rather than da capo form, and expanded the two-bar or four-bar interlude preceding the trio into a full break strain of eight or sixteen measures. Most importantly, he changed the conception of the trio from a soft, lyrical strain that had traditionally contrasted with the louder and more rhythmically forceful march strains to a grand climactic ending. He achieved this by playing the trio first softly, followed by the break strain which included an antiphonal rela-

tionship between the treble and bass, a repeated rhythmic pattern, and forte dynamics; a repetition of the trio, still piano; again the break strain, and finally the trio, played fortissimo. Another technique that Sousa adapted to heighten the drama of his marches was to revert to the earlier practice in march composition of using only a single key change, which in his marches moved exclusively to the subdominant at the trio.

Sousa's conception of the march form ideally succeeds only on the theatrical or concert stage. The time which a bystander has to hear the music performed by a band as it marches past is too brief to permit a complete performance of a Sousa march, and a complete performance is necessary in order to receive the full impact of the dramatic design. The influence of the theater on Sousa's march style is indicated in his statement on composition: "The chief aim of the composer is to produce color, dynamics, nuances and to emphasize the story-telling quality."[14] The idea that a march should tell a story was a concept entirely outside the scope of march composition until Sousa. The traditional march provided a good melody, a strong beat, and its form permitted continuous repetition, a practice which ruled out any "story-telling quality." Sousa, however, used a variety of dynamic, melodic, and rhythmic contrasts, which he manipulated to create the suspense and tension which he released in his grand, climactic finales.

A major influence on Sousa's march style did in fact come from the American musical theater. March music had long accompanied the formation of figures and evolutions on the theatrical stage, the practice dating back several centuries in European dance history.[15] Called military drills in the nineteenth century, such formations were danced by both women and men, and remained a common feature of theatrical productions into the twentieth century. The popularity of such drills in the musical theater experienced an upsurge with the sensational success of *The Black Crook* (1866) in which women performed carefully staged drills designed to permit the display of legs. Called the "Amazon march," it became a standard feature of theatrical productions and "the dance form," Gerald Bordman writes, "that most seriously rivaled classic ballet until the waltzes of *The Merry Widow* (1907) swept it away."[16] The Amazon march was further popularized with the arrival from England in 1868 of Lydia Thompson, who, with her troupe of young, blond women, established the burlesque as one of the most popular American theatrical forms of the next seventy years.[17] Dressing her company in tights and male clothing, she incorporated the drills and high kick that showed off the leg to such advantage,[18] and in the process established a tradition which is still continued by the Rockettes at Radio City Music Hall.

The military drill experienced another upsurge of popularity in the musical theater through the presentation of the military drill as a burlesque of the then currently popular militia companies. The innovation was first introduced in the farce-comedy, *The Mulligan Guards Ball* (1879) created by Edward Harrigan, Tony Hart, and David Braham. The march song, which combined lyrics with a strong martial beat, accompanied the performers in their singing and stepping.[19]

Indirectly, Gilbert and Sullivan's *H.M.S. Pinafore*, which opened the same year as *The Mulligan Guards Ball*, contributed to the development of the march song in the musical theater. The importance of Gilbert and Sullivan's influence lay not in the march song itself, but rather the great success with ensemble singing which Arthur Sullivan presented in a style emphasizing rhythm rather than tuneful melody.[20] That factor has particular importance because of its apparent influence on Sousa's compositional style, Sousa being the first composer to successfully present comic opera in a format emphasizing the march song.

Gilbert and Sullivan and, to a lesser extent, Jaques Offenbach provided perhaps the most important influence on the music of Sousa. Paul Bierley, in fact, has speculated whether Sousa might not have chosen a career in musical theater had he not been offered the position of director of the U.S. Marine Band.[21] Sousa's major instrument was the violin, and he both performed in and conducted several theater orchestras, including that of Ford's Theater in Washington, D.C., and the Washington Theatre Comique.[22] In 1879, the same year as the debut of *H.M.S. Pinafore*, Sousa became director of the Amateur Opera Company in Washington and, succumbing to popular demand for the Gilbert and Sullivan opera, the company mounted its own production with Sousa's orchestration. The company took the production to New York where it was performed at the Broadway Theatre for a period of seven weeks. According to Sousa, Gilbert and Sullivan heard one of these performances, and Sullivan commented favorably on Sousa's orchestration.[23]

Sousa composed seven operettas before his first success with *El Capitan* in 1897. Reviewers noted the heavy emphasis on the march song in *El Capitan* by criticizing the operetta for being nothing more than a "combination of a lot of marches."[24] That a certain novelty, however, was present in Sousa's music is indicated by still another critic who observed that Sousa had followed "his old method and given new rhythms in everything." It was this factor, the critic claimed, which had helped make *El Capitan* the "greatest success known in years."[25]

Sousa's style in the music of *El Capitan* was essentially the same as that of his individual march compositions. The concept of the song in relation to Sousa's marches, however, should not be thought of in melodic terms alone, but rather, as in Gilbert and Sullivan, as sung harmony. Unlike David Braham's march songs for the *Mulligan Guards*, whose melodies possessed the tunefulness of an Irish jig or American quickstep, Sousa's melodies emphasized a more marked accent and frequent leaps, which made them, like those of Arthur Sullivan, difficult to sing.[26] It has been noted that Sousa's melodies are more easily played on the violin (his own instrument) than on the cornet.[27] The point is an interesting one with respect to the influence of the musical theater on Sousa's march style, for marches composed for the brass band were traditionally written for the cornet as lead melodist, the cornet using the human voice as its aesthetic ideal.[28]

 Gilbert and Sullivan's operettas, which popularized the grand ensemble finale, provided one important influence on Sousa's conception of the march. Richard Wagner provided another. Sousa placed Wagner first on his list of the nineteenth century's great opera composers and considered Wagner's orchestration—as well as that of Richard Strauss, Elgar, Dvorak, and Tschaikovsky—to be most similar to his own.[29] He paralleled the dramatic mood of the compositional works of these composers to that of romantic drama in which, he writes, "it is not incongruous to see a comedy scene immediately follow a tragic one. . . . It does not shock me to see laughter follow tears in the romantic drama."[30] Sousa frequently programmed Wagner not only, as Charles Church claims, because Wagner's music was ideally suited to wind band transcription, but also because of its great dramatic appeal. Theodore Thomas, whom Sousa also admired, described the appeal of Wagner's emotionalism for late nineteenth-century audiences:

I have always believed in climaxes, also in giving people the most recent musical productions, and Wagner is the composer who satisfied both these essentials. . . . He represents the modern spirit, and his effective scoring makes the desired climax. Wagner excites his hearers, especially the younger generation, and interests the less musical.[31]

Sousa indicated the same sentiments in his explanation of the programming of Wagner's *Tannhäuser* overture:

I have made "Tannhaeuser Overture" as popular as "The Stars and Stripes." I played the "Tannhaeuser Overture" in a little town of three thousand, and they enjoyed the "Tannhaeuser." If I had not got these people stirred up by the pleasure of listening to and enjoying the "Tannhaeuser," they would have been too much down in the dumps to ask for a Sousa march. My two most popular pieces are the "Tannhaeuser Overture" and the "Stars and Stripes." . . . At Fargo (we were then at Winnipeg) I got a telegram saying: "In the name of a hundred citizens of Fargo, will you kindly put the "Tannhaeuser" on your program? Don't put it No. 1, because we want the house to be quiet." I put it No. 6 on the program. Everyone wanted to hear "Tannhaeuser," not because it was "Tannhaeuser," but because they loved it; it appealed to them; and I think I have done more missionary work for the better class of music than all the rest of them together. I think so. Wagner was a brass band man, anyway.[32]

 The appeal and popularity in the 1890s of both Wagner's and Sousa's music are understandable within the context of the general excitement, energy, and intense nationalism which so characterized the last decade of the nineteenth century. The belief in evolutionary progress that developed in that century was thought to have culminated in the 1890s, the Columbian Exposition held in Chicago in 1893 perhaps being the most impressive celebration of that idea. As John Higham has noted, the 1890s witnessed a period when "women became more manly," and "men became more martial." By then the Civil War had become an event of the past, and a cultivation of militarism had begun which would culminate in the Spanish-American War:

Meanwhile, flag ceremonies, such as the newly contrived pledge of allegiance, entered the school houses of the land. Patriotic societies multiplied as never before. In function they resembled the cheerleaders, who were becoming so prominent a part of the big football spectacles and who lifted the massed ranks of students into a collective glory. The link between the new athleticism and the new jingoism was especially evident in the yellow press: William Randolph Hearst's *New York Journal* created the modern sports page in 1896, just when its front page filled with atrocity stories of the bloody debauchery of Spanish brutes in Cuba. At the same time the new music produced such martial airs as John

Philip Sousa's masterpiece of patriotic fervor, "The Stars and Stripes Forever."[33]

In 1896, Rupert Hughes provided this comment on Sousa's music: "The music is conceived in a spirit of high martial zest. It is proud and gay and fierce, thrilled and thrilling with triumphs. . . . The glory of Mr. Sousa is that he was the first to write in this style, that he has made himself a style."[34] In 1901, the *Morning Leader* printed this statement: "Sousa is more than a mere band composer, he represents the energy and blatant assertiveness of America. His music is idiomatic of his race. To a great extent he is the Rudyard Kipling of music— the Kipling of slang and daring idiom."[35] And one London critic wrote: "Here ('Stars and Stripes') is the very quintessence of military music. . . . In short, Sousa in his music really represented not only himself but his country. . . . I am convinced that his marches are in reality the most valuable contribution that American music has yet made to the world."[36]

Such commentaries on Sousa and his music have significance not only because of their reference to the nature of Sousa's style, but because they also point to the emergence and celebration of a composer of march and dance music as a distinct personality. March music, as well as dance, had existed as a repertoire whose composers were generally unknown to the public. The names of approximately twelve hundred composers of march music were gathered for this study and, of those few names recognized today, almost all composed in the last decade of the nineteenth century. For most of the century, march and dance music were advertised by genre and title first, and by composer or arranger second. The widely accepted practice of arranging in the nineteenth century appears to have evolved because of the strong link with oral tradition in music history. Specifically, the practice prevailed of adapting an already existent melody or tune, often identified by a single work or title, to fit a variety of texts or purposes. *Dixie* serves as a good example, the name of its composer, Dan Emmett, still being generally unknown to most people.[37] The *Musical Courier* reported in 1880:

It is singular that the great majority of those who listen with pleasure to the strains of a waltz, a polka, or a galop, have no idea of what is the title of the composition, or the name of the author. Indeed, the musicians are often no better informed than the audience, since most of them are in the habit of reading the notes without noticing the name of the piece or the composer on the printed sheet.[38]

In 1895, a change in such composition had been observed:

When we look back to—say twenty years—we cannot recall many composers whose names are identified with march writing. . . . Within the past decade, however, everything has changed and we see that composers of fine marches have taken the front rank and are holding it against all comers. It is but necessary to mention such names as Tobani, Sousa, Herman, Reeves, Puerner, Innes, Brooks, Reed and many others, to realize what rapid strides we have made in this direction. When any of the composers named sits down to write a new march he has a definite purpose before him; he does not borrow the ideas from others or wholly use a melody already constructed, unless he is to elaborate upon it by working it up into a new theme.[39]

The compositional practices of late nineteenth-century writing seem to have emerged, as they had throughout the century, not from consultation with established procedures, but from a process that was to some degree unconscious. Sousa, like other march composers of the period, was a part of that process. As noted earlier, the rigidity of form that Sousa's marches have come to represent is a judgment granted them by historical hindsight. At the time in which Sousa developed his style, the looseness and malleability which had characterized the march form throughout the nineteenth century were still very much in existence, and, in fact, made possible the means by which the particular stylistic and structural developments of late nineteenth-century marches, such as those of Sousa, could occur.

Much of the stereotype of rigidity attributed to the march derives from the idea of the regularity of beat, rhythm, and tempo found in march music. But while regular, the nature and quality of the beat and rhythm in nineteenth-century march music varied considerably. Much attention, for example, is given to the change in rhythms of the 1890s influenced by the music of black Americans. What many do not realize, however, is the novelty also granted to the rhythms composed by John Philip Sousa.[40] The kind of rigidity associated with the march appears to have come more from its association with the military and its emphasis on uniformity and precision of movement, than from any inherent quality in march music itself.

March music was the nineteenth century's popular music, a music which seems to have had one foot in each of what H. Wiley Hitchcock has defined as the vernacular and cultivated traditions. The particular example of nineteenth-century American march composition, however, suggests a reworking of Hitchcock's definition, one in which the vernacular tradition, such as that of the folk ballad, is expanded to regard musical form and structure as belonging to the community, which grants the individual performer-composer only limited ways in which to establish an identity within that form and structure. In contrast, the cultivated tradition which distinguishes between the performer and composer, grants individual composers the license to change that form and structure in any way they choose. Popular music—in this case, march music—possesses qualities of both categories to varying degrees. Like that of the cultivated tradition, a distinction occurs between the composer and performer, and composers have some freedom to express their individual personalities; but, like the vernacular tradition, there is still a sense in which the form is communal and composers are expected to conform to that communal understanding. The history of nineteenth-century march writing shows a movement from an association closer to the vernacular tradition at the beginning of the century to one closer to the cultivated at the end of the century. The emergence of the march composer as a distinct personality in the 1880s provides an example of that shift. John Philip Sousa is, of course, one example, and Charles Ives is still another, Ives's highly individualistic style setting him squarely within the cultivated tradition. Rather than adapting features of the American popular tradition to the ideals and principles of the European classical tradition, Ives accepted American compositional and performance practices as he found and heard them and incorporated them directly into his music. He went one step further; he took the spirit of those practices and made them the ideals and principles of his own writing. Rather than the "harsh discords" of street band playing observed by John Sullivan Dwight or the "excruciating manner" of brass band performances and "senseless fashion" observed in the *Metronome*, Ives noted on his manuscript for the *Fourth of July:* "they didn't always play right & together & it was good either way."[41] Ive's works contain numerous examples revealing his roots in the musical genres popular at the close of the century: "We Are There!" and "Son of a Gambolier," both march songs; *Country Band March, Circus Band March*, and *March Intercollegiate*, obviously marches; *Over the Pavement*, based in part on street dance rhythms; and *The Gong on the Hook and Ladder*, written in the spirit of the annual fire company parade, an event where "nobody always seemed to 'keep step,' but they got there just the same."[42]

Jonathan Elkus has observed that given Ives's nostalgic ties to the events and forms of his childhood, Sousa's marches were composed too late for them to have been part of that experience

50

and an influence on Ives's writing. Ives's fondness for the traditional street band quickstep is indicated in his music by his frequent quotation of Reeve's *Second Connecticut Regiment Quickstep*, of which he wrote: "as good a march as Sousa or Schubert ever wrote, if not better!"[43] Ives's associating Sousa with Schubert needs to be emphasized here, for while Ives's ties may have been with the traditional march, his own works indicate the influence of the practices that had emerged in march composition during the 1890s. *The Intercollegiate March* (1895), for example, contains a separate introduction, the regularity of sixteen-measure strains, and a sixteen-measure break strain before the trio in Sousa's antiphonal style. But his ties with the earlier quickstep are also clear. Instead of Sousa's "story-telling" concept, the march uses the traditional da capo form which, in the humorous spirit of the band tradition, "wrench(es) us a not-very-nice half step" back from the A major of the trio to the A-minor triad which begins the introduction.[44]

About 1910 the popularity of the march began to decline, the march to become in the twentieth century a music of tradition rather than a viable expression of popular taste. That role was to be assumed most immediately by jazz, whose rhythms had first been anticipated in ragtime. Perhaps, then, it is not without significance that the first performance of the *Stars and Stripes Forever* took place in 1897, the same year as the first sheet music publication of ragtime, William H. Krell's "Mississippi Rag." The *Stars and Stripes*, which the twentieth century would come to consider the classic example of the American march, in a sense provided the grand finale of a music whose era was ending, while the new "temper" of ragtime, as Isaac Goldberg has written, had begun to "undermine, as new rhythms always undermine, the order of things-as-they-were."[45]

Notes

1. John W. Moore, *Complete Encyclopedia of Music* (Boston: Oliver Ditson & Co., 1852; 1854), p. 559.

2. Both my experience and observation with this concept of a "march identity" appear similar to Thomas Kuhn's observation that the paradigm can operate without "a formulation of rules and assumptions," that scientists can still be guided by the paradigm, even though they cannot give a full interpretation, identification, or rationalization of it. Kuhn makes special reference to Michael Polanyi's argument "that much of the scientist's success depends upon 'tacit knowledge,' i.e., upon knowledge that is acquired through practice and that cannot be articulated explicitly." Thomas S. Kuhn, *The Structure of Scientific Revolutions*, 2d ed., Foundation of the Unity of Science (Chicago: University of Chicago Press, 1970), XI (no. 2): 44.

3. Pauline Norton, "March Music in Nineteenth-Century America" (Ph.D. diss., University of Michigan, 1983). See pp. 123-76.

4. David L. Stackhouse, "D. W. Reeves and His Music, Part I," *Journal of Band Research* 5, no. 1 (Spring, 1969): 19.

5. Henry A. Pochmann, *German Culture in America* (Madison: The University of Wisconsin Press, 1957), pp. 63, 322; "Promotion of the Arts," *Musical Magazine* 3, no. 62 (May 22, 1841): 160; *Journal of the Fine Arts. Formerly The Message Bird* (new series), no. 28 (September 1850): 447; John Mueller, *American Symphony Orchestra* (Bloomington: Indiana University Press, 1951), p. 33; Frederic Louis Ritter, *Music in America* (New York: Charles Scribner's Sons, 1890), p. 337; Nicolas Slonimsky, "Plush Era in American Concert Life," in Paul Henry Lang, *One Hundred Years of Music in America* (New York: G. Schirmer, Inc., 1966), p. 111; George P. Upton, "Musical Societies of the United States and Their Representation at the World's Fair," quoted in Joseph Mussulman, *Music in the Cultured Generation* (Evanston: Northwestern University Press, 1971), p. 77.

6. The demand for higher wages was in part provoked by the great increase in the cost of living that occurred at the end of the century. Robert Grant, for example, published a series of articles in 1895 in which he discussed the admittedly difficult but possible way in which a man could live like a gentleman on $10,000 a year. Only a decade earlier, Stowe Persons points out, Grant and his family had maintained four maids for a total of $62 in wages a month on an annual budget of between $6,500 and $7,500 a year. Stowe Persons, *The Decline of American Gentility* (New York and London: Columbia University Press, 1973), p. 102.

7. *Metronome* 10, no. 3 (March 1894): 3.

8. *Musical Courier* 1, no. 8 (March 27, 1880): 119.

9. *Musical Courier* 1, no. 11 (April 17, 1880): 157.

10. Glenn Bridges, *Pioneers in Brass* (Detroit: Sherwood Publications, 1965), p. 28.

11. James Ferguson has observed the growth in the popularity of the concert band at the end of the nineteenth century in his study of the Vicksburg, Mississippi, Silver Cornet Band. He divides the history of the band into three distinct periods: the first, marked by the association of the band with the Vicksburg fire company in the years 1871-84, in which it performed almost exclusively in parades; the second, beginning in 1885, when it performed at military drills and field competitions; and the third, its most successful period, when it existed primarily as a concert organization, a period which began in 1893 after the decline in popularity of military activities. James Smith Ferguson, "A History of Music in Vicksburg, Mississippi, 1820-1900" (Ph.D. diss., University of Michigan, 1970), pp. 135-36.

12. Walt Lewis, "Stray Notes," *Metronome* 3, no. 2 (February 1887): 3.

13. *Metronome* 12, no. 7 (July 1896): p. 9.

14. John Philip Sousa, *Marching Along* (Boston: Hale, Cushman and Flint, 1928), p. 332.

15. One of the best-known examples occurred in the grand ballet of Balthasar de Beaujoyeulx's *Ballet Comique de la reine* (1581).

16. Gerald Bordman, *American Musical Theatre* (New York: Oxford University Press, 1978), p. 19.

17. Cecil Smith, *Musical Comedy in America* (New York: Theatre Arts Books, Robert M. MacGregor, 1950), p. 30.

18. Ibid., pp. 30-33; Bordman, *American Musical Theatre*, p. 25.

19. In David Braham's march song, *The Mulligan Guard*, the drums began the music with a six-bar introduction, followed by an eight-bar section for fife and drum, and twelve bars scored for orchestra. Singing was scored for sixteen bars, after which the marching began. Following a second verse, and an orchestral interlude of eight bars, the Mulligan Guard presented "arms" to an accompaniment of drum rolls. The meter changed from 2/4 to 6/8 for an eight-bar jig played by the "target excursion band." The music concluded with a sixteen-bar chorus in 2/4, to which the Mulligan Guard sang and marched. Stanley Appelbaum, *Show Songs from the Black Crook to the Red Mill* (New York: Dover Publications, Inc., 1964), pp. 14-16.

20. Gervase Hughes, *The Music of Arthur Sullivan* (New York: St. Martin's Press, Inc., 1960), pp. 94, 119, 128-29.

21. Paul E. Bierley, *John Philip Sousa: A Descriptive Catalogue of His Works* (Urbana: University of Illinois Press, 1973), p. 9; Paul E. Bierley, *John Philip Sousa: American Phenomenon* (Englewood Cliffs, New Jersey: Prentice-Hall, Inc., 1973), pp. 120-21.

22. Bierley, *American Phenomenon*, p. 35.

23. Ibid., pp. 41, 129; Sousa, *Marching Along*, p. 64.

24. John Lathrop Mathew, "El Capitan, A Comic Opera by Sousa," *Music* 10 (May 1896): 166.

25. Ibid, p. 164.

26. Hughes, *Arthur Sullivan*, pp. 88, 92.

27. Bierley, *Catalogue*, p. 31.

28. Bower Church, noted cornetist of the late nineteenth century, purportedly studied with a vocal instructor in order to learn to breathe and phrase properly. Albert Weldon, in advertising his services as a cornet teacher, offered to teach "legato tonguing, embellishments of all kinds, expression, and song playing." Practically, however, the voice also served as a suitable model for the cornet, since the compass of each was approximately the same. Bridges, *Pioneers in Brass*, pp. 21, 84.

29. Sousa, *Marching Along*, p. 180.

30. Ibid., p. 275.

31. Ibid., pp. 130-31; *Theodore Thomas, A Musical Autobiography*, ed. George Upton (Chicago: A. C. McClurg & Co., 1905), 2:15-17.

32. "Sousa and His Mission," *Music* 16 (July 1899): 274-75.

33. John Higham, "The Reorientation of American Culture in the 1890s," in *Writing American History* (Bloomington/London: Indiana University Press, 1970), p. 84.

34. Charles Fremont Church, Jr., "The Life and Influence of John Philip Sousa " (Ph.D. diss., Ohio State University, 1942), p. 309.

35. Ibid., p. 187.

36. Francis Toye, London *Morning Post*, 1932, quoted in Church, "Sousa Life and Influence," p. 314.

37. Hans Nathan, *Dan Emmett and the Rise of Negro Minstrelsy* (Norman: University of Oklahoma Press, 1962), pp. 247-74.

38. *Musical Courier* 1, no. 16 (May 24, 1880): 221.

39. *Metronome* 6, no. 6 (June 1895): 3.

40. The distinctively light, springing quality of Sousa's rhythms prompted a dancing masters' association to select Sousa's *Washington Post* march to introduce their new dance, the two step, the most popular dance of the 1890s. Church, "Life and Influence of John Philip Sousa," p. 102; Sousa, *Marching Along*, p. 117.

41. Jonathan Elkus, *Charles Ives and the American Band Tradition: A Centennial Tribute* (University of Exeter, American Arts Documentation Center, 1974), p. 22.

42. John Kirkpatrick, *Charles E. Ives: Memos* (New York: W. W. Norton & Co., Inc., 1972), p. 62.

43. Ibid., p. 102.

44. Elkus, *Charles Ives*, p. 20.

45. Isaac Goldberg, *Tin Pan Alley* (New York: Frederick Ungar Publishing Co., Inc., 1961), p. 138.

Photo Essay

Sousa's father, John Antonio Sousa, was a Portuguese immigrant and musician with the U.S. Navy when he met his future wife, Bavarian-born Maria Elisabeth Trinkhaus. In 1854, they moved with their first two children to Washington where the father, Antonio, joined the U.S. Marine Band. That year was also the year of John Philip Sousa's birth. Washington had a music school run by John Esputa, Jr., a violinist and cornetist who also served in the Marine Band, and it was from him that the young Sousa received a sound musical education. It was his father, however, who was primarily responsible for encouraging Sousa to pursue his career in music. According to Sousa, his father enlisted him as an apprentice in the Marine Band in 1868 upon discovering that his son was planning to run away from home to join a circus band as a violinist. He died shortly before Sousa signed a contract with David Blakely in 1892, the arrangement that was to mark the beginning of the phenomenal success of the Sousa Band. — *U.S. Marine Band.*

The first page of the full score of *The Stars and Stripes Forever,* in Sousa's hand. The piano score was completed on Christmas Day, 1896. This full score, written in Boston, is dated April 26, 1897. The march's official premiere was given in Philadelphia on May 14, 1897, at the unveiling of a new statue of George Washington. There is evidence, however, that it was first performed publicly, as yet untitled, in Augusta, Maine, on May 1. — *Music Division, Library of Congress.*

Sousa with his band at Coney Island, circa 1900.—
Brown Brothers, Sterling, Pennsylvania.

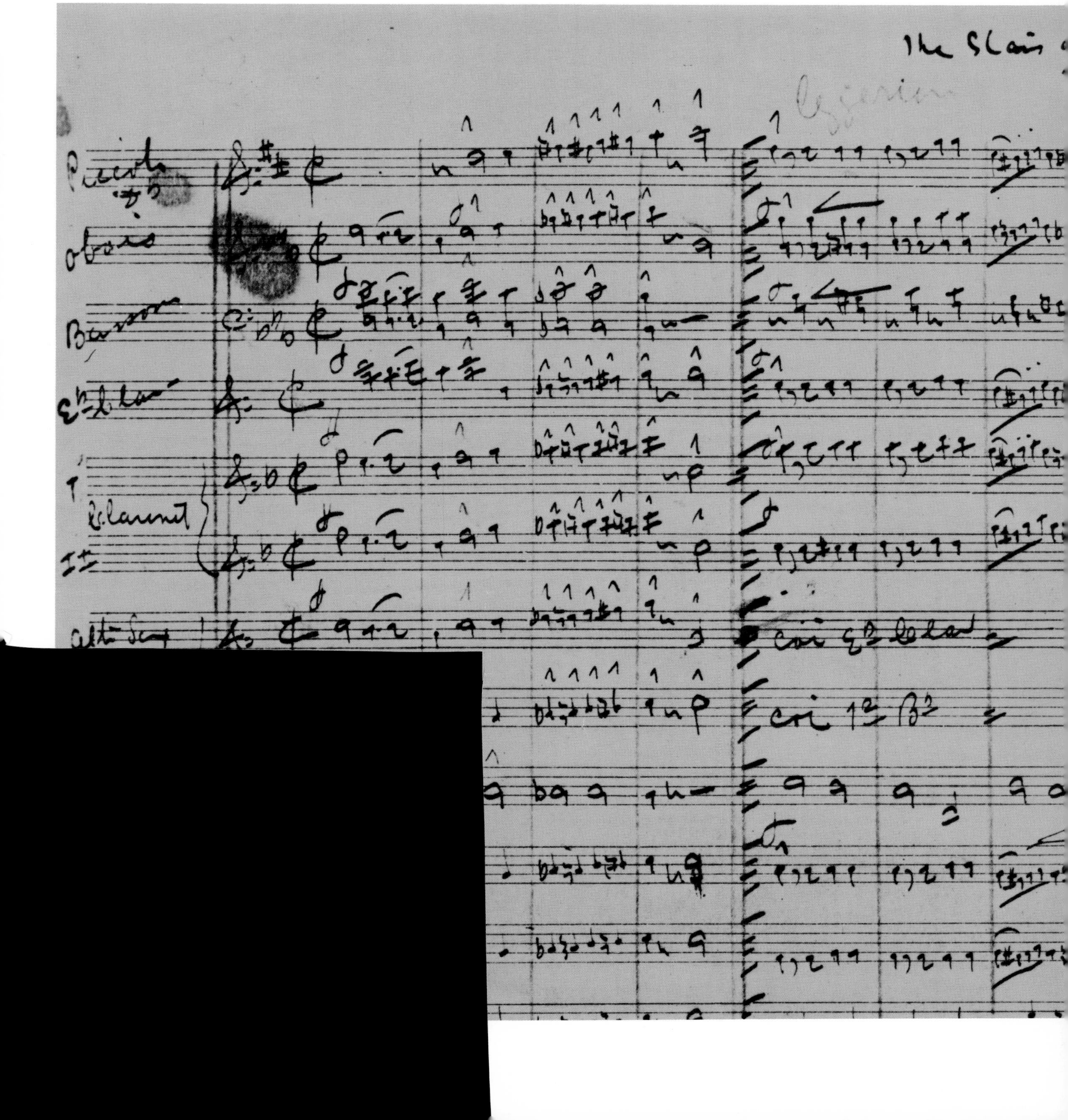
Oboes
Clarinet

This is one of many letters Sousa received requesting membership in his band. Here, besides testifying as to his musical competence, the applicant states that the possibility of having his wife with him "to take this trip west and see her folks . . . would probably make the terms more reasonable." Wives, including Sousa's, rarely accompanied the band on tour, and Sousa discouraged the practice. — *Blakely Papers, New York Public Library.*

New York, Feb. 23d

Mr. Sousa, Dear Sir, I would like to become a member of your band for the coming season — Namely — Chicago, Manhattan Beach, St. Louis. I am a member of Brooks Band, playing 2d Slide Trombone at Nantasket, and again at Pittsburg. At present I am at the Olympic Theatre, Harlem, N.Y. I am a good musician and acquainted with all classes of music. My wife is a St. Louis lady, and it would give us untold pleasure to take this trip west and see her folks. The consideration of this fact would probably make the terms more reasonable. I would be pleased to have you make an appointment with m I feel certain you will be pleased with me both as musician and gentleman.

Most Respt. Yours

Louis Rogasey
220 E. 127th St
N.Y. City

A program cover for a U.S. Marine Band concert during one of the two tours Sousa was able to make with it. After repeated denials of permission to take the band on tour, permission was granted personally by President Harrison in 1891, when, as Sousa reports in his autobiography, he told him: " 'Mrs. Harrison tells me that you are anxious to make a tour with the band. I was thinking myself of going out of town, and'—with a smile—'it would be tough on Washington if both of us were away at the same time. I have thought it over, and I believe the country would rather hear you than see me; so you have my permission to go.' "

The tour was managed by David Blakely, and so exhausted Sousa that he had to take a trip to Europe with his wife to recuperate. But it was the beginning of a collaboration with Blakely that, the next year, resulted in Sousa's leaving the Marine Band to form his own, under Blakely's management.—*David Blakely Papers, Rare Book and Manuscripts Division, The New York Public Library, Astor, Lenox and Tilden Foundations (hereafter cited as Blakely Papers, New York Public Library).*

A program cover for a concert of Sousa's own band. Sousa left the Marine Band in 1892 to form his own band under the management of David Blakely. This most fruitful partnership of composer-conductor and businessman ended with Blakely's sudden death in 1896, but by then, Sousa's independent success was assured. — *Blakely Papers, New York Public Library.*

Starting in 1893, Sousa began to appear regularly each summer at Manhattan Beach in Brooklyn, New York. This chromo-lithograph of a panoramic aerial view of the resort appears on the back cover of a program of events for the 1896 season. — *Music Division, Library of Congress.*

The cover of a concert program for Sousa's second tour of Britain in 1901. As his band began its tenth year, Sousa could look back on eighteen semiannual American tours, starring appearances at five major expositions in the United States (Chicago, San Francisco, Atlanta, Philadelphia, and Buffalo), and two abroad (Paris and Glasgow), with an average of 500 concerts a year and a total of 250,000 miles of travel. — *Music Division, Library of Congress.*

SOUSA AND HIS BAND

LONDON.
COVENT GARDEN THEATRE, at 8.30.
THE EMPIRE THEATRE, at 3.
Commencing November 23rd, 1901.

Cover of the published piano arrangement of *The Picador March*, 1889. Harry Coleman of Philadelphia published this march with a most elaborate black and white cover illustration. Coleman was not Sousa's first publisher, but he did much to popularize him in his early years, to Sousa's great glory and Coleman's enormous profit. A naive businessman before he left the Marine Band to work under David Blakely's management in 1892, Sousa sold Coleman outright, for a flat fee of twenty-five to thirty-five dollars, some of his most popular marches, including *Semper Fidelis*. — *Music Division, Library of Congress.*

The cover of the piano arrangement of *The Invincible Eagle,* 1901. By this time, Sousa had an arrangement more beneficial to himself than the one with Coleman. Sales of all kinds of arrangements of this highly popular march brought him substantial royalties. This cover advertises no less than eighteen arrangements for instrumental forces ranging from full orchestra ($1.00) to zither solo (40 cents). — *Music Division, Library of Congress.*

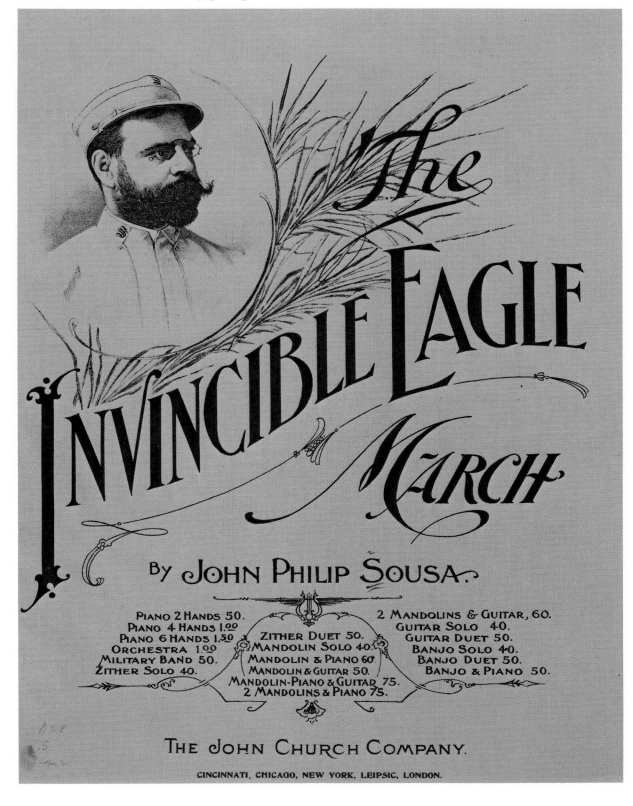

The cover of the piano-vocal score of Sousa's operetta, *The Free Lance*, composed in 1905 and given its premiere the following year. This elaborate comedy involves disguises and international intrigues. The character represented here is the protagonist, Sigmund Lump of Graftiana, a goatherd and, before a sorceress bereft him of his hair and, hence, his strength, a former mighty bandit chief, who assumes the guise of a prince. After he is discovered and condemned, the sorceress enables him to save himself by reversing the depilatory procedure. In the end, all the right people fall in love, and Sigmund becomes ruler of two countries. — *Music Division, Library of Congress.*

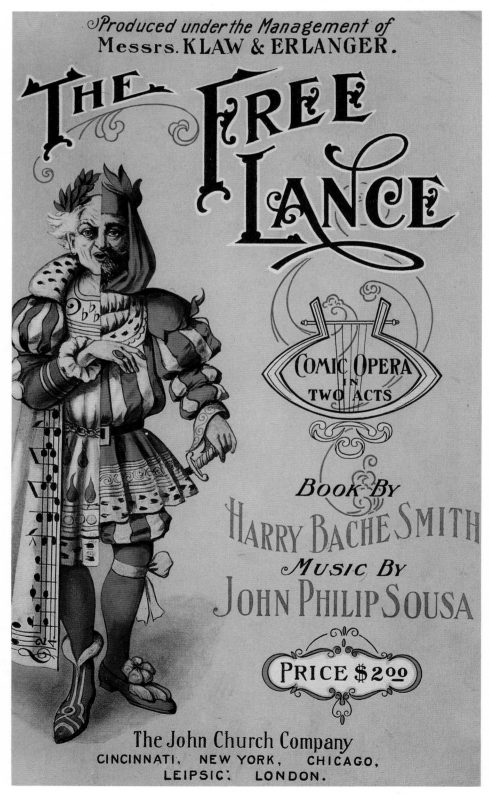

Composed in 1895 while Sousa was at Manhattan Beach, his operetta *El Capitan* received its premiere in Boston the following year. It was Sousa's most popular stage work. As he did with other of his operettas, Sousa extracted music in composing his march of the same title. — *Blakely Papers, New York Public Library.*

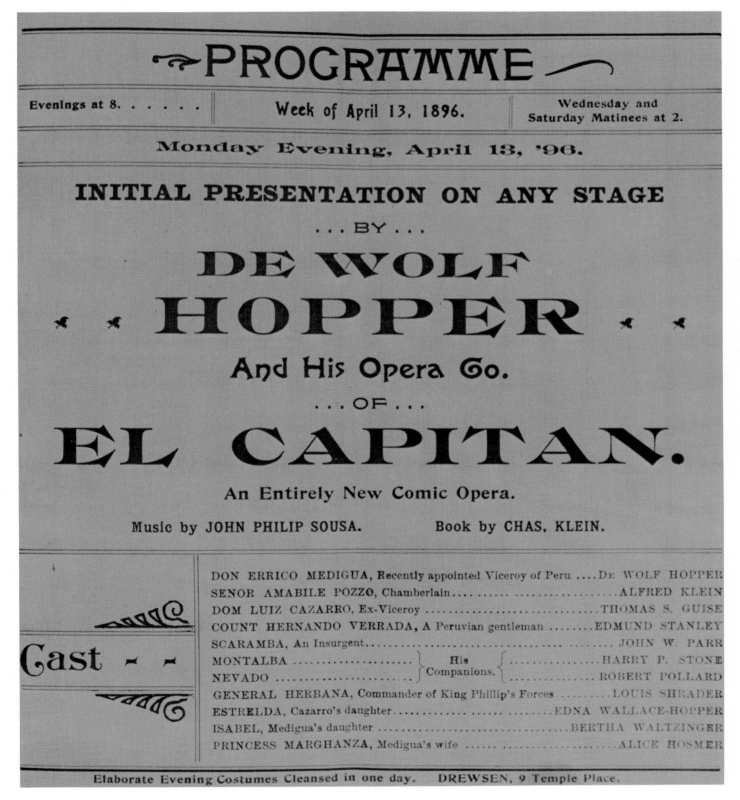

PROGRAMME

| Evenings at 8. . . . . . | Week of April 13, 1896. | Wednesday and Saturday Matinees at 2. |

Monday Evening, April 13, '96.

INITIAL PRESENTATION ON ANY STAGE

...BY...

DE WOLF HOPPER

And His Opera Co.

...OF...

EL CAPITAN.

An Entirely New Comic Opera.

Music by JOHN PHILIP SOUSA.   Book by CHAS. KLEIN.

Cast

DON ERRICO MEDIGUA, Recently appointed Viceroy of Peru ....DE WOLF HOPPER
SENOR AMABILE POZZO, Chamberlain.................................ALFRED KLEIN
DOM LUIZ CAZARRO, Ex-Viceroy.................................THOMAS S. GUISE
COUNT HERNANDO VERRADA, A Peruvian gentleman.........EDMUND STANLEY
SCARAMBA, An Insurgent...JOHN W. PARR
MONTALBA .... } His { ....HARRY P. STONE
NEVADO .... } Companions. { ....ROBERT POLLARD
GENERAL HERBANA, Commander of King Phillip's Forces.........LOUIS SHRADER
ESTRELDA, Cazarro's daughter.............................EDNA WALLACE-HOPPER
ISABEL, Medigua's daughter..............................BERTHA WALTZINGER
PRINCESS MARGHANZA, Medigua's wife ....ALICE HOSMER

Elaborate Evening Costumes Cleansed in one day.   DREWSEN, 9 Temple Place.

Sousa and his band at Willow Grove Park, Philadelphia, in 1905. Sousa appeared at this major musical center for many summers following his first engagement there in 1901. — *U.S. Marine Band.*

Sheet music cover for "I've Made My Plans for the Summer," 1907. One of the many songs for which Sousa was lyricist as well as composer. A boy meets a girl and asks her for a date; later he asks her to marry him. Each time, she puts him off: "I've made my plans for the summer,/ I'm dreaming of happy days;/ When I'll hear the roll of the drummer,/ The music the big band plays;/ With wooing and cooing at twilight,/ And shooting the chutes after dark,/ From me to you,/ That is what I'll do,/ Down at Luna Park." — *Music Division, Library of Congress.*

Pages from Sousa's sketchbooks. Sousa's method of composing *The Stars and Stripes Forever* was exceptional in that he developed the piece in his mind without making preliminary sketches. Typically, he sketched sometimes quite fragmentary musical ideas in notebooks, later using whatever he thought worth developing to make finished pieces. Both books contain much material he never used.

The smaller sketchbook is a convenient size for carrying in one's pocket when travelling. He was observed to sketch and even compose quite fully realized pieces on trains.

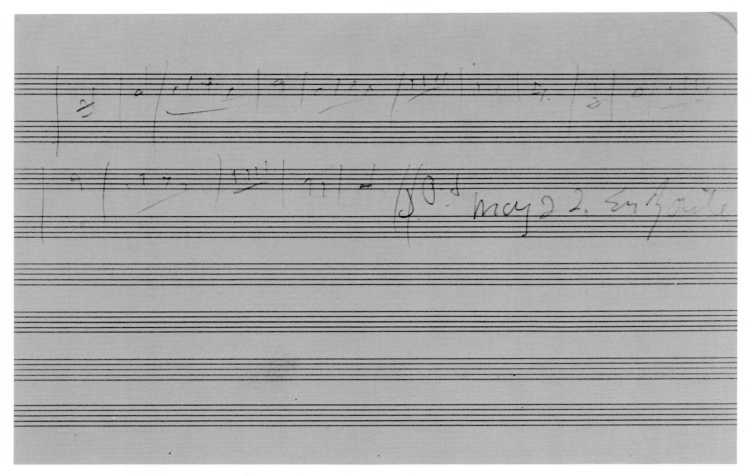

The larger one was probably kept in his study. The page shown contains a tune dated May 1917, when he finished his march *Wisconsin Forward Forever* at his home in Sands Point, Long Island. The inscription "Solid Men to the Front" appears in this sketch and, later, in the manuscript of the march, as its original title; but he crossed it out and used it as the title of one of his best World War I marches, written the following year. — *Music Division, Library of Congress.*

Maud Powell, violinist (1868–1920), and Estelle Liebling, soprano (1880–1970), were among the soloists who appeared with the Sousa Band. Sousa was able to use his unique ensemble to perform works originally intended for full symphonic orchestra. His use of soloists extended the variety of possibilities for programming. Maud Powell, an outstanding virtuoso in her day, had studied in Ger-many with Joseph Joachim and performed in New York under Theodore Thomas before touring Europe with Sousa in 1903. In the same year, Estelle Liebling, having made her European debut, appeared with the Metropolitan Opera. In later years, she became a distinguished peda-gogue as a professor at the Curtis Institute and then as a private vocal teacher in New York. — *U.S. Marine Band.*

A postcard photograph of Sousa inscribed by him in 1905, with a musical quotation from his march, *The Diplomat* (1904). — *Music Division, Library of Congress.*

Draft, in Sousa's hand, of two concert programs for the same day, a matinee and an evening performance. This typically varied program ranges from Wagner's "Entrance of the Gods into Valhalla" to excerpts from Gilbert and Sullivan's *Mikado.* The only compositions by Sousa that appear are his humoresque, "A Stag Party," and his "La Reine de la Mer" waltzes. However, Sousa interpolated many additional pieces on his programs, including many of his most popular marches. — *Blakely Papers, New York Public Library.*

Program for a Sousa Band concert, heavily annotated, showing the many unannounced additional numbers Sousa interpolated in his concerts. An astute showman, Sousa knew how to judge his audience. If he felt a heavy number was in danger of losing listeners, he could wake them up with a showstopper. Or, at such times as an occasional piece seemed appropriate, he could offer his audience an unprogrammed work, as he did, for example, after the death of President McKinley. Then, he is reported to have moved his listeners to tears with an unexpected rendition of "Nearer My God to Thee" followed by a tolling funeral bell. — *Music Division, Library of Congress.*

SOUSA AND HIS BAND

Lieut.-Commander John Philip Sousa, Conductor

Miss Mary Baker, Soprano
Miss Florence Hardeman, Violinist
Mr. John Dolan, Cornetist
Mr. George J. Carey, Xylophone

1. Rhapsody, "The American Indian" (new) . . . . *Orem*
   (On themes recorded and suggested by Mr. Thurlow Lieurance)

2. Cornet Solo, "Scintilla" . . . . *Perkins*
   Mr. John Dolan

3. Suite, "Camera Studies" (new) . . . . *Sousa*
   (a) "The Teasing Eyes of Andalusia"
   (b) "Drifting to Loveland"
   (c) "The Children's Ball"

4. Vocal Solo, "The Crystal Lute" . . . . *Sousa*
   Miss Mary Baker

5. (a) Her Majesty at Westminster, from "The King's Court," by *Sousa.*
   (b) March, "Semper Fidelis" . . . . *Sousa*

   INTERVAL

6. "A Study in Rhythms" (new) . . . . *Sousa*
   (Being a manipulation of a group of classics)

7. (a) Xylophone Solo, "The March-Wind" . . . . *Carey*
   (b) March, "Comrades of the Legion" (new) . . . . *Sousa*

8. Violin Solo, First Movement from F Sharp Minor Concerto . . . . *Vieuxtemps*
   Miss Florence Hardeman

9. "Dale Dances of Yorkshire" . . . . *Wood*
   (Traditional and newly arranged)

   NATIONAL ANTHEM

72

A program for a Sousa band concert, July 14, 1894. Sousa's concerts included featured soloists, including the two singers that appear here. Original programmatic works and suites and fantasies for band by Sousa also played an important part in his concerts. Composed in 1890, this dramatic series of scenes from the highly popular novel *Ben Hur,* by Lew Wallace, was a tour de force of orchestration, and, while a piano arrangement was published in 1892, Sousa kept his instrumental tricks a closely guarded secret. — *Blakely Papers, New York Public Library.*

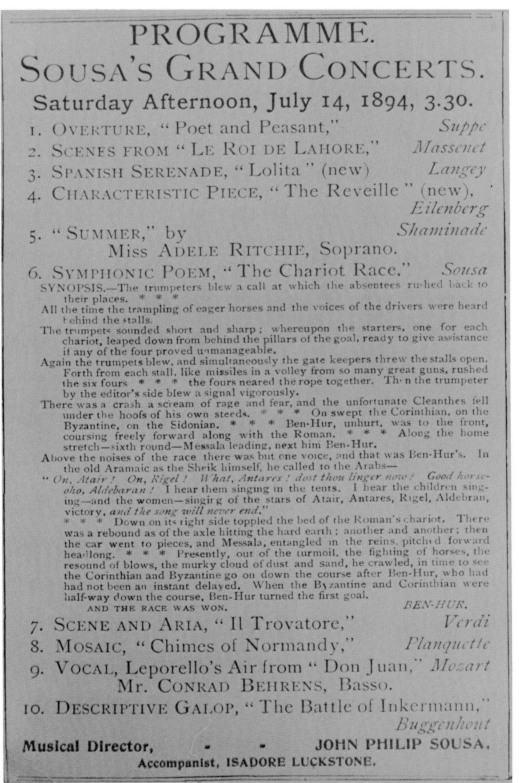

Informal snapshots of Sousa and his band on tour from family photo albums. — *Courtesy of John Philip Sousa III.*

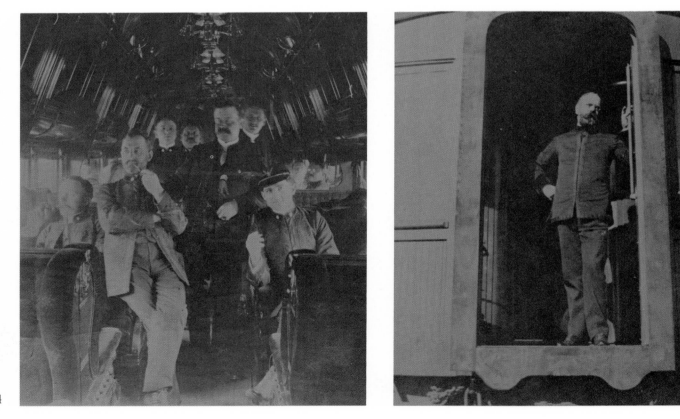

Beginning in the January 1934 issue of *Jacobs' Band Monthly,* there appeared a series of illustrated reminiscences by Herbert L. Clarke, the famous cornet virtuoso and longtime soloist with Sousa, of the around-the-world tour of Sousa's Band. It was, in Clarke's words, "the greatest and longest professional tour ever attempted by a first-class musical aggregation, a tour that commenced in the middle of August, 1910, and continued until the middle of December, 1911." The photographs were taken by the author's brother, Edwin G. Clarke, then general manager of Sousa's band.

"On the Hurricane Deck—*R.M.S. Tainui.* At the right, Captain Moffat, frankly British, and Mr. Sousa, deceivingly French—the rest, members of the bandmaster's party with the exception of the ship's officer, who, true to the best nautical tradition, has appropriated three of the ladies to himself." — *From Jacobs' Band Monthly, April 1934.*

"Landing from A. P. & O. Liner at East London, South Africa. With no dock and the continually obtrusive restlessness of the Indian Ocean to contend with, this method of transferring to a tug boat and thence to dry land was the experience of all those who debarked at East London. These baskets were built for three. Count this load! But what is a little discomfort to musicians *en route?* If there wasn't some of it, they wouldn't feel comfortable, if you get our meaning." — *From Jacobs' Band Monthly, June 1934.*

"In Hobart, Tasmania. As slinky as they make them, when it comes to looks, and class for class, an automobile runs a bad second to a horse rig. Compare the average taxi to one of these." — *From Jacobs' Band Monthly, September 1934.*

The cover of a Sousa band souvenir booklet, 1926, and a page showing Sousa being made a chief of the Star Blanket Band of Indians in the File Hills Indian Reserve, Western Canada, in 1925. In later years, he was so honored on three occasions. Twice, he received honorary doctorates. — *Music Division, Library of Congress.*

1892 SOUVENIR 1926 | 10c

SOUSA AND HIS BAND

Lieut.-Commander John Philip Sousa, Conductor

Sousa at the National Music Camp, Interlochen, Michigan, in the summer of 1931. On his left, is Albert Austin Harding, conductor of the camp's band. On his right is Joseph E. Maddy, president and musical conductor of the camp. — *From Jacobs' Band Monthly, September 1935.*

The Sousa March: A Personal View

by Frederick Fennell

I heard the first performance of John Philip Sousa's *The Black Horse Troop* when I was eleven years old. My father had taken me to a concert by Sousa's Band at the Public Auditorium in Cleveland, Ohio. At the end of the concert Sousa turned and faced the audience. This was obviously a signal, for the whole of Troop A of the Ohio National Guard Cavalry—The Black Horse Troop—walked their horses up the aisles and onto the stage. Standing at attention behind the Band, they faced the audience as Sousa led his musicians in the first performance of the march. Their reception as they made their way to the stage was wild enough, but the tumultuous applause for all at the conclusion of *The Black Horse Troop* was like nothing I had ever heard. It was probably Sousa's 125th march.

By the time that I—and about 699 other high school students—had the privilege of playing two concerts which he conducted with the National High School Band and Orchestra at the Bowl at Interlochen, Michigan, in July 1931, Mr. Sousa was no longer the exceptionally gifted physical conductor who had once ignited audiences everywhere to flaming acclaim and of whom no less a judge of performance than his contemporary, the distinguished actor Otis Skinner, declared that he was "the best actor America has ever produced."[1]

But the mere fact that he was John Philip Sousa was sufficient to mesmerize us all and draw the largest crowd imaginable to the National Music Camp's Interlochen Bowl. Those of us there who did the playing at the rehearsals and concerts had not the slightest interest in, let alone any real ability to judge, his conducting technique. He made what we thought were the right motions, and when he did we played our hearts out for him. In this last summer of his life he was seventy-seven years old and comparatively frail, but he was "Our Sousa," the "King of the March."[2]

The youth of America became very involved with band performance during the last years of Sousa's life. He was their obvious idol. We young school musicians were beneficiaries of the great band movement's desire to follow Sousa's example. We had the benefit of good instruction at public support, could play in a good group at an early age, and our instruments were provided by the school we attended—all of which did not exist when John Philip Sousa was a lad. But there it was, the great bursting forth of all those school bands as the result of the labors of so many.

Sousa was drawn inevitably into all of this as the honored guest conductor of enormous bands massed in his honor. He gave his name to causes that would enhance musical opportunities for young people. Among those exemplary leaders within music education who were drawn to him was the Director of Bands at the University of Illinois, Albert Austin Harding (1880-1958). He took what Sousa had done to make the indoor sit-down concert band artistically acceptable, expanded it, and eventually thrust that concept throughout schools in most of the forty-eight states. Sousa responded to Harding's devotion to bands and to his expertise and musicality by visiting the Urbana campus and guest conducting Harding's superb Illinois Concert Band.

Their friendship—together with the impact on music education that Joseph E. Maddy had made with the National High School Orchestra and the summer music camp that was built to house it at Interlochen, Michigan, where Harding was conductor of the band—led to two visits to Interlochen by Sousa. I was there for the second visit, described above, and for this occasion he honored all Interlochen campers with a march written just for us; number 136, his last. He called it *The Northern Pines* (1931). The preparation that preceded his arrival for dress rehearsals was done by Harding who was quick to notice several details in style, so well known to him, to be in need of adjustment, such as dynamic shadings and ensemble accents. These were subsequently approved by Sousa and incorporated into the printed edition. One time, Mr. Harding also suggested that it was more in the Sousa style to have the trombones join the solo cornets at the octave for the melody in the first half of the second strain rather than to play their inactive harmonic role. When he went back to the trombone section and picked up somebody's instrument and played the suggested change, Sousa smilingly approved. Sousa conducted the premiere of *The Northern Pines* on Sunday afternoon, July 27, 1931. Harding had assigned me the honor of playing bass drum for the occasion.

Such are my personal and youthful observations of Sousa. Much has been written about him by others, and Sousa's autobiography was published in 1928, four years before his death. Aptly titled *Marching Along*,[3] it is a rambling account of a fascinating life, somewhat frustrating to one awaiting any words from Sousa on how he wrote marches. The book is 365 pages long, 357 of which have passed before he ever mentions the subject. Then, however, he provides the following statements:

Marches, of course, are well known to have a peculiar appeal to me. . . . The march speaks to a fundamental rhythm in the human organization and is answered. A march stimulates every center of vitality, wakens the imagination. . . . But a march must be good. It must be as free from padding as a marble statue. . . . How are marches written? I suppose every composer has a somewhat similar experience in his writing. With me the thought comes, sometimes slowly, sometimes with ease and rapidity. The idea gathers force in my brain and takes form not only melodically but harmonically at the same time. It must be complete before I commit it to paper.[4]

At age seventy-four and with 115 of his 136 marches already written, Sousa's manifesto is a statement by a man totally in control of the medium that suited him best. Benevolent circumstance had placed him in a time and society where his gifts could make it all happen.

But his words, however candid, are no match for his marches—except, perhaps, for that single phrase that a march "must be as free from padding as a marble statue."

The style of his marches was singular. The time which Sousa had spent as a violinist with touring companies and in theater pits in Washington and Philadelphia had brought him into the closest kind of contact with the popular music of his youth. A seven-year slice of that time had been spent first as an apprentice and then as a musician in the U.S. Marine Band.[5] The sounds of marches had been all about him, perhaps since the time he could remember having heard anything. But it does not seem that he fell under the spell of any particular international style as a result of his early days in the military; nor does it seem that the ceremonial routine of that life left any strong marks on his earliest march compositions.

Once he was freed from his military commitment, Sousa was drawn to the theater, the leading musical activity of the day. He had been "moonlighting" there during his time off from the Marine Band.

Sousa's basic training in violin, piano, and composition while in Washington[6] provided him with the tools he would use eventually in the theater. Songs were among his first compositions,[7] and words had always interested him too. Because of the innate flair for showmanship that would soon make him and his Band a top international attraction, theater and Sousa made a superb match.

How all of those early professional experiences found their way into Sousa's marches is, of course, impossible and unnecessary to trace by specific example. But it is reasonable to assume that as he played he sorted what worked from what did not and made more than a mental note, for instance, of the charm and clarity he surely heard in the scores of Arthur Sullivan, and of the effervescence and drive he must have experienced while playing for Jacques Offenbach in the orchestra at Philadelphia's Centennial Exhibition.

High among Sousa's gifts were his obvious talents as a composer and conductor. It is here, perhaps, that his theater experiences were to serve him most directly. His work at the podium, beginning at age twenty, offered the priceless opportunity to hear everything from that most desirable and productive elevation. He could choose the best of what he saw and heard, carefully avoiding imitation; he was an original and he knew it.

Sousa discovered very early in his life as a composer that what he had to offer through his marches was a music that people really wanted to hear and sometimes to dance to and for which they were ready to pay; these were to remain inseparable touchstones to success throughout his life. Once his marches in their basic pattern had established him as the March King,[8] he chose to reign in this realm only, in spite of his long interest and initial success in musical theater.[9]

Sousa's mature description of a good march as being "as free from padding as a marble statue" fits the exemplary ones we know from France, Italy, Germany, England, Norway, or Austria. And while his gift and its fruits were unique and extraordinary he must have assimilated a broad range of what had gone before and what was happening all around him as well. From among all the possible influences I have always sensed the presence of the lighter character of Austrian marches from pit or parade ground to be present in his early achievements, notably *Our Flirtations* (1880) with which it may also be said that the Sousa march was born. It was also the year he became leader of the Marine Band,[10] a very significant event in his life.

From the outset of his career as a composer of memorable marches he obviously lived up to his later specifications for the writing of something "as free from padding as a marble statue." *Our Flirtations* was followed chronologically by *Sound Off* (1885), *The Gladiator* (1886), and *The Rifle Regiment* (1886), three of his very best achievements. Each of these continued to reveal a composer with something to say that was worth "marching" to.[11]

The Gladiator was Sousa's first real hit and he knew it; it is a fabulously swinging march that has everything. He was to borrow from it for the rest of his life. A few of its very attractive resources include an introduction and first strain in the minor mode (as does *Sound Off* from 1885), great use of the reeds throughout, a judicious piccolo concept in the trio, a break strain in the minor, and a rousing finale with all the melody brass in unisons or octaves—and no stinger (final chord). Sousa was obviously headed in the direction of the street.

Semper Fidelis (1888), unquestionably one of the greatest of all regimental marches, leaves no one in doubt as to its purpose: it is for marching and it is Sousa's perfect "marble statue." It is the ideal march for the street or for regimental review. He had been conducting for eight years when he wrote it "one night, while in tears, after my comrades of the Marine Corps had sung their famous hymn at Quantico."[12]

Providing appropriate music for the parade ground has long been the principal purpose for the existence of the military band and those units of fifers, drummers, pipers, and buglers attached to it in military establishments throughout the world. Regimental review calls for a no-nonsense, solid, one-two cadence undergirding simple tunes that are usually orchestrated in equally no-nonsense, block-buster fashion. The object of the regimental march is to move lots of organized pairs of feet forward and at a pace and with a spirit that elevates the occasion to those moments of pride and purpose without which probably no unit can function as intended.

In the overview of his enormous output it is obvious, however, that Sousa conceived the majority of his marches for sit-down performances, for toe tapping rather than foot marching while, at the same time, it is unmistakably clear that Sousa's music is for the feet rather than for the head.[13]

In the last decade of the nineteenth century the full force of Sousa's musical personality extended to its international dimension. He had two years left with the Marine Band, during which David Blakely came into his life as manager for two important tours. At the end of the second tour Sousa was ready to leave the Marines and reach for the money Blakely offered him to form his own band.

Up to this point Sousa was anything but a good business man. He had the poorest kind of contract with his first publisher, Harry Coleman, making Coleman rich while accepting a meager outright payment of thirty-five dollars for each of his early marches. His financial success only began with the Blakely contract and the astute and experienced management it provided. Their brief but highly productive time together ended with Blakely's sudden death in 1896. The contract caused Sousa the anxiety of a court suit that ruled mostly in favor of Blakely's widow.[14]

Sousa's marches and his personality as a conductor, however, had altered his status completely. Sousa was obviously very good for business, management notwithstanding, for it was he whom the people came to see and hear, no matter how good the Band was. Sousa's day was band day in the United States. It was the time of the horse-drawn vehicle and the electric street car, of the amusement park and the seaside pier, of the railroad and the side-wheel steamer. Everything that was John Philip Sousa could be considered a fair representation of what America was—or thought it was—to a large part of the world.

His marches, generously sprinkled throughout his programs as encores to the mostly light music he chose to play wherever he went, became what can easily be assumed to be an honest reflection of the taste of the general public in our country during the first three decades of the twentieth century. His was the pop music of his day; he was the rock super star; his Band was the big money group that the people lined up to hear and paid top dollar just to be near. They were probably the only first-class musical group that performed in some of the places where they traveled. But he went everywhere as an entertainer to carry out that demanding, rewarding, and (to him) necessary pursuit. The symphony orchestra and the opera company would wait their turn to dominate the musical scene and the entertainment world as had the bands in Sousa's time.

His Band also flourished because, it is said, he always paid the highest wages and, therefore, could hire the best musicians. In securing such services, in some instances for several seasons, he was buying more than mere technical expertise. He was also acquiring high professionalism, expert musicianship, artistic loyalty, and, most of all, experience. He depended on these men to bring to his Band their superior tonal quality and a sympathetic expressiveness in their playing, to grasp immediately the stylistic character of the music as played by the Sousa Band—especially his marches. Rehearsals, we are told, were rare after the few that launched a new season.[15]

Sousa frequently mentioned in press interviews that contact with the public was critical to creativity as he knew it. The next two of his marches to be considered here both evolved from extended visits to very public places. I can well imagine that the great man—however sophisticated at this point—was often very excited before he met the Band at the train that took them where they were going. Frequently, this is still the case for those who make their living as twentieth-century troubadours.

The first of these marches is *Manhattan Beach* (1893). It was the money—obviously very good money—that was available to be earned at such a facility and at exciting gatherings like the Cotton States Exposition in Atlanta that kept Sousa's Band together in its earliest days. And while the receipts guaranteed his survival it was the presence of all those people and what their enthusiasm for him fed back to his creative juices that kept him composing march after march, each one as logical a link in a chain of musical pleasure as one can imagine.

In its late nineteenth-century heyday, New Yorkers flocked to the Manhattan Beach Hotel, a nearby and well-known Brooklyn summer resort. Foremost among the musical attractions appearing in concert at the amphitheater there in the summer of 1893 was the brand new John Philip Sousa Band. The hotel has long been gone but the spirit of what must have been quite a place lives on in this exciting Sousa march.

And while the Band's players were probably enjoying the diversions of Manhattan Beach, Sousa was busy composing the march he would take with him to their next engagement that same fall at the Cotton States Exposition in Atlanta; the score of *King Cotton* is dated "28 July 1895 Manhattan Beach, N.Y." The business of having a group that people really wanted to hear, together with his great acceptance as a leading musical personality could only have urged him on in his endless quest to please. He did have a seemingly endless reservoir of smashingly simple musical ideas which flowed from him on call. *King Cotton*, for instance, has that same infectiously happy sounding drive which makes *The High School Cadets* and *Manhattan Beach* such successful pieces of music, as well as that vital added ingredient for many listeners as it swings along in the six-eight meter. Each of his marches had its own individual character, its own musical personality. By now Sousa had really hit his stride; the next two marches would be *El Capitan* and *The Stars and Stripes Forever* (both in 1896).

The one would bring him fame, lasting and unlimited, establishing an indelible association with the American people and those high principles on which the republic was founded. This would extend beyond any geographical center. *The Stars and Stripes Forever* would also far transcend the borders of the customary five- by seven-inch march-size paper on which it was printed, reaching out beyond those confinements to touch the heart and spirit of each succeeding generation. It has its own special consideration in this volume through the penetrating study written by James R. Smart, "Genesis of a March: *The Stars and Stripes Forever*."

The operetta *El Capitan* (1896) marked Sousa's return to the theater, a triumphant rejoining of that natural combination. And for our purpose in this march overview, the *El Capitan March*—like all the marches that precede it—is just a little different, though positively out of the same Sousa march mold. This was another vital factor in his galloping conquest of the public. A new Sousa march was always new, although to some listeners it might have sounded at first like something they had heard before; as it played on it would grow less familiar but they would still find those satisfying characteristics that had made the other marches so memorable.[16]

By the time that Sousa had seen the beginning of the twentieth century he had produced a mountain of marches—fifty-seven by exact count—and he was only forty-six years old. His touring had become international, and his literary and theatrical projects also consumed much of his time. March production held at about one a year, and in 1906 he produced *The Free Lance*. His leanest year ever was 1908 in which *The Fairest of the Fair* was his only composition in any form. But, if it was to be that kind of year, Sousa could not have come up with a more perfect example of his view of the march at any time in his career than is this single gem.[17]

He wrote the march for the Band's engagement that fall at the Boston Food Fair.[18] The holograph score's final page was signed: "John Philip Sousa, Camp Comfort, Saranac Lake, Adirondack, New York, July 8, 1908."

Another year passed before *The*

Glory of the Yankee Navy (1909) was written to the same high standards, if not to the acclaim, of *The Fairest of the Fair*. Then there is a lull in top-notch creativity lasting for about six years. But when the First World War reached out to involve the United States Sousa volunteered his services to train bands for the Navy in which he served as a dollar-a-year officer until the armistice.

The exemplary march to come from this period was *The U.S. Field Artillery March* (1917) written at the request of artillery officer Lt. George Friedlander, whom Sousa had met at lunch in company with Secretary of the Navy Josephus Daniels. This unusual combination of diners provided Sousa with the chance to take a very good tune that was not his and to make of it one of his greatest marches. What neither Sousa nor Friedlander knew about the artillery song suggested to Sousa and presumed by all to be a traditional song, was that it had been composed in 1908 by another artillery officer, Lt. Edmund L. Gruber. Liking the tune, Sousa simply gave it his treatment and the result, far beyond what Lt. Friedlander had hoped for, was another booming Sousa success![19]

A new publisher appeared in the Sousa repertory just before the twenties when he entered into a contract with the Sam Fox Publishing Company. Since the Blakely contract of 1892, Sousa's principal publisher had been the John Church Company (now Presser). As a newcomer to the Sousa success, Mr. Fox was the lucky recipient of a series of vintage marches, beginning with *Sabre and Spurs* (1910) and moving on to *The Gallant Seventh* (1922), the best regimental march Sousa had written since *Semper Fidelis*.

This was followed by the concert-oriented and novel *Nobles of the Mystic Shrine* (1923), which is unique in that it has a part for the harp and its introduction and entire first strain are in the key of B-flat minor. There are violent outbursts of sound in keeping with the "Turkish music" character of its intent. Percussion instruments, the triangle, and the tambourine are integral to the music's texture as all such colorful oriental sounds are part of Shrine marching music. Sousa wrote this for his fellow Shriners of Almas Temple.

He also contributed two of his best "equestrian" marches to this series, *The Black Horse Troop* (1924) and *Riders for the Flag* (1927). The horse lover in Sousa was a vein that ran very deep,[20] and when he could no longer ride after he broke his neck in 1921, he could still pour his affection for the animal into these two outstanding examples of a march for riders. *The Black Horse Troop* is a classic among Sousa's 136 marches. It possesses a great dignity that belongs to it alone, and its proportions are as gracefully balanced as the beautiful black steeds for whom it was written and who stood at attention behind the Band at the march's premiere performance. It is vintage Sousa with characteristics that hark back to *Semper Fidelis* and *The Washington Post*, but its own bold profile is there for all to hear.

Having completed this brief survey of Sousa's career and marches, I would like to discuss some of his works in greater detail from a conductor's point of view.

How does one write about a Sousa march? The idea has baffled me for years as I have strived, futilely I fear, to provide reading guides to record listeners.

While Sousa was fully aware of his credibility as a writer, he mostly avoided—save for *The Stars and Stripes Forever*[21]—any discussion of the creative process. When in his autobiography, Sousa asks how marches are written, the conductor and the scholar have to respond in genuine desperation by asking how marches are studied. I have seen but two full scores of Sousa's marches, photocopies of the holographs of *The Black Horse Troop* and *The Fairest of the Fair*.[22] While they are treasures to see, all of us who seek to conduct, edit, or talk about them would be able to do our work quickly and more fully if printed copies in full score had been published as has been true for any other piece of music worth considering in the first place. Lacking this, I have long resorted to distributing on my living room floor a single copy of each part arranged in ensemble formation. Moving about from one part and section to the next, with a small stool for resting, I can study the music both from an overall view and by detailed observation of each part. It is a tedious but necessary business which the full score obviously provides with such ease for all other musical forms, including today a growing amount of concert band music.

Those of us who conduct Mr. Sousa's "marble statues" have also tried to absorb them through repeated performances and rehearsals; by listening to them at concerts, parades, reviews, and on recordings; and by practicing the individual parts for the instruments we play. All of these are experience, to be sure, but within them lie that incompleteness of information, those seeds of bad performance habits, and that certain dullness of routine that frequently rob these wonderful little pieces of their emotional and stylistic potential as music.

I begin my study with *Our Flirtations* (1880), which was composed in the year that Sousa became Leader of the Marine Band and is one of his most charming marches—light in character, transparent in texture, captivating in its rhythmic swing. It is a model for the many that were to follow. It is theater pit Sousa,[23] more Austrian than German in character. The lightness of the first strain's melody invites appropriate counter figures borrowed rhythmically and melodically from the final bar of the introduction:

Sousa's marches begin by getting everybody's attention, and *Our Flirtations* sets that

pattern, too. These solidly scored attention getters were no place for the safe-minded Sousa to take chances, for he almost always began his marches squarely on the first beat of the first bar. The prebar flourish would come later, but for now he was consistently given to downbeat introductions in multiples of the two-pulse. This beginning is a solid four-bar, four-octave fortissimo statement that leaves nothing in doubt:

As the quiet first strain unfolds past its middle, listeners are led carefully where the composer wants to take them and where, it is assumed, they are happy to go. This fundamental observation of one aspect of his technique in writing these miniature essays states, as well, one of the basic reasons for his immense success with his general public. He gave them what they had grown to expect. And as the first strain of *Our Flirtations* moves toward its twelfth bar Sousa raises the listener's attention to his enriching harmony, to be followed by a vitally rhythmic and highly dynamic conclusion to the march's initial statement:

The graceful melodic figure which skips along in the reeds of the band marks the music as conceived for them. Sustaining harmonic trombones, countering euphoniums, rhythmic horns, and tubas with quiet percussion lead to the conclusion already described and dominated by the brass. In these sixteen bars Sousa has provided a tune, a counter tune, simple yet rich harmony, rhythmic-harmonic accompaniment, and an interesting crescendo to contrasting new material in a convincing climax—sixteen bars any composer might well have been pleased to write. They look and sound composed, the result of a combination of talent and intellect—and inspiration.

In addition to leading the listener in the manner described, the composer has also knitted a single rhythmic figure (a) into the fabric of the first strain and has then made it the principal idea (b) of the second strain:

Whether known to them or not, average listeners cling to these tonal-rhythmic consistencies as they hear their way through the music, and these are the people for whom Sousa wrote his marches.

The second strain of *Our Flirtations* is in deliberate contrast to the first, for it plays at the fortissimo dynamic all the way, that being the nature of the material with its simple and effective imitation between the upper brass and reeds and like instruments of midrange. It would eventually become his style sometimes to write second strains with contrasting dynamics:

The trio's subdued first strain, like the airiness of the first strain of the march, is in contrast to the music that precedes it and is, as well, a continuation of his theater pit experiences heightened here by extensive use of trills (harmonized) in the melody and given, of course, to the reeds of the band:

Trills and ornaments of this nature are characteristic of Sousa's early marches, those before 1910, including that most famous trill trio of them all, *The Stars and Stripes Forever.*

The initial strain and first trio of *Our Flirtations* are definitely indoor sit-down music, their essentially delicate character not being rooted in the parade ground. This primary element of band music was to become a part of the Sousa style in marches up ahead.

The break strain[24] in *Our Flirtations* is sixteen forceful bars of contrast to the trio's beginning:

Its tune, solidly blocked in bass line octaves while others accompany and counter it in mostly afterbeat patterns, is aural preparation for the all-out final fortissimo statement combining the trio material with an attractive arching countermelody on euphoniums and trombones:

Sousa's choice of the six-eight meter for *Semper Fidelis* guaranteed it a certain swing,[25]

but when that meter becomes the drive for his attractive use of what appears at first to be the key of G major in solid harmony, aided by repetition, and capped by the white-key scale on G, the swing gains its remarkable momentum in a big hurry. Listeners are actually ten bars into the piece before the composer offers them a C-major chord—the key of it all. It all seems very simple and it is very effective:

The music that follows in contrast to this makes marchers and listeners comfortable while the composer readies his repeated offering of the main tune topped off with a trumpetlike flourish that happily surprises the first time it is heard. Any portion of the trumpet's (or bugle's) functional harmonic series that is employed in music of the genre usually brings instant identity with things military. Again, Sousa leads his listeners and in this instance focuses their attention on the military purpose of this march:[26]

And when strain one has run its second playing, Sousa picks up on the spirit of the trumpet flourish to take the marcher-listener into the second principal idea (second strain) by way of those secure and effective devices known as a crescendo and a rising C-major scale. We may have heard or played these measures hundreds of times but, in my case, they never fail to cause me to rise to Mr. Sousa's attractive aural bait; it must be the same for others. One can only assume that it is the combination of talent, musical intellect, and an innate sense for balancing variety that tells a Sousa that his second musical idea in a march like this one is more effective when it is in contrast to the first than when it is either similar to it or the same. Here, when the initial contrast is paced to longer note values, equal and driving—set in solid bedrock pylons of harmony—the listener and marcher are treated to every security, dressed up in the best Sousa fashion. It, too, then has its contrasts and restatements (including a reminder of the trumpeting idea) leading to a primary Sousaism: one strategically and startlingly placed chord to surprise the average listener. This occurs in *Semper Fidelis* as the second strain is about to be concluded:

Using the ancient and effective device of deceiving listeners momentarily by (in this case) slipping the A-minor chord under the melody (to which it is compatible) he then "startles" them

with the immediately louder and very forcefully executed harmonic combination described above and displayed in Example 11. This kind of harmonic "exoticism" obviously became an audience pleaser and he set it up for them by framing it within music's most effective ally—silence. This attempt at a nontechnical description of how Sousa wrote one segment of a march may further be portrayed as "momentarily deceiving" so as to then "comfort and satisfy."[27]

Sousa was very adept at this basic process in writing the music he chose to compose for the audience he obviously lived to please; the device may be found in almost every Sousa march.

To conclude the first half of *Semper Fidelis*, he continued to be a good composer in his reuse of familiar material by returning again to the trumpet flourish, this time played going down instead of up in continual fulfillment of his regimental march commitment.

Sousa's most original contribution to the march idiom comes next by way of the content, form, and character of the trio of *Semper Fidelis*. He began it in the most effective manner, devoting its introduction entirely to an eight-bar cadence for the snare-field drums alone:

(x = hit drumsticks together)

It is a marvellously simple idea! It spawned a variety of other similar and anonymous drum cadences—some still developing—sometimes called "street beats," but to the writer's knowledge, this is the first one to have been written down, generally accepted, and incorporated into a military band march.[28] He borrowed it from a book he had compiled and composed two years earlier to aid in the training of players. He called it *The Trumpet and Drum*.[29]

When he adopted this music as the first half of the *Semper Fidelis* trio he obviously thought the top-line melody could stand alone. The trumpet's part as the principal musical idea in this music used only the four notes that are the easiest to blow on a natural trumpet (no valves) pitched in the key of F:

Sousa then began to construct his unusual march edifice above and below it, first adding this foundation of scales in the tubas with rhythmic punctuations from the drums:

These lines then became the bottom layer of a delicious four-layer musical cake.[30]

On top of this and above the trumpet tune he added this intriguing layer of offbeat sounds from the clarinets:

The whole fabric of the music was then interlaced by this compellingly powerful counter tune in the trombones:

When put together this is what a slice of this layer-cake march looks like:

91

For the final strain, with its composer still "Always Faithful" to the regimental purpose of this really great march, he provides yet another compelling and appropriately simple tune that allows his buglers to trumpet away at their fanfares (now expanded to a fifth partial above the four used in the first half of the trio); the trombones scale their way throughout this simplest, this minimal harmonic material. While the drums beat their way into the first trio, the music employs only two chords, but in no way does it seem to be as uninteresting as that low chord count might suggest. Much has been accomplished with the triads of F and C major (with the seventh of the C major added to the second half of the trio).

But as the march is drawing to its close Sousa reaches back to the exactly comparable spot in its second strain to serve up, one last time, his favorite chord for harmonic emphasis (see Example 11). And when he is done he is finished—no break strain, no stinger or repetition of the final chord being any part of his concept of this superbly constructed piece of music. It is, as he must have known, "a really inspired march" and it speaks with glowing eloquence for the whole Sousa output.

Had he stopped here he would surely have had an unquestioned high place among the composers of music on-the-march. Happily, there would be so many more, such as *The Thunderer*, or *The Washington Post* which turned out to be Sousa's double-edged essay in the form—popular as a march, of course, but almost equally so for a time as dance music for the two-step.

Among Sousa's continuing developments in march composition is a noticeable variety in texture, *The Washington Post* being as different from *The Thunderer* as that march is from *Semper Fidelis*. Even more different from all of the marches he wrote between 1880 and 1890 is *The Corcoran Cadets* (1890). It is Sousa's eighth-note march, more for sit-down playing than for the field or street and certainly not for the dance floor. It is

as though he set out deliberately to compose a piece in duple time that would be produced with absolutely minimum resources, yet be rhythmically neat, texturally clean, harmonically and melodically satisfying, and (for him) stylistically unique. He succeeded.

The High School Cadets (1890) is as contrasting a kind of march from *The Corcoran Cadets* as Sousa would write in a single year. The contrasts are stylistic and, like *Corcoran*, it is fashioned from very simple rhythmic and melodic elements. By them he leads listeners through two fetching strains to a quiet and sonorous trio in G-flat. The whole of its form is uncomplex; imitation is basic; there is no introduction to the trio, no break strain, no stinger, and the trio's second strain winds up with some of the most wide-open, free-swinging band music I know. Sousa's use of the trombones to intone the first three notes only and then other fragments of the melody while the rest of the tune keepers carry on with the melody makes all the difference. The simplicity of this final strain simply gets to me, and its appeal to everything in me that made me feel that—somehow—I had to become a conductor will always reaffirm that critical decision. It is a feeling I got in high school; the realization that the two great upbeats to every phrase in the last strain were made for percussion!

On one vividly memorable occasion it struck again and with a big impact. In the fifth week of Serge Koussevitzky's private class in conducting at the 1942 session of the Berkshire Music Center, I had just finished a busy week of lessons with the maestro during which I had filled my head with an exciting study of Stravinsky's *Histoire du Soldat*, conducted Haydn's Symphony no. 88, and played percussion along with my classmates and the Berkshire Music Center Orchestra in the first U.S. concert performance of the Shostakovitch Seventh Symphony. Pretty heady stuff, and I was into it all the way.

It was Sunday and my wife, Dorothy, our close friend, Robert L. Swan, and I ventured up the highway toward Pittsfield stopping at a restaurant that looked inexpensive yet inviting. The heady conversation continued over the sounds of a pop tune coming from the then inevitable jukebox. But suddenly there came from it—of all sources—the unmistakable and arresting opening bars of *The High School Cadets*. As the end of the record approached, with the sounds I knew were coming, dining ceased while Mr. Sousa moved into my head in company with Stravinsky, Haydn, and Shostakovitch. I fed a dime into the slot and pushed the button for two more plays; it was nothing less than terrific. The feeling has never really left me.[31]

The introduction to the *Corcoran Cadets*, like that of *Our Flirtations* of a decade earlier, is eight bars of octaves-unisons that also establish a simple rhythmic premise that is then projected into the first strain. The five-note figure with which this begins *is* that rhythmic premise, and it appears there in various guises eleven times to set the scene for what is perhaps Sousa's most tightly knit, rhythmically integrated, and sparsely conceived piece, from the first note to the last:

Sousa's second idea is similarly compact and repetitious:

Three literal statements of this idea drive home rhythmically a simply repetitive point. The harmonic and dynamic contrast expected in the trio is fulfilled, but it, too, is ruled by the march's integral concept, this identical eight-bar figure consuming twenty-four of the strain's thirty-two bars:

Still concerned with his introductory rhythmic idea, Sousa's break strain, though moving the rhythmic motive:

from the first beat of the bar to the second, uses it five insistent and extremely effective times to conclude the bridge leading to the final statement, thus bringing to a climax the composition's impressive rhythmic unity. Like every piece of music, it is meant to be heard, not written about, but if heard with some awareness of its simple yet superb construction within the four-square confines of the traditional march form, listening to it may be just that much more rewarding. It is very unusual Sousa.

Manhattan Beach is a mere sixty-eight bars long without repeats. Lean and driving, it is almost brash for Sousa. With brevity ruling its very concise form, he needs only the minimum four-bar introduction, two sixteen-bar highly complementary strains, no introduction to the two-part trio, no break strain, and a very convincing no-stinger ending! The tune of the trio is utterly plain rhythmically and is one of Sousa's simplest, its harmony hovering continually around the subdominant G-minor triad and darting off to wherever seems appropriate. Its Alberti basslike insides given to the clarinet section is a striking feature, one he used again twenty-nine years later in the first trio of *The Gallant Seventh*.

Both strains of the *Manhattan Beach* trio are fashioned from large note values. These, together with the forward-thrusting action of the introduction and the spritely character of the first strain, make this sit-down march take right off. Each march has its own tempo, especially those marches not specifically intended or used for regimental review, which this one was not, and thus as it moves along it fits the gay character of the kind of place for which it was named, and very probably reflects a happy personal relationship with Sousa's Manhattan Beach audiences.

El Capitan (1896) is a fair compendium of already familiar Sousaisms run through the creative sieve and set down with evident discipline. His loyal toe-tapping, two-pulse appreciators marching down familiar streets in the first two strains are suddenly introduced, and with no warning, to one of Sousa's rare switches in a basic march rhythm. The lilt of the triple pulse in the six-eight meter with which the march begins simply gives way to the duple bounce of two-four. When heard for the first time, an intriguing rhythmic reaction is the result. The march could well have ended with the full cadence of the second

ending that precedes it with its forceful fortissimo termination. Slipping this change in under the cover of the starkly reduced pianissimo dynamic, Sousa has as effectively deceived his listeners as he had faithfully led them on so many other occasions. He did it again ten years later in another great march, his longest, *The Free Lance*, (1906).

The instruments which constituted the Sousa Band (basic to what we use today) and for which he wrote his marches have proceeded in their evolution to the high level of today's mass-manufactured and well-produced machines of music.

The Band's principal instrument seems always to have been the cornet, the evolutionary tale of which is too long to relate.

The three-valve cornet, with its power to project the sound of its chromatically negotiated two-and-a-half-plus octaves, was the inevitable carrier of the tune for music played mostly in the open air. A long line of virtuosi, who emerged as its premier players, became the public's darlings in the era of bands such as Sousa's. The lyricism and musical pyrotechnics displayed by the featured cornet soloist were expected by the public, and Sousa always tried to satisfy his audience with the best available performers.

Before the obvious need for the publisher to provide something more was satisfied, it was the part written for the solo B-flat cornet from which all of us were expected to conduct, and the printed music so specified. This impossible condition is far from totally relieved in this eighth decade of the twentieth century.

The B-flat cornet's predecessor among the brass melody instruments was the shorter high-ranging cornet in E-flat that led and topped the sound of the American brass band instruments played over the shoulder at the time of the Civil War. Later, when the bell of the instrument was repositioned up and in front during the post-Civil War silver cornet band era, the E-flat instrument lived on briefly in Sousa's and other composers' marches but disappeared when Sousa abandoned it.

By the time he scored *El Capitan*, the solo B-flat cornet was king among his brasses and, when joined by a second and third voice playing triad harmony, the customary functions of the cornet section were clearly established as joint tenancy of melody and harmony. A more rhythmic role was assigned to the trumpet in Sousa's concept of that instrument as a counter soprano to the cornet among the Band's brasses. It differs from the cornet (supposedly of conical bore) as to its cylindrical tubing, the character of the mouthpiece cup, and the tonal concept and playing style provided by the performer. Its sonority, contrasted with the cornet's may be considered as more brightly projected. It has always been a fanfare instrument, serving royalty and enjoying that patronage. Coupled with kettledrums it has always enjoyed its role in the orchestra.[32]

It was the trumpets' fanfare function that Sousa liked. Their appropriate use in rhythmic figuration was what set them apart from his three-voiced melodic and harmonic lines for cornets. *El Capitan*'s cornet and trumpet parts in the final strain of the trio demonstrate these differences:

As the nineteenth century was winding down, Sousa composed another of his great marches and fashioned a catchy title to go with it. *Hands Across the Sea* (1899) was a good and welcome idea, since the Spanish-American War had recently become history.[33]

It has been selected for comment because of its strong rhythmic vitality. Its introduction is a vivid example of explosive Sousa:

After this everything continues to go someplace and keep moving with great vigor. That carefully planned repetition of an idea (frequently observed) is here, too, and it leads listeners harmonically through Sousa's first ideas, even deceiving them as to where he is by avoiding all the chords they expect to hear until he finally provides them as he plunges into the second strain. It, too, keeps driving ahead with enormous rhythmic thrust avoiding any letup in the solid fortissimo dynamic which has ruled since bar one; but here the listener is on solid Sousa soil.

That strong two-beat attention getter which so swingingly marks the last strain of *The High School Cadets* is here, too, used just a bit differently to lead the music to its trio. Here the dynamic has changed for the first time to piano as Sousa begins to spin out a very simple tune, seemingly designed to grow:

After thirty-two bars of this quiet contrast, he comes at the listener with a solid break strain that is as effective as it is simple,

leading to this simple bit of contrapuntal play that he so frequently built into these musical bridges:

The final strain is a happy melange of compatible musical ideas, all in fortissimo, that continues to build and to carry the march's excitement to the end. Sousa is true to his simple imitative material in the final two bars of the bass line:

In its dynamic proportions it is not the usual Sousa; of the 150 measures in *Hands Across the Sea*, 119 are fortissimo. Something is lost when these balances are changed.

The Fairest of the Fair (1908) is among the very best of Sousa's pieces—mature, inspired, positively composed, revealing not only his expected melodic gift, but displaying as well

genuine craftsmanship in its composition. The introduction's four very attractive bars (beginning with a prebar flourish) are such a good idea that he uses them five more times, twice to conclude the first two strains, then once again to end the twenty-bar break strain in a novel setting for reeds and percussion:

As we have seen was his fashion, all of this transpires within the simplest of harmonic means supported by engaging rhythmic energy and solid orchestration. Here he displays that remarkable sense of pacing that seems to be the special gift of the writer of ballads. We hear again that Sousa knows just where to arrest or to activate the tapping toe. His change of pace at the trio when the busy activity of the march to that point gives way to the larger note values is just the change that is needed. The sonorous A-flat major tune with its expressive ornamentation and rich supporting harmonies carries the listener willingly through a series of rises and falls. And when he has come to the end of these musical elevations, the composer returns his listener safely to the solid finish which then invites the attractive interlude between the trios.

The U.S. Field Artillery march is set in duple time, beginning with another of those Sousa explosions in A-flat that get everybody's attention and let them know from the first note that they are about to hear something they will want to remember. The most intriguing factor in the evaluation of this march masterpiece is how perfectly the Sousa in it fits the Gruber which it surrounds, as I mentioned earlier. All of it simply belongs together, Sousa rising so remarkably to the vitality and drive that both the words and music of

"The Caisson Song" (as it is properly called) so effectively generate. The first strain's unrepeated thirty-two bars contain unusual harmonic and rhythmic variety for an initial Sousa statement:

Then, as if to gather listeners after this (for him) rambling excursion, the second strain is solidly simple, rhythmically contrasting, and the ideal bridge to the featured song in the trio. Inasmuch as it is a song, Sousa had the words printed beneath the music of the solo cornet part. Their performance at top voice by all in the band except those playing a minimum accompaniment adds an important performance dimension to this initial setting of the song. Then the master of the break strain goes to work on a compatible rhythmic figure:

and develops it for twelve bars of gathering harmonic and rising dynamic excitement until the whole thing explodes with one of Sousa's most effective uses of that favorite "surprise" chord:

97

He likes the idea so much that after stretching it out twice he then hits the listener with six short bursts of the same chord and works his way right back to "The Caisson Song" for its final full-throttle conclusion by the whole band. Marches more wide open or exciting than *The U.S. Field Artillery* are not easy to find.[34] Once again, as in that other swinging finale of *The High School Cadets*, when Sousa is through he has no need for that traditional final note and it should never be added.

In *The Black Horse Troop*, after the solid introduction, the first strain, and the first half of the second episode he offers—for the only time this way—a charming eight-bar bridge:

It is quietly scored (piano) to feature his trio of mellow cornets and to expose as well the lyric quality associated with the Sousa Band reeds. The percussion, save for the quiet chinging sound of cymbals, is absent until the whole band joins again for a truncated statement of the opening of the second strain. It is the work of a skilled and inspired sculptor of those pad-free "marble statues." So, too, is the singing quality of his melody for the trio. It is one of his most expressive melodic lines, dynamically subdued and harmonically rich.

The connecting bridge between the two final playings of the trio that follows the beautiful initial exposition of that melody is more than a break strain in its character. It does fulfill the function described throughout this paper as a break strain, but its content, its musical energy, and—again—its functional dignity grant it a dimension that its composer seems to have reserved for this very special march. Here are sixteen bars of mature band music as good as Sousa ever wrote, providing the listener and the player with all of those individual dividends I have attempted to isolate in these observations of his marches:

He had one more for horsemen; *Riders for the Flag* is the lighter counterpart to the solid dignity of *The Black Horse Troop*. It combines the bounce of *The Washington Post* with the layer-cake construction of *Semper Fidelis*, a fair distillation of both. And, of course, there is the constant undercurrent of that riding rhythm of horses' hooves that the six-eight pattern matches so effectively. *Riders for the Flag* has regimental march characteristics from its trio onward, beginning with cavalry bugle call figures joined by euphonious countermelodies and an unusual use of the reeds of the band in the trio's first playing. Sousa gives their chordal punctuations the rhythmic spacings usually reserved for the cymbals and bass drum:

When the final statement of all the elements in this very convincing mixture of sounds is concluded, Sousa closes the march with a four-bar tag that always surprises everybody. His humorous and appropriate quote here from the   99 last four bars of the old bugle march "You're in the Army Now" is the only coda Sousa added to any of his marches.

Throughout our view of the Sousa march we have seen that its composer was a strict observer of custom and order. Rarely did he attempt to color his marches with props or borrowed tunes. But when he decided to shed his traditions, he went all the way—to New Mexico. The march he wrote for that state begins like many other Sousa marches, but that is the end of tradition in this piece. What follows is a musical history of New Mexico (recently granted statehood) embracing with appropriate effects the music of the Indian, the cavalry, and the Mexican. All of these diverse elements are then joined in happy fusion until the finale, the state's official song, 'O, Fair New Mexico."

Some might call it camp, but I am sure that its composer was serious about every note. Among its departures from usual Sousa are odd-numbered phrases and unpredictable musical lines. These, together with the use of nonmilitary band percussion add to the novelty. The first strain, for instance, has thirty-six bars (not thirty-two) and it is strongly two-part with its first twenty bars devoted to materials I have never seen in any of his marches. The second strain, though in the thirty-two-bar pattern, somehow registers as apart from the customary results of that order.

Next comes Sousa, Indian style, in a sequence lasting a rare forty-two bars in which all the clarinets of the band play the jagged, non-diatonic tune, punctuated by war drums:

Finally, when "O, Fair New Mexico" brings all together, the most unusual and different of all the Sousa marches is finished.

With the fourteen marches selected for this discussion of some aspects of his work, Sousa is revealed as a composer who was absolutely serious about composition in the march form. He composed to entertain, not to educate. The legacy of the march as he found it in the street and on the parade ground is what he chose to live with. Enriching its body and content he otherwise left it pretty much as he found it. He had not one hair of the experimenter in the moustache he wore to his grave; his marches reveal a constant outpouring of ingenuity, presenting a variety of approaches to a positively four-square form.

The cramped confinement of march-size paper, originating in the five- by seven-inch format to fit a soldier's music pouch or the pocket of his tunic, has dictated every element in a march ever since the military band began. Function, function, function—this is what Sousa patiently accepted, inasmuch as he seems to have found it a very adequate means of expression.

The obvious paper limitation does raise this question: Why did Sousa not adopt the continental practise with its·return to the beginning and termination at the trio, just to gain more playing time? A probable answer might be that he just did not hear his marches that way, as a look at the end of almost every second strain will show. His final strains are final. I cannot imagine a da capo in *The High School Cadets* or *The Stars and Stripes Forever*. Clapping the palms together as frequently as possible was also another design in Sousa concerts; 2¾ minutes were long enough for a march.

These creations had to sell for him on the street and band stand, and in the ballroom, the parlor, the amphitheater, and the concert hall. In his world of performance there was no room for the cerebral development of abstract musical ideas; these he left to others while he was busy entertaining a waiting public that obviously adored everything he did.

Human as he was he made his share of miscalculations, too, such as his view of jazz and its future.[35] He lived to see his Band die—to see all such bands die—and there is no recorded observation known to me of his reaction to this. The development of the motor car, the rise of jazz, the financial depression, the perfection of the vacuum tube, and the coming of radio are among the principal causes for the demise of the professional concert band as Sousa and others knew it. Difficult though it would be to fortify the statement with the customary mountain of data, it seems fair to say that the bands of America, for the seventy-five-year period that brought us from the Civil War to the Great Depression, made pioneer and positive contributions to the growth of music up to the present. Sousa, the great catalyst, came and passed; his marches remain.

Yes, John Philip Sousa was an American phenomenon, a composer with the gift to write simple music that, whatever else it may or may not be, is a music of anticipation—anticipation and fulfillment. That is what *The Stars and Stripes Forever* is all about—the anticipation in the second break strain and then the fulfillment of the great final trio. It is a measure of the man and his belief in himself as well as an indication of his devotion to the art, that he continued to produce march after march, never fearing that the next might fail.

Notes

1. Paul Bierley, *John Philip Sousa: American Phenomenon* (New York: Appleton, Century, Crofts, 1973), p. 133. Paul Bierley has assembled the most comprehensive overview of Sousa the conductor and all who wish to know this in detail are referred to this book, particularly Chapter IV, "Sousa's Philosophy of Music."

2. We did not know it then, and neither did his public, but Sousa had suffered a broken neck in 1921 when he was thrown from a horse. Recovery was limited and so, too, was his conducting style after this accident which immobilized his left arm for any action resembling the former colorful Sousa style; he could swing the arm but not lift it. At the outset of my career as a conductor well-meaning advisors always informed me that I should be much less active in my motions: "After all, Frederick, Sousa hardly moved at all!"

3. John Philip Sousa, *Marching Along* (Boston: Hale, Cushman and Flint, 1928).

4. Ibid., pp. 358-59, excerpted by the author.

5. Bierley, *Phenomenon*, p. 33.

6. Ibid., pp. 28, 29, 34.

7. Paul Bierley, *John Philip Sousa: A Descriptive Catalogue of His Works* (Urbana: University of Illinois Press, 1973), p. 172.

8. He said he had been crowned by an anonymous writer in "some obscure Brass Band Journal, published in England."

9. Bierley, *Phenomenon*, pp. 45, 62, 64-65.

10. He was the Band's seventeenth leader, 1880-92. All dates for Sousa's marches are based on the Paul Bierley *Catalogue*.

11. *The Rifle Regiment* was a very successful extension of form for him with its twenty-bar introduction that was incorporated into the first strain. Both were repeated; one of the few times Sousa went back to bar one. *On Parade* (1892) is among his very best, too, in every way, and like the customary continental march it makes the full da capo, repeating the introduction and the first and second strains to be completed where the trio begins. This, to me, is Sousa's most underrated march. *Guide Right* (1881) is known to me only from the Eastman Wind Ensemble-Hunsberger recording (Philips 9500-151). It has echoes from the brass band era and hints from Vienna as equal parts of its charm.

12. Bierley, *Catalogue*, pp. 69, 70.

13. I owe the source of this oft-used phrase to Deems Taylor, able and articulate observer of the musical scene, in *Of Men and Music* (New York: Simon and Schuster, 1944), p. 59. Paul Bierley, *Phenomenon*, p. 154, states that the Sousa Band marched only seven times during the thirty-nine years of its existence, and on those occasions some significant national event was celebrated. Sousa obviously worked very tirelessly to promote the Band as a concert-giving ensemble equal to any, while ironically achieving his fame through the writing of music inseparably associated with the Band's other and original function—moving marching units down streets and across parade grounds. Except for *The Stars and Stripes Forever*, American school bands rarely play his marches today, indoors or out.

14. For a detailed account see Margaret L. Brown, "David Blakely, Manager of Sousa's Band," in this volume.

15. Bierley, *Phenomenon*, p. 162.

16. Another American composer who was a master of music in the lighter vein was Leroy Anderson (1908-1975) whose similarly inexhaustible connection with the muse also produced music that invariably struck the listener as familiar on the first hearing.

17. Bierley, *Catalogue*, p. 174.

18. Ibid., pp. 42, 44.

19. Ibid., pp. 76-77.

20. "A horse, a dog, a gun, a girl, and music on the side. That is my idea of heaven." A quote from Sousa in Bierley, *Phenomenon*, p. 110.

21. For this see James R. Smart, "Genesis of a March: *The Stars and Stripes Forever*," in this volume.

22. Courtesy University of Illinois Bands and the Music Division, Library of Congress.

23. The march was written for a musical comedy which Sousa conducted. He was with the company in St. Louis when he received the invitation to become leader of the Marine Band.

24. The term, known to bandsmen, might also be called a bridge or interlude.

25. Duple- and triple-metered marches both swing but there are those who feel that the six-eight gait has the more effective projection of the pulse for a large number of marchers, mostly because its third and sixth beats are just that much closer to beats one and four when the marcher's foot touches the ground. But more important than the meter is the number of pulses per minute that establishes a marching cadence which drill instructors and marchers can live with. Invariably, it is too fast for a comfortable stride (104 steps per minute).

26. Beethoven's dramatic focus of attention, using the trumpet call on these same notes in *Fidelio*, is a classic use of the trumpet's functional harmonic series.

27. The technical harmony term for the chord is the German sixth which always resolves to the tonic chord in its second inversion.

28. F. E. Bigelow's classically simple march, *Our Director*, is one that follows this pattern. It dates from 1895.

29. John Philip Sousa, *The Trumpet and Drum* (Washington: 1886), pp. 114-17; reprinted 1954 by W. F. L. Drum Co. (Chicago, Illinois).

30. The trio of *The Stars and Stripes Forever* is also a layer-cake construction. Its melody, however, includes all of the notes of its A-flat major scale plus some notes that are altered, whereas the *Semper Fidelis* melody resource was dictated by those four "easy-to-play" notes on the natural trumpet (or bugle).

31. The performance was by the American Legion Band of Hollywood, California, on a ten-inch, 78 rpm Decca record.

32. The cornet's disappearance from most bands in the United States is probably the result of the trumpet's preeminence as the great horn for jazz.

33. Sousa felt inspired to write this march at this time in history as he was living it and gave it this title after reading a play in which he "came across this line—'a sudden thought strikes me—let us swear an eternal friendship.' " See Bierley, *Catalogue*, p. 50.

34. Mayhew Lake scored it for Sousa and the march was a brilliant commercial success. In his reluctance to accept first the phonograph and then the radio Sousa missed his greatest financial bonanzas, but reject them he did. His tardy move to radio is one I remember. His Band was sponsored by the Hoover Vacuum Cleaner Company; using *The U.S. Field Artillery* trio as one of the early singing commercials the voices sang along. All I remember of the words were those sung to the last nine notes, "for it beats, as it sweeps, as it cleans" in substitution for the "Caisson" words "that those caissons go rolling along." For a thorough review of Sousa and the phonograph see: James R. Smart, *The Sousa Band: A Discography* (Washington: Library of Congress, 1970).

35. Sousa, *Marching Along*, pp. 357, 358.

This flyer announces the itinerary for the Sousa Band for February and March 1896. The eighth semi-annual grand transcontinental tour ran from January through July. In the two months covered here, we find Sousa giving seventy-four concerts in fifty-eight days while travelling from coast to coast.
Blakely Papers, New York Public Library.   ▷

1896   EIGHTH SEMI-ANNUAL TOUR.   1896

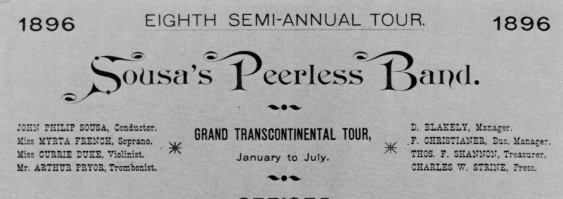

Sousa's Peerless Band.

JOHN PHILIP SOUSA, Conductor.
Miss MYRTA FRENCH, Soprano.
Miss CURRIE DUKE, Violinist.
Mr. ARTHUR PRYOR, Trombonist.

GRAND TRANSCONTINENTAL TOUR,
January to July.

D. BLAKELY, Manager.
F. CHRISTIANER, Bus. Manager.
THOS. F. SHANNON, Treasurer.
CHARLES W. STRINE, Press.

...OFFICES...

Carnegie Music Hall, New York.   *186 Monroe St., Chicago.*

FEBRUARY

Sun.	2	CHICAGO, III.	-	Matinee	-	Haymarket Theatre
Sun.	2	"	"	Evening	-	Grand Opera House
Mon.	3	JANESVILLE, Wis.	Matinee	Meyer's Opera House
Mon.	3	MADISON,	"	Evening	-	University Hall
Tues.	4	MINNEAPOLIS, Minn.	Mat. & Eve.	Lyceum Theatre
Wed.	5	DULUTH,	"	Mat. & Eve.	Lyceum Theatre
Thur.	6	ST. PAUL,	"	Mat. & Eve.	Grand Opera House
Fri.	7	FARGO, N. D.	-	Mat. & Eve.	Fargo Opera House
Sat.	8	En Route
Sun.	9	BUTTE, Mont.		Mat. & Eve.	Grand Opera House
Mon.	10	HELENA,	"	-	Mat. & Eve.	-	Auditorium
Tues.	11	SPOKANE, Wash.	-	Mat. & Eve.	-	Auditorium
Wed.	12	TACOMA,	"	-	Evening	-	Tacoma Theatre
Thur.	13	SEATTLE,	"	-	Mat. & Eve.	-	Seattle Theatre
Fri.	14	VICTORIA, B. C.	-	Mat. & Eve.	-	Victoria Theatre
Sat.	15	OLYMPIA, Wash.	-	Matinee	-	-	Opera House
Sat.	15	TACOMA,	"	-	Evening	-	Tacoma Theatre
Sun.	16	SEATTLE,	"	-	Evening	-	Seattle Theatre
Mon.	17	PORTLAND, Ore.	-	Evening	-	1st Reg't Armory
Tues.	18	"	"	-	Mat. & Eve.	1st Reg't Armory
Wed.	19	SALEM,	"	-	Evening	-	Reed Opera House
Thur.	20	En Route
Fri.	21	FRESNO,	Cal.	Evening	-	Barton Opera House
Sat.	22	LOS ANGELES,	"	Mat. & Eve.	-	Hazard Pavilion
Sun.	23	SAN DIEGO,	"	Evening	-	Fisher Opera House
Mon.	24	LOS ANGELES,	"	Evening	-	Hazard Pavilion
Tues.	25	SAN. BARBARA,	"	Mat. & Eve.	-	Opera House
Wed.	26	BAKERSFIELD,	"	Matinee	Niederaur's Op. House
Wed.	26	TULARE,	"	Evening	-	-	Old Rink
Thur.	27	SAN JOSE,	"	Mat. & Eve.	-	Auditorium
Fri.	28	SAN FRANCISCO,	"	Evening	-	-	Pavilion
Sat.	29	"	"	Mat. & Eve.	-	-	Pavilion
MAR.	1	"	"	Evening	-	-	Pavilion
Mon.	2	STOCKTON,	"	Evening	-	Yosemite Theatre
Tues.	3	SACRAMENTO,	"	Mat. & Eve.	Met. Opera House
Wed.	4	CARSON, Nev.	-	Matinee	-	-	Opera House
Wed.	4	RENO,	"	-	Evening	McKissick Op. House
Thur.	5	OGDEN, Utah,	-	Evening	-	Grand Opera House

MARCH

Fri.	6	SALT LAKE, Utah,		Evening	-	-	Tabernacle
Sat.	7	"	"		Matinee	-	-	Tabernacle
Sat.	7	PROVO,	"		Evening	-	-	Tabernacle
Sun.	8	LEADVILLE, Colo.	Evening	-	-	Opera House
Mon.	9	DENVER,	"		Evening	-	Broadway Theatre
Tues.	10	"	"	Mat. & Eve.	Broadway Theatre
Wed.	11	COLO. SPRINGS	"	Matinee	-	-	Opera House
Wed.	11	PUEBLO,	"	Evening	-	Grand Opera House
Thur.	12	HUTCHINSON, Kan.	Matinee	-	-	Opera House
Thur.	12	WICHITA,	"	Evening	-	-	Auditorium
Fri.	13	KANSAS CITY, Mo.	Matinee	-	-	Auditorium
Fri.	13	ST. JOSEPH,	"	Evening	-	-	Tootle Theatre
Sat.	14	OMAHA, Neb.	-	Mat. & Eve.	-	Boyd's Theatre
Sun.	15	CHICAGO, III.	-	Matinee	-	Haymarket Theatre
Sun.	15	"	"	-	Evening	-	Hooley's Theatre
Mon.	16	ANDERSON, Ind.	-	Matinee	-	Grand Opera House
Mon.	16	RICHMOND,	"	-	Evening	Bradley Opera House
Tues.	17	XENIA,	Ohio,	Matinee	-	-	Opera House
Tues.	17	DAYTON,	"		Evening	-	Grand Opera House
Wed.	18	SPRINGFIELD,	"	Matinee	-	Grand Opera House
Wed.	18	COLUMBUS,	"	Evening	-	High St. Theatre
Thur.	19	PITTSBURG, Penn.	Evening	-	Carnegie Music Hall
Fri.	20	PHILADELPHIA,	"	Evening	-	-	Academy
Sat.	21	"	"	Mat. & Eve.	-	Academy
Sun.	22	WASHINGTON, D. C.	Evening	-	The Lafayette
Mon.	23	BALTIMORE,	Md.	Evening	-	-	Music Hall
Tues.	24	HAGERSTOWN,	"	Matinee	-	-	Opera House
Tues.	24	CHAMBERSBURG,	"	Evening	-	-	Opera House
Wed.	25	CARLISLE,	Penn.	Matinee	Sentinel Opera House
Wed.	25	HARRISBURG,	"	Evening	-	-	Opera House
Thur.	26	SHAMOKIN,	"	Matinee	G. A. R. Opera House
Thur.	26	HAZLETON,	"	Evening	-	Grand Opera House
Fri.	27	PITTSTON,	"	Matinee	-	-	Music Hall
Fri.	27	SCRANTON,	"	Evening	-	The Frothingham
Sat.	28	BETHLEHEM,	"	Matinee	-	-	Opera House
Sat.	28	ALLENTOWN,	"	Evening	-	-	Academy
Sun.	29	BROOKLYN, N. Y.	Evening	-	Montauk Theatre
Mon.	30	PATERSON, N. J.	Mat. & Eve.	-	New Armory

Address Letters three to five days in advance of date, care SOUSA'S BAND.

NOTE.—New England and Canadian Tour commences April 24th. Manhattan Beach, June 14th to Sept. 6th.

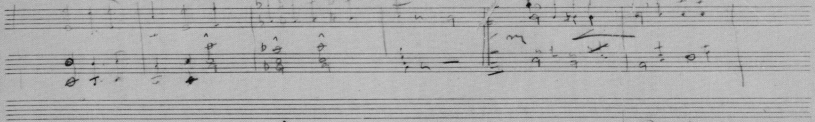
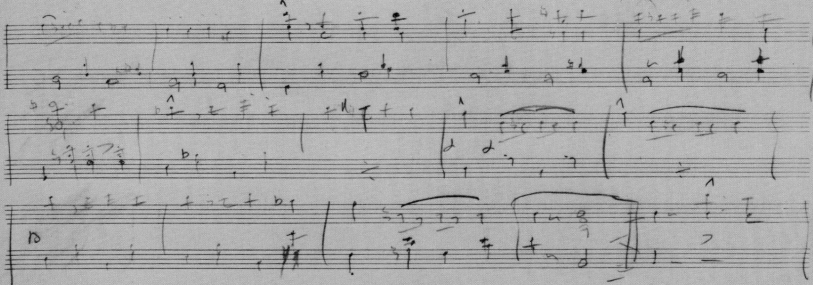
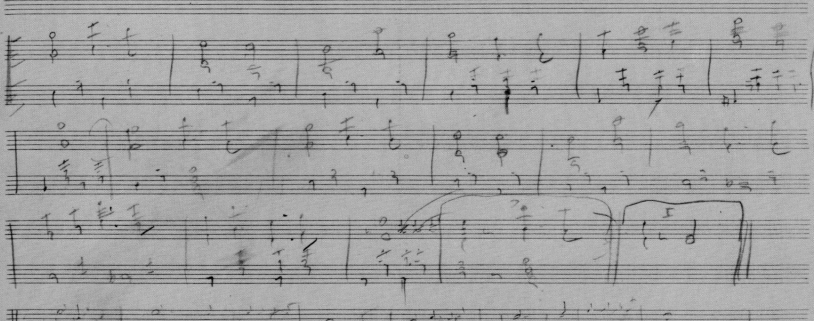
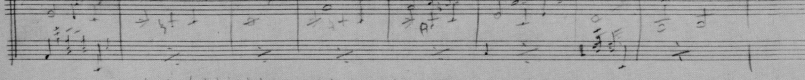
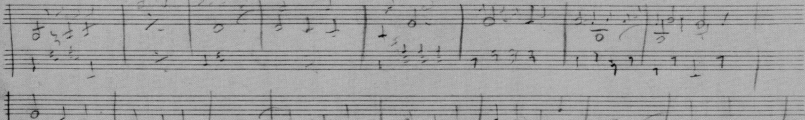

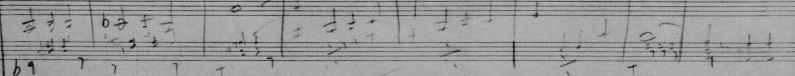

Genesis of a March:
The Stars and Stripes Forever

by James R. Smart

Sing out for liberty, and light,
Sing out for freedom and the right,
Sing out for Union and its might,
O patriotic sons.

John Philip Sousa

The Congressional Cemetery in Washington, D.C., is far removed from the well-worn track followed by the tourist trade. Yet, this simple graveyard is the last resting place of many of America's famous men and women. Among the graves of political and military figures, of statesmen and educators, housewives and laborers, is the Sousa family plot. There one finds a stone engraved, "John Philip Sousa, U.S.N.R.F." Two additional engravings indicate, however, that something more than an officer of the Naval Reserve lies here. At the head of the stone is a wreath lying on a music director's baton. At the foot is inscribed a tune covering a brief four measures of notation. The baton implies that this man was a musician, a conductor in fact. The four-measure melody indicates that he was also a composer. But more than this, it shows that here lies the man who wrote one of the most famous of musical compositions, a work known the world over. The melody is the first four bars of the trio section of *The Stars and Stripes Forever*. Out of the large body of musical works composed by John Philip Sousa, no more fitting choice for an epitaph could have been selected. Not only is this march his most famous work, it is one that he said many times was his finest composition. It was his favorite child and the only one to whose composition Sousa openly and publicly referred. Considering his comments today, one is almost inclined to believe he was in awe of this march, which he said was produced by some powerful impulse beyond his direct control. Paul Bierley, in his catalog of Sousa's works, quotes the following from a 1923 band program:

Someone asked, "Who influenced you to compose 'Stars and Stripes Forever,'" and before the question was hardly asked, Sousa replied, "God—and I say this in all reverence."[1]

This piety might seem startling in someone who spent a good part of his life writing martial music, but Sousa was, as Bierley points out, a religious man who told a reporter in 1922, "The music that becomes valuable in the world's repertoire is formed by the combination of a man with a power beyond himself."[2] Sousa, of course, was far from being the only composer to hold such a belief, but he was one of the few to state it openly. That he did so is indicative of the fact that he was entirely serious in his approach to composition. He viewed all his works—marches as well as descriptive suites, operettas, and all the rest—as serious creations.

We are fortunate in that Sousa was born at just the time most suitable for developing his particular gifts—an era of great bands and band music, which he himself brought to its zenith, and an era of tremendous nationalist excitement. Sousa's childhood was lived surrounded by the patriotic and musical trappings of the Marine Band, of which his father was a member, and he was an eyewitness to the stirring scenes of Washington at the end of the Civil War. He wrote later of the May 1865 Grand Parade up Pennsylvania Avenue by victorious Boys in Blue: "Surely no boy of eleven would miss that spectacle. It is as vivid today as if it all happened only yesterday."[3] (Sousa described the Grand Parade in detail in his semiautobiographical novel, *Pipetown Sandy*.) The flag, freedom, pageantry, the American eagle, patriotism—all these were woven into the fiber of John Philip Sousa at an early age, as they were into many other young men of the time. These impressions colored their outlook generally and surfaced again during the Spanish-American War of 1898. The years immediately preceding that war, the first major conflict with a foreign power since 1845, were years of fiery patriotism and even of jingoism. Patriotic newspaper propaganda found a ready response in the hearts of Americans of the mid-1890s when the cry *Cuba libre* rang through the land. All of this must be taken into account when discussing the works of Sousa, especially *The Stars and Stripes Forever*.

Sousa turned forty-two years of age in the fall of 1896. Behind him were some of his finest compositions, including the marches *Yorktown Centennial*, *The Gladiator*, *The Rifle Regiment*, *Semper Fidelis*, *The Thunderer*, *The Washington Post*, *The High School Cadets*, *The Liberty Bell*, and *King Cotton*, and the recently completed operetta, *El Capitan*. He was already called the March King, and these compositions, as well as such descriptive pieces as *Sheridan's Ride* and *The Last Days of Pompeii*, had brought him national acclaim. Encouraged by this success, in 1932, at age thirty-seven, he resigned from the Marine Band, which he had led since 1880, to form his own concert band. By 1896 he had led the new Sousa Band on four cross-country tours, from Maine to Oregon, had played extended engagements at the 1893 Columbian Exposition, and had spent summers playing at such resorts as the then famous Manhattan Beach. Throughout these years Sousa remained active as a composer and finished his successful operetta, *El Capitan*, whose first production he supervised personally. David Blakely, manager of the Sousa Band and the person chiefly responsible for persuading Sousa to organize it, realized that Sousa was nearing exhaustion. Blakely suggested a vacation before the beginning of the 1896-97 tour in December, and on September 17, 1896, Sousa and his wife left New York for their first trip abroad.

Sousa must have felt confident that he could leave final arrangements for the tour in Blakely's hands. The two men had worked closely together for four years, since the Band was formed and their first contract signed in 1892. According to that contract, Blakely was to arrange all the tours and pay Sousa both a salary and a percentage of the gross profits. Sousa agreed to pay Blakely half the receipts on sales both of all music he had written up to that time and of any music he might write during the five-year life of the contract.[4] It must

have been with considerable shock and sadness, then, that Sousa read, in a four-day-old copy of the Paris *Herald*, that Blakely had dropped dead in his New York office on November 7, the day after Sousa's forty-second birthday. Sousa was then in Naples, Italy, but realizing that the entire 1897 tour and the rest of his carefully laid plans were now in jeopardy, he decided to cut short his vacation and return to New York. He and his wife left Naples for England almost at once, traveling through Genoa and Paris. On November 18 they sailed from Liverpool on board the White Star liner *Teutonic* and landed in New York City on the afternoon of November 25 (not December 25 as is sometimes said). Sousa's arrival was mentioned in the "Theatrical Gossip" column of the New York *Times* for November 27, 1896: "Sousa arrived Wednesday on the *Teutonic*. His vacation abroad was brought to a sudden close by the death of Band Manager Blakely."

His abrupt departure from Europe, under sad and anxious circumstances, may have produced in Sousa that reflective mood so often associated with serious creative work. The voyage itself was described by the composer several times, and in slightly different versions. In *Marching Along*, a book of reminiscences published in 1928, he wrote:

As the vessel steamed out of the harbor I was pacing the deck, absorbed in thoughts of my manager's death and the many duties and decisions which awaited me in New York. Suddenly, I began to sense the rhythmic beat of a band playing within my brain. It kept on ceaselessly, playing, playing, playing. Throughout the whole tense voyage, that imaginery band continued to unfold the same themes, echoing and re-echoing the most distinct melody. I did not transfer a note of that music to paper while I was on the steamer, but when we reached shore, I set down the measures that my brain band had been playing for me, and not a note of it has ever changed. The composition is known the world over as *The Stars and Stripes Forever* and is probably my most popular march.[5]

Two additional references by Sousa to this event

should be quoted. One was in the 1923 band program mentioned earlier:

On board the steamer as I walked up and down the deck, back and forth, a mental band was playing *Stars and Stripes Forever*. Day after day as I walked it persisted in crashing into my very soul. I wrote it on Christmas Day, 1896.[6]

Sousa referred to the voyage again in an interview published in the October 30, 1915, issue of *New York Review*, also quoted by Bierley:

In a kind of dreamy way I used to think over the old days at Washington when I was leader of the Marine Band . . . when we played at all public official functions, and I could see the Stars and Stripes flying from the flagstaff on the grounds of the White House just as plainly as if I were back there again.

Then I began to think of all the countries I had visited, of the foreign people I had met, of the vast difference between America and American people and other countries and other peoples, and that flag of ours became glorified . . . and to my imagination it seemed to be the biggest, grandest, flag in the world, and I could not get back under it quick enough.

It was in this impatient, fretful state of mind that the inspiration to compose *The Stars and Stripes Forever* came to me, and to my imagination it was a genuine inspiration, irresistible, complete, definite, and I could not rest until I had finished the composition. Then I experienced a wonderful sense of relief and relaxation. I was satisfied, delighted with my work after it was done. The feeling of impatience passed away, and I was content to rest peacefully until the ship had docked and I was once more under the folds of the grand old flag of our country.[7]

There are several points to be noted in these most interesting accounts. In the first, Sousa reports that "I did not transfer a note of that music to paper while I was on the steamer, but when we reached shore, I set down the measures that my brain band had been playing for me, and not a note of it has ever changed." In the second account, he says "I wrote it on Christmas Day, 1896." In the third, however, he says that "I could not rest until I had finished the composition. Then I experienced a wonderful sense of relief and relaxation." Was the march, then, written down as soon as "we reached shore," on November 25; or a

month after landing, on Christmas Day, 1896; or, as implied by the last quote, during the voyage? It may be, as Bierley suggests, that Sousa composed the piece in his head during the voyage and only wrote it down later, after landing. This theory would remove the most serious contradiction in Sousa's accounts. Some have assumed from the first quote that Sousa landed, dashed to his hotel, and wrote out the march in the heat of inspiration. But this apparently did not happen, and in fact Sousa at no time claimed that he wrote the music *immediately* after he "reached shore."

It appears to have been Sousa's custom when composing marches, first to sketch out themes in (usually) pencil and to sign and date them. Depending on his schedule, Sousa evidently tried to do some sketching every day. Among thousands of preserved sketches are some written while on the train, often marked en route, and others written on the backs of envelopes, on hotel stationery, and even on menus, a la Franz Schubert. Having chosen melodies for various sections of the march in progress, Sousa would then write out the piece in a pencilled piano score which sometimes, but not always, was signed and dated. If this gave a satisfactory result, he would then rewrite the piano score in ink and sign and date it. The final step in the process was the writing out of the complete band score in ink, which also would usually be signed and dated. It should not be supposed that these steps necessarily followed one another in close sequence.

Turning now to *The Stars and Stripes Forever*, it is interesting to note that not a single sketch for this march has been located. This bears out the composer's contention that the march was conceived as an entity, although we must point out that sketches for numerous other marches have not been located either. Until 1977 it was thought that the only surviving holograph manuscripts of this march were the piano score in ink and the full band score, also in ink. The piano score is written out so neatly that many years ago a publisher had it reproduced, and copies were distributed to many libraries and college band departments. This piano score is dated "Xmas '96" and supports Sousa's statement, "I wrote it on Christmas Day, 1896." In view of Sousa's usual practice of first drafting the piano score in pencil, and in view of the neatness of the ink score, scholars have suspected that there must have been at least one earlier draft. And in 1977 the first page of a piano score in pencil was discovered by this author, among a large collection of unidentified Sousa manuscripts on deposit at the Library of Congress. Unfortunately, page two was not found with it, the page that might have carried the date, and efforts to locate that page have so far been unsuccessful. The pencil score is untitled and is a typical early draft, i.e., the bar lines are freely drawn, the notation shows signs of haste, no staff or key signatures are used, and harmonic fill is indicated but not fully written out. There is little doubt that it was written before the ink score of Christmas Day. The question is, how much earlier? As we have already said, Sousa arrived in New York City on November 25, not December 25. Far from having to rush to his hotel in order to have the composition completely written out in ink within a few hours, the composer had no less than thirty days in which to complete the ink piano score. One can imagine several sequences of events. Sousa may have finished the pencil draft immediately after landing in New York and the ink score on December 25, and later considered the ink score the real composition. Or, Sousa may have allowed the composition to "ferment" for thirty days, and both the pencil and ink scores may have been written out on Christmas Day. We must also consider the confusion which must have greeted Sousa's arrival in November, with his own future uncertain and the upcoming tour in jeopardy. Both demands on his attention and his own inner

turmoil may well have made creative work difficult for several weeks. The new tour, which Blakely had arranged before Sousa's vacation, was due to open on December 27. Its approach may have been the catalyst that finally forced Sousa to sit down and write out the new march. Thus, this writer believes it was on Christmas Day, 1896, thirty days after Sousa's landing in New York, that not only the ink piano score, but the pencil score too, came into being.

The pencil piano score is untitled. The ink score has the title, slightly corrupted as *The Star and Stripes Forever*. While this slight error is understandable, what does seem odd is that the title is written in a much paler ink than the rest of the score. Could it have been added after the score was finished? Is it possible that as late as December 25, 1896, exactly thirty days after arriving in New York City, Sousa had not decided upon a title for the march? While the composer has told us a great deal about the conception of the music for this march, he has not said a word about just when the title came to him. It is known that Sousa frequently did not name his marches until after they were composed, and that on some occasions the title first given to the march was changed before the work was published. It would not have been unusual, therefore, for Sousa to ponder for a time before selecting a title for his new march. Based upon evidence to be presented below, it seems likely that Sousa did not fully decide upon *The Stars and Stripes Forever* as a title until the spring of 1897.

The phrase "Stars and Stripes" was a familiar name for the flag of the United States and may go back to the first design of the flag. It had already been used numerous times as the title, or part of the title, of a musical composition. Even the full phrase, "the stars and stripes forever," had been used several times before.[8] Paul Bierley points out that this form was used by William J. Lemon for a Civil War song published by the firm of Lee and Walker in Philadelphia in 1861. Since Lee and

Walker were Sousa's early publishers, Bierley surmises that the composer saw a copy of the song in their office and that the title stuck in his memory.[9] Perhaps so. It seems even more likely, if indeed any influence was required at all, that Sousa would have come into contact with Frank L. Armstrong's "marche militaire," *The Stars and Stripes Forever*, published in Philadelphia by the Music Syndicate Publishing Company in 1895, only a year before Sousa's march was written.[10]

Sousa's *The Stars and Stripes Forever* is cast in the tripartite form used for most post-1900 marches. Sousa had been using this form with increasing frequency during the 1890s and was soon to use it almost exclusively. In this march it consists of a four-bar introduction; an A section of sixteen bars, repeated, and a B section of similar length, also repeated. Then follows the large trio section—a melody of thirty-two bars, repeated twice. The first two times the trio is played it is followed by a bridge or episode section of twenty-four bars, which we will designate X. Thus the entire march can be diagramed as: Introduction-A-A-B-B-trio-X-trio-X-trio. The vigorous introduction and both sections A and B are outstanding examples of the verve and elan that Sousa could inject into the march form. The A section is remarkable chiefly for its rhythmic vitality and the emphasis on stacatto playing. The B section on the other hand is unusual in that its melody would have served many other composers as a trio melody, i.e., a broad, singing tune with many half notes and a subdued rhythmic background. In this section Sousa hit upon a device that cleverly and effectively conceals the fact that the clarinets and other woodwind instruments are playing the melody in unison with the brass. Where the brass had descending half notes, the woodwinds break their line by octave leaps. These octave leaps put an emphasis on the weak beats of the measure and lead one to believe the woodwinds are playing a syncopated rhythmic figure instead of the melody.

There is no doubt that the major factor in the wide appeal of *The Stars and Stripes Forever* lies in its magnificent trio section. Its melody of thirty-two bars' length is particularly fine, even for Sousa. This tune has been compared, in style, not in content, to the great melody composed by Edward Elgar for the *Pomp and Circumstance* march no. 1. One can readily believe that Sousa would have agreed wholeheartedly with Elgar's famous statement, "Such a melody comes to a composer but once in a lifetime." Sousa's tune is enhanced by an underlying rhythmic figure that is rare in march composition. It consists of a bass that emphasizes the offbeat, instead of the one-two, one-two, or left-right, left-right of the traditional march. The bass plays on "one" as we might expect, but then instead of playing on "two," plays on the final upbeat of the measure, the pickup to the next bar. This results in a syncopated bass line. This figure is used with the first two phrases of the melody (measures 69 through 83 and 85 through 95), except for the weld that joins the two. Only during the final six bars of the second phrase does this figure break down and the bass revert to the conventional one-two pattern. Together with this bass figure, the drums, cornets, and a few other instruments are also playing an unusual rhythm, almost a Spanish dance. These give the trio melody an intriguing kind of rhythmic support, probably unique in march literature:

Another important feature of the trio is its two countermelodies. As the march is played today, these melodies are added one at a time at each of the trio's two repetitions. But according to the original printed parts as well as the holograph band score, they were both to be added to the first repetition as well as the second, and both repetitions were to be played grandioso. One of the melodies is the famous piccolo obbligato (usually 109 played by the entire piccolo section) which brings to mind fife and drum music of revolutionary war days. While the lower woodwinds and the euphoniums are playing the main trio melody in a subdued manner, the ear is drawn irresistibly to this brilliant piccolo passage, one of the most famous in music literature. The other countermelody, in modern performances played only with the second repetition of the trio, is given to the trombone section. Unfortunately, the composer's directive that this part of the march be played grandioso has led some conductors to allow all instruments, particularly the percussion, to play so loudly that the two countermelodies are swallowed up in the din. Here is the beginning of the trombone tune:

The final section of the march to deserve special mention is the episode or bridge passage inserted between repetitions of the trio. While such passages are common in marches of this type, the one for *The Stars and Stripes Forever* is no less then twenty-four bars in length, far longer than usual. The apparent simplicity of this episode, with much of the band playing in unison, belies its extraordinary effectiveness. Its opening staccato notes strike the listener like machine gun bullets, and these are followed by a fanfarelike motif shooting upward like a skyrocket, which then falls back through a descending chromatic scale. This latter figure is repeated twice, each time on a higher degree of the scale. The fanfare motif of this section is itself repeated, building up tension that is finally released as the last "rocket" effect settles to the ground through a long descending passage leading back to the trio. This skyrocket effect adds further to the patriotic, Fourth of July atmosphere that permeates the march.

We now have before us at least a quick sketch of the unique character of the work

that began to ferment in Sousa's mind during that fateful voyage of 1896. In our effort to piece together the chronology which led to the final version of this extraordinary march, we turn again to the three manuscripts which have survived—two piano scores, one in pencil (incomplete) and one in ink, and a full band score in ink. In length, the surviving first page of the pencil score matches the first page of the ink piano score exactly. Both pages end at the beginning of the first episode after the trio, suggesting that Sousa copied the ink score from the pencil version. Comparing these pages more closely, we find only minor differences between them. The ink score, although its bar lines are freely drawn like those of the piano score, includes clef signs (only on the opening brace) and key signatures, while the pencil score has neither. On the other hand, the pencil score has some harmonic fill sketched in, and one can see the trombone melody written lightly over the opening of the trio melody. The ink score has neither of these. These and other minor differences between the two piano scores may be largely functional. The pencil manuscript seems to have been hastily written as the composer tried to get his thoughts down on paper in a logical form. Such ideas as the trombone theme and harmonic fill just mentioned would have been worked out in detail only in a full band score and we would not expect them to appear in a finished piano version. Thus, the ink manuscript seems to represent a finished version, a score for piano two hands that one could set up on the music rack and play. This may have been, in fact, the manuscript that Sousa sent off to his publisher as the piano "arrangement." It is practically identical with the solo piano version printed by Church in 1897. And one can see on the ink score circled numbers in pencil which probably indicated to the printer where the music should be divided into pairs of staves on the printed page. Finally, there are some rhythmic changes in both piano scores which seem to represent second thoughts on Sousa's part. Some appear to have

110

been made after the ink piano score had been finished, perhaps even months later, after the full band score had been completed.

The pencil score breaks off just as the trio section reaches the first episode, so we are, unfortunately, unable to see whether Sousa included sketches for the piccolo obbligato. Neither this obbligato nor the trombone melody appears in the ink piano score. Again, this is not surprising and reflects the different functions which the two scores served. It was considered impossible for a solo pianist to play these additional parts, and they were not included in the published version for solo piano. Many years later Vladimir Horowitz exposed the error of that assumption.

Thus, by the end of Christmas Day, 1896, we believe, Sousa had sketched in pencil all the essential ideas for the full band score arrangement of the march and had finished the piano score in fair copy. Two days later he left New York for the 1897 tour, with both manuscripts in his traveling bag.

The tour began in New York City on December 27, 1897.[11] After leaving New York, the band swung through the South as far as New Orleans, then it curved northward through Mississippi, Tennessee, Illinois, Kentucky, Ohio, Indiana, and on to Chicago. It continued through Kansas, Colorado, and into Southern California. After a short stay in Los Angeles, the band turned up the coast to Seattle, then across the northern states back to New York and finally up into New England. By this time it was spring 1897, and on April 25 and 26 the band was in Boston for three concerts. While there, Sousa finally sat down in his hotel room and finished, we are not sure when he began it, the band score for *The Stars and Stripes Forever*. We should point out that since December 27, 1896, the band had been on tour continuously, playing as many as three programs a day, with only three days off during the entire period. Even those days—February 18, March 1, and March 9—were spent traveling between cities by train. This means

that Sousa would have had very little time to begin the band score. The chances are that it was written out entirely in Boston. There are certainly no signs in the manuscript that any part of it was written on board a moving train. We can assume, therefore, that the entire score was written out on April 25 and/or 26 in Boston. As usual, Sousa completed the manuscript and signed it after the closing measure: "John Philip Sousa April 26th 97 Boston Mass." He then turned the score over to his copyist so that instrumental parts could be extracted.

In view of the popularity of this march and the many arrangements made over the years, it may be instructive to give Sousa's original instrumentation:

Piccolo (D flat)	Alto saxophone	Three trombones
Two oboes	Tenor saxophone	Euphonium
Two bassoons	Baritone saxophone	Tuba
Clarinet (E flat)	Three cornets	Percussion
Two clarinets (B flat)	Four horns (E flat)	

Since 1897 the usual makeup of military and concert bands has changed, and the instrumentation of older music has often been adjusted for modern bands, For instance, few bands now use cornets, which have been replaced largely by trumpets, and other instruments such as the bass clarinet and flugelhorn have been added. Consequently, one rarely hears *The Stars and Stripes Forever* played just as Sousa wrote it. The U.S. Marine Band in Washington, which still employs cornets, probably comes as close to an authentic performance as any band today.

Sousa wrote out the full band score in Boston on the basis of ideas he had sketched into the pencil piano score four months earlier. The band score does show a few changes from both earlier piano versions, but the changes are minor and only amount to clarifications of the original conception. The first of these changes can be seen at bars nine and ten of section A. Both of the piano scores and, originally, the band score too had for these measures:

111

The piano scores were not changed, and the 1897 Church edition for solo piano was printed with the above rhythm. But in pencil, in the full score, Sousa changed the rhythm to the following:

So concerned was the composer that the copyist (and the printer) not mistake his meaning that he notated it carefully in pencil above the piccolo part and just in front of his signature. Similar adjustments to the rhythm can be found here and there throughout the manuscript. One of the most interesting changes cannot be seen in the band score. In that manuscript, as in the piano scores, the opening eight bars in the bass instruments were written in descending half notes. But the original 1897 printed parts for these instruments show the line as:

At some point after turning the band score over to his copyist Sousa had the passage changed. It was never rewritten in the holograph band score.

To sum up, the two piano scores and the band score show a number of changes in rhythm and, to a lesser extent, in harmonic fill from the earliest versions. Some of these changes were decided upon after the piano scores had been written out but before the band score was finished. Others were made after the band score had been completed, and at least two of these were not transferred to either piano manuscript and did not appear in the printed piano arrangement. In one instance Sousa seems to have decided to change an important bass line after the full band score had been completed. Apparently the parts were changed and sent off to the publisher but the change was never written into the holograph band score. None of these changes indicate, however, that Sousa ever had doubts about the principal melodies of the march. We believe the manuscripts amply bear out the composer's contention that the music (i.e., the melodies) conceived on board the *Teutonic* was never changed after he first wrote it down.

It happened that in the spring of 1897 the city of Philadelphia was preparing a grand celebration for the unveiling of a new statue of George Washington in Fairmont Park. An imposing list of dignitaries scheduled to attend the celebration was headed by William McKinley, president of the United States. By chance or by design, the Sousa Band's itinerary would bring it to Philadelphia on May 14th and 15th for three concerts, just in time for the big event on the 15th. The band had already visited Philadelphia twice on that tour, on January 1st and 2d and again on April 9th and 10th, and it may have been on one of these earlier visits that Sousa promised the city fathers that, in honor of the occasion, he would unveil his newest march as they were unveiling the statue. In any case, on May 9, 1897, the Philadelphia *Inquirer* notified its readers that the Sousa Band would play a new Sousa march at its upcoming concerts; it then continued, "The name of the new march will be announced May 14."[12] Accordingly, concert advertisements in newspapers on the 14th stated in bold type, "Sousa's latest march will be produced at each concert." And so it is usually considered that the premiere performance of the march that would eventually resound throughout the world took place on

Friday, May 14, 1897, in the hallowed old Academy of Music in Philadelphia. News accounts of the concert all state that the march was being heard for the first time. But was this really the case?

Between the date of the completion of the band score and May 14, a period of seventeen days had elapsed. During that period the band had played no less than twenty-eight concerts in over twenty different cities and towns. Now it would probably not require a good copyist more than two or three days to write out the band parts, and considerably less time if several worked together, and any number were available in the band. Also, is it unreasonable to suppose that Sousa would have wanted to rehearse the march before playing it in Philadelphia, especially on such an auspicious occasion? But there was one difficulty. There was little, one may even say no time available for a private rehearsal with the band so heavily engaged in giving concerts and traveling. The only solution, it seems to this writer, would have been for the band to read through the march once or twice during a concert before the Philadelphia engagement. It should also be remembered that the march would have been played from manuscript parts, not from printed parts, and this would have made rehearsal all the more crucial. Manuscript parts can be difficult to read, certainly more difficult than printed parts, and there was the ever present danger of errors in copying. Is there any evidence to support a claim that the march was played in public before May 14?

On May 2, 1897, the Augusta (Maine) *Journal* carried an effusive report on a concert played by the Sousa Band the previous day. The article continues:

A *Journal* reporter found him [Sousa] in the special train, just after the concert busy looking over some music. . . . It was a piece of his new march which was played as the first encore Saturday—a march that has not been named. Mr. Sousa says that he hoped to formally announce it in Augusta, but certain restrictions prevented. It ws superb anyway, and it did not matter much what the name was.

There are several points to be made from this report. In the first place, it was a *new* march and the only marches Sousa had written since the beginning of 1896 were the march in the operetta *El Capitan*, already produced and certainly named many months earlier than May 1, and *The Stars and Stripes Forever*. The reporter also says that the composer had wanted to formally announce the new work in Augusta but that "certain restrictions prevented" his doing so. These certain restrictions might well have included a promise by Sousa to the Philadelphians that theirs would be the first city to hear his new creation. We believe that Sousa took advantage of this Augusta concert, and perhaps other concerts during the interval, to rehearse the new march, placing it on the programs as an untitled encore. This seems eminently reasonable and, in this writer's opinion, hardly to be doubted. In the absence of contrary evidence, then, we can say that the first public performance of *The Stars and Stripes Forever* took place during a concert in Augusta, Maine, on May 1, 1897. The official premiere, however, was certainly the May 14 concert in Philadelphia.

Critical opinion at the premieres was almost, but not quite, unanimous. As we have seen, the reporter from the Augusta *Journal* thought the work "superb," though he does not say why. A few dissenters found it unnecessarily raucous. The following is a sampling of opinion from a number of cities, beginning with reviews of the official premiere.

Philadelphia *Public Ledger*:

The concert of John Philip Sousa's Band at the Academy of Music last evening served to introduce to the public for the first time in any concert his new march "The Stars and Stripes Forever." Judging from the enthusiastic reception accorded it, evidenced by the fact that he was made to repeat it twice, Mr. Sousa's newest composition will be as popular as most of his marches. The piece has an ambitious title and is something on the Jingo order itself, but it has the merit of originality and is devoid of any imitation of the national airs. Sousa's musical offspring naturally have a family resemblance and "The Stars and Stripes Forever" is embellished by the wealth of fanfare and clatter of cymbals a la Cairo which are his hall-mark. It is of a martial nature throughout and stirring enough to rouse the American eagle from his crag and set him to shriek exultantly while he hurls his arrows at the aurora borealis. [In Sousa's scrapbook a clipping of this review is preserved and on it he has underlined the words "It is of a marital nature." One wonders if the composer felt that this was an uncalled for remark.]

Philadelphia *Item*:

The brand new Sousa march, however was quite an event. It was excellent. It created a furore. None of us were satisfied until the band, good-naturedly enough, had played it three times over. I predict its popularity. In some respects it is the best Sousa has yet given us—not even excepting the Washington Post and the stirring finale to the second act of El Capitan. [This review was signed by J. Raymond Parke and is one of the very few musical reviews of the 1890s whose author received credit.]

Philadelphia *North American:*

Sousa gave one of his popular concerts at the Academy of Music last evening when the program included his new march "The Stars and Stripes Forever" which had not been heard here before. It caught the fancy of the audience at once, and had to be several times repeated.

Unidentified clipping, but from Philadelphia:

In it [the new march] he has introduced some Wagnerian effects[13] and the great vigor of the entire composition makes them appropriate and pleasing.

Musical Courier, May 9, 1897:

Music in Philadelphia: Sousa's new march, The Stars and Stripes Forever, was played for the first time at his concert on Friday evening at the Academy. It is original and has a fine marital spirit, though possibly a little too flamboyant and warlike for your peace-loving correspondent. [Signed by M. Fletcher.]

Following the Philadelphia engagement, the Band resumed its tour and, of course, continued to program the new march.

Unidentified clipping, from Washington, D.C., May 17, 1897:

The initial production in this city of John Philip Sousa's latest march at the Lafayette Square Opera House last night was the success of the evening. . . . The fervid reception it met with caused the bearded bandmaster to blush to the very roots of his rapidly disappearing hair.

Washington *Post,* May 17, 1897:

John Philip Sousa, composer and bandmaster, gave his last concert of the season at the Lafayette Square last evening, presenting a pleasing selection of new numbers and his new march "The Stars and Stripes." Washington people are critical, and there was nothing lacking in the size of the audience, but the new march took with everybody. The first recall was enthusiastic, the next was in the nature of an ovation, and when the patriotic selection had been played a third time, the plaudits were as warm and as long continued as Mr. Sousa probably ever received in this or any other city. The new march undoubtedly has the catchy qualities that characterize most of the Sousa marches, and which set people beating time with their feet hands umbrellas and walking sticks. Above all it was rendered by the band in a manner that completely charmed the audience. . . . It was a pretty idea to bring out thirteen soloists for the conclusion of "The Stars and Stripes Forever" suggesting the thirteen original states.

Washington *Evening Star*, May 17, 1897:

Sousa, of course, always draws a crowded house, but when a new composition from his versatile and graceful pen is announced the result is a packed auditorium, and this was the case last evening. The new number, a march entitled "The Stars and Stripes" took at once and at its first presentation secured an enthusiastic recall; the second time it was given an ovation, and on its third presentation received more applause than any of Sousa's have for many a day. The new march is catchy in the extreme—it would not be a Sousa march if it were not—and is of that variety that makes feet, umbrellas and fingers keep time involuntarily. Aside from its pleasing qualities in this respect the trio is probably the finest piece of work the popular bandmaster has ever done in the march line, there being three distinct themes worked together in the nicest way imaginable.

Unidentified clipping, Baltimore, probably May 18, 1897:

but the hit of the evening was made by Sousa's own march—heard in Baltimore for the first time. The music is bright and catchy and is distinctly "Sousa" in its sound, as all of the composer's productions are characterized by its originality.

Baltimore *Sun,* May 18, 1897:

Much interest was shown in the first performance of the new two-step, "The Stars and Stripes Forever." It is built on the same lines as the earlier marches and lacks in no way their wonderful rhythm. The fervid reception it met with caused the bearded bandmaster to blush with pardonable pride to the very roots of his rapidly disappearing hair. [See:

Unidentified clipping, Washington, D.C., May 17, 1897, for a similar statement.]

Toronto, Ontario, *Daily Mail and Empire*, May 26, 1897:

There were many United States citizens present, and in response to a request from them Mr. Sousa gave his rather noisy march "The Stars and Stripes Forever."

Unidentified clipping, Toronto, probably May 26, 1897:

For an encore, Sousa's new march "The Stars and Stripes Forever" was given, but many were glad it was not "for ever" because the din was awful, and it would hardly be fair to judge the March King's latest composition by hearing it within four walls.

Unidentified clipping, Boston, probably June 14, 1897:

The final concert for the benefit of the Emergency Hospital was given at the Boston Theatre last evening by Sousa and his magnificent band. . . . The new march by the conductor "The Stars and Stripes Forever" was enthusiastically received and emphatically redemanded.

Unidentified clipping, Boston, probably June 14, 1897:

A feature of the program was a new march by Sousa "The Stars and Stripes Forever." It was played with spirit and feeling and was applauded to the echo. Musically it is more ambitious than many of the composer's works, yet while it has the swing and "go" which mark all his works, it lacks something of the "catchy" quality so noticeable in the most popular ones, and is not quite so pleasing.

In one of the Washington reviews, the reporter states that the trio section contains three themes that are "worked together in the nicest way imaginable." No other reviewer seems to have noticed this. It may have been that the Washington reviewer had inside information. On the day of the concert Sousa was interviewed by an anonymous reporter and the account appeared in the papers on May 16th. In this interview he is reported to have said:

I am more than pleased with the success that has attended its [the new march's] first productions. I believe in the march, and think it is, perhaps, better developed than any of its predecessors. It was composed last November, while we were

crossing from the other side and is intended to convey the feelings of the homeward-bound American.

The special feature of the new march is its melody, patriotic and martial, and yet it does not infringe on any national air . . . the main idea of the composition consists of three original themes, representing three sections of the country, and these are worked up so as to end with a climax which brings all three into prominence.

A somewhat fuller account can be found in the early July 1, 1897 issue of the *Musical Age*. There Sousa tells the reporter:

The march was written when I was in Europe last summer, and finished on board ship coming home. One never feels so patriotic as when under a foreign flag, you know. I have often heard people say that in a foreign country the sight of the Stars and Stripes seems the most glorious in the world.

My idea was to climax the march with three themes—one representing the North, a broad sweeping theme; the South with its languorous beauty and romance; and the West, a strong, pushing melody carrying all before it. These themes were to blend harmoniously, but were to be used independently if necessary.

There are some confusing elements in the above quotation. In the first place, Sousa was not in Europe in the summer, he was there in the fall. In the second place, we have several Sousa statements, some already quoted, indicating that the march was conceived on board ship and written down in New York, not begun in Europe and finished on ship. But most of all, his explanation of the three themes is difficult to reconcile with the music itself. True, the trio melody so well known to everyone is a "broad, sweeping" one that fits the North criterion. It is also true that during the last time through the trio, the trombones have a new countermelody that should be brought out clearly and which can well be termed a "pushing melody carrying all before it" as is called for in the Western theme. But where is the "languorous" melody representative of the South to be found? Was Sousa referring to the famous piccolo obbligato played during the second time through the trio? "Brilliant" would seem to be a more appropriate term for this passage than "languorous." No, search as

115

one may, there is no melody in the trio that can by any stretch of the imagination be evocative of languorous beauty and romance. All of this North, South, West business smacks of afterthought. There obviously are three themes in the trio as we have already pointed out. On the spur of the moment, pestered by a reporter, Sousa came up with the first explanation that came to mind. Besides, why not a fourth melody for the East? Sousa was only too ready to provide reporters with such picturesque tales as this one.

All of the performances thus far mentioned appear to have been played from manuscript parts written out by the Band's copyist. However, Sousa wasted no time in sending the music to his publisher, the John Church Company of Philadelphia. Presumably he sent the ink piano score, or possibly some other piano version first, as the company must have received the music no later than early April, before the band score had been finished. This assumption is based on the fact that on May 14, 1897, the very day the march was officially premiered, the Copyright Office received and registered *The Stars and Stripes Forever* in a variety of printed arrangements including piano; piano duet; piano six hands; banjo; banjo and piano; banjo duet; mandolin; mandolin and piano; two mandolins and piano; guitar; mandolin and guitar; two mandolins and guitar; mandolin, piano, and guitar; zither; and zither duet. These arrangements, which would have required some time to make, were presumably the work of employees of the publishing house. The band arrangement, which Sousa completed on April 26, was registered June 5 when the printed band parts were sent to the Copyright Office. On July 1 an orchestra version was similarly registered by means of printed parts.

As the Sousa Band continued its tour, it introduced the new march to a large audience. As soon as the printed parts were published, we can be sure that many other bands began performing the piece. But this was not the only way that the march was disseminated across the country during 1897. It was also recorded.

By the end of 1897 there were eight recordings of *The Stars and Stripes Forever* on the market, three issued by the Columbia Phonograph Company and five from the Berliner Gramophone Company. Owing to the scarcity of documentation for recordings made during the formative years of the industry, we are able to date only one of these eight items. On May 27, thirteen days after the premiere of the march, a recording was made in the Washington, D.C., studio of the Berliner Gramophone Company. The band performing is identified only as "Military Band" and, contrary to the custom of the Berliner Company, the leader of the band did not inscribe his name into the master record. There were several bands active in the Washington area at that period, notably Will Haley's concert band and the U.S. Marine Band. Possibly it was one of these that made the recording and for reasons now obscure the Berliner Company did not wish to name the group. It certainly was not the Sousa Band, because on May 27 it was performing in Ogdenburg, New York, in the afternoon and in Watertown in the evening. Berliner issued the recording as No. 61Y.[14] It was a seven-inch diameter disc with a playing speed of about 70 rpm and a playing time of little more than two minutes. The performance had to be truncated to fit the record and in this version we hear: Introduction-A-B-trio-X-trio (grandioso).

Another recording issued by Berliner was made by the Sousa Band itself. It was issued as No. 61V, but unfortunately the disc has neither a date nor place inscribed on it. As I pointed out some years ago in *The Sousa Band: A Discography*,[15] there is evidence to indicate that the Band made no recordings for the Berliner Gramophone Company until August 1897 and that these recordings were made in New York City. While the band could have recorded for Berliner in Washington during its brief visit in May, it is not likely that Berliner would have recorded the march by the above-named "Military Band" in addition. In the absence of other information, we may assume as the most likely possibility that the band recorded the new march in August under the leadership of Assistant Conductor Henry Higgins, who duly inscribed his name on the disc. This recording by the Sousa Band is of historical interest. The Band plays the new march with a vigor and precision lacking in the earlier "Military Band" recording. It also manages to fit in a bit more of the march on the little Berliner disc. The recording includes: Introduction-A-B-B-trio-X-trio (grandioso).

At least three other recordings of *The Stars and Stripes Forever* were issued by the Berliner Gramophone Company before the end of 1897. One of these was made by the Metropolitan Orchestra and issued as No. 1491. It was probably recorded in November. Since records 1473 and 1476, both made by the Metropolitan Orchestra, are known to have been recorded on November 9, it is likely that No. 1491 was recorded shortly after that date. The remaining two Berliner recordings were made by banjo soloists William P. Collins and Vess Ossman. Collins is known to us through his many solo recordings and duet recordings with Joseph Cullen, made for both Berliner and the Columbia Phonograph Company. (Both Cullen and Collins resided in Washington for a time.) Collins's recording was issued as Berliner 470. Vess Ossman was one of the greatest of early banjo players and recorded prolifically. His recording, which cannot be accurately dated, was issued as Berliner 470Z and includes: Introduction-A-A-B-B-trio-X-trio. The recordings by the Metropolitan Orchestra and by William P. Collins were not available to this author for study.

As far as can be determined, all other recordings of *The Stars and Stripes Forever* issued on the commercial market in 1897 were published by the Columbia Phonograph Company. The first of these in importance and perhaps also in chronology was recorded by the Sousa Band and issued as cylinder 532. It is presently impossible to date accurately a wax cylinder made by the Columbia Phonograph Company. Far less is known about their operations before 1900 than is known about the Berliner Gramophone Company. Further, Columbia's means of reproducing from a master cylinder were so limited that a work was customarily recorded six, eight, or even twelve times to provide a large number of masters to be used in making duplicates for sale. The list of Sousa Band recordings in the Columbia catalog for June 1897 stops with cylinder 531. Assuming this catalog was printed in May, however, as it probably was, we would not expect it to include recordings made during May. It is quite possible, therefore, that the Sousa Band recorded *The Stars and Stripes Forever* for Columbia in its Washington studio on the afternoon of May 16, just before its evening concert. This, of course, is pure supposition, but if it is accurate, cylinder 532 of *The Stars and Stripes Forever* would be the earliest recording of the march made by the Sousa Band itself. Unhappily, no copy of this recording was available to this writer for study. In view of the immense popularity of the march in the years immediately after 1897, the Sousa Band would surely have rerecorded it for Columbia in 1898 and 1899. But all of these would have been issued under the number 532, and there is no way today to assign a recording with that number to one of these years specifically.[16]

The final two recordings of the march which we are quite sure were issued before the end of 1897 were also Columbia cylinders, one by the Columbia Orchestra, cylinder 15107, and one by Vess Ossman, cylinder 3831. The June catalog ends with cylinders 15096 for the Columbia Orchestra and 3824 for Ossman, so that, as in the case of the Sousa Band recording, both of these were probably made within weeks of the printing of the June catalog. Neither was available for study.

This series of early recordings of *The Stars and Stripes Forever* reflected the immense popularity of John Philip Sousa and the Sousa Band and also served to further popularize Sousa's latest march. In April 1898 the outbreak of the Spanish-American War, with its parades and patriotic fervor, gave added impetus to the growth of the popularity of this great march. Early in 1898 Sousa wrote words for it, not only for the trio theme but for sections A and B as well. This choral version was first performed as part of "The Trooping of the Colors," a pageant that Bierley describes as a "grandiose and patriotic extravaganza."[17] It was subsequently published as *The Stars and Stripes Forever Song*. While the text is not on the plane of the music, it is quite good and in performance can be very effective. Nevertheless, the work has never been popular in this form and performances are rare. The complete text is printed in Sousa's *Marching Along* and in Bierley's catalog of Sousa's works.

Within a year of its premiere, *The Stars and Stripes Forever* had become one of the most popular marches ever written, and it has remained so to this day. Not only bands large and small, but symphony orchestras have the work in their repertories. Arturo Toscanini, Serge Koussevitzky, Arthur Fiedler, and Eugene Ormandy are just a few of the great symphony orchestra leaders who have performed and recorded it. And who can forget the dazzling display of technique shown by Vladimir Horowitz, the great pianist, in his virtuoso performances of *The Stars and Stripes Forever* on the concert stage? The U.S. Marine Band plays the work regularly in its Washington concerts and, as this writer was informed, plays it on every concert while touring.

In short, *The Stars and Stripes Forever* is one of the world's most popular pieces of music. It is known in practically all countries. It has probably suffered from more bad performances and worse arrangements than any other composition. It was the basis for a successful ballet by Hershy Kay and gave its title to a 1952 motion picture built loosely around Sousa's life. On May 12, 1937, as the coach carrying King George VI of Great Britain to his coronation rolled out of Buckingham Palace, American audiences could hear, behind the voice of the radio announcer, the Band of the Coldstream Guards performing, not a British march, but *The Stars and Stripes Forever*.

In the summer of 1915, while the Band was giving concerts at the Panama-Pacific Exposition, Sousa was notified that the Music Teachers' Association of California had adopted a resolution petitioning Congress to make *The Stars and Stripes Forever* an official "air" of the country. Sousa wrote in his reminiscences: "The idea did not appeal to me for, though Congress is a powerful body, it cannot make the people sing. If *The Stars and Stripes Forever* ever becomes a national air it will be because the people want it and not because of any Congressional decree."[18] Congress apparently did not act on the petition, and the matter was dropped for a number of years. In the early 1930s, when debates over a national anthem were in progress, the subject of Sousa's march was again raised. Resolutions designating *The Stars and Stripes Forever* as the national march were introduced in Congress in 1932 and 1933 but were not acted upon.

The petition and the two proposed Congressional resolutions, though unsuccessful, are indicative of the esteem in which Sousa's march is held by countless Americans. Apart from its musical value, the march has become a national symbol. After the National Anthem there is probably no other patriotic composition so beloved of the general public. And unlike the National Anthem and "America," both of whose tunes are by foreign composers, *The Stars and Stripes Forever* is entirely our own.

Notes

1. Paul Bierley, *John Philip Sousa: A Descriptive Catalogue of His Works* (Urbana: University of Illinois Press, 1973), p. 71.

2. Paul Bierley, *John Philip Sousa: American Phenomenon* (New York: Appleton, Century, Crofts, 1973), p. 121.

3. John Philip Sousa, *Marching Along* (Boston: Hale, Cushman and Flint, 1928), p. 13.

4. Margaret L. Brown, "David Blakely, Manager of Sousa's Band," in this volume.

5. Sousa, *Marching Along*, p. 157.

6. Bierley, *Catalogue*, p. 71.

7. Ibid., p. 72.

8. Other compositions with the same title as Sousa's march include a work by Charles Grobe published in 1882.

9. Bierley, *Phenomenon*, p. 72.

10. Bierley also reports that Sousa said in a 1919 interview that his publisher suggested that the last word of the title be dropped. Bierley, *Catalogue*, p. 72.

11. My thanks to Paul Bierley for generously providing me with the Band's itinerary.

12. I can think of no cogent reason for the delay in announcing the title of the new march except that Sousa had not fully decided upon it. Nevertheless, by May 9 he had already sent the music to his publishers. Perhaps the Church company was still trying to persuade him to drop the word "forever" from the proposed title.

13. One wonders what "Wagnerian effects" the reviewer had in mind.

14. The letter *Y*, apparently according to the custom of the Berliner Company, designated the third recording—or take—of the march. The other two takes were probably made the same day but it is not known whether they were published.

15. James R. Smart (Washington: Library of Congress, 1970).

16. Variations in the spoken announcements at the beginning of Columbia wax cylinders may provide a key to a method for dating them; however, not enough information has been compiled at the present time to enable us to use this method.

17. Bierley, *Catalogue*, p. 102.

18. Sousa, *Marching Along*, p. 305.

SOUSA'S
GRAND CONCERT
BAND.

JOHN PHILIP SOUSA.
CONDUCTOR
D BLAKELY MANAGER
CARNEGIE HALL NEW YORK
SEASON 1896

David Blakely,
Manager of Sousa's Band

by Margaret L. Brown

The business correspondence of David Blakely was found in the shed of the old Low Mansion in Bradford, Vermont, when Jessie Blakely Low sold the house nearly fifty years after Blakely's death. She was his eldest daughter and the widow of Walter Carroll Low. This article is based primarily upon the Blakely collection, which was given to the New York Public Library in 1955.[1] As the business nature of its content makes necessary mention of salaries, wages, and profits, it should be remembered that the purchasing power of the dollar during the 1890s was about ten times that of the 1980 dollar.[2]

David Blakely established an office in New York City during the summer of 1889. He was already fifty-five years old, and all his life had considered himself a journalist. He was also a moving spirit behind the formation of the Minneapolis Mendelssohn Club in 1881 and its director for three years. He then resigned to aid in the formation of the Minneapolis Philharmonic Society and to become its director. By this time he was well qualified for such work. In addition to the Mendelssohn, he had been training men's choruses in Des Moines and Omaha. All three groups participated in the Emma Thursby concerts on her 1884 tour. The press comment after each performance was extravagant in its praise of Blakely as director and conductor.[3]

It was customary then for bands and orchestras to play in the larger cities at festivals lasting from three days to a week. One of the most popular conductors for such occasions was Theodore Thomas. In 1883 he brought his Orchestra to Minneapolis for its first spring Festival there. Blakely, because of his position as conductor of the Mendelssohn Club, became the local manager for the affair. As such he gained invaluable experience as well as a tidy profit. The Festival was repeated in 1884 and 1885.[4] By this time Blakely was confident of what he could do,

and knew that what he wanted was to bring the famous Gilmore Band to Minneapolis for the first time. The first official tour of the Gilmore Band under Blakely's management was made in the spring of 1886.

Patrick Sarsfield Gilmore[5] had become well established as a military band leader during the Civil War. In the twenty years since, his fame was such that he was regarded as king of the bandleaders in the United States. Two of the choicest long engagements in the country were his for as long as he wanted them. These were July and August at the Manhattan Beach Hotel in Brooklyn and the next six weeks at the annual St. Louis Exposition. The other eight and one half months he divided among festivals and other expositions.

By the time he went to New York in 1889, Blakely had developed a tour routine that was handled by his permanent staff of two. Usually Frank Christianer dealt with the local managers and Howard Pew kept the books. Printing and transportation were in the hands of one or the other, varying with different tours. There were also half a dozen others known as "advance men" who would precede the Band on the road by about a week or ten days to check up on the local advertising. These men were temporary employees who were often rehired each season.

Except for minor changes, the printing for all tours was the same. There were lithographs of the Band leader, the Band itself, and the soloists accompanying it. There were posters of three sizes with local time and place information strips to be added. Cuts of the leader and certain soloists were supplied for newspaper articles.

Soloists accompanying all the tours Blakely sent out while in New York were engaged through Henry Wolfsohn. Occasionally, they were well known singers, but usually Blakely preferred to spend less for relatively unknown artists, reasoning that the public really came to hear the Band, so why waste money on something that did not help the receipts at the box office?

These receipts were, of course, the real reason for the tours. Blakely always hoped that the local managers would guarantee him a fixed amount, then divide the net after local expenses into approximately 75 percent for the Band and 25 for the local management.[6] Whatever the division, Gilmore found touring to be more profitable than long engagements. He always received one half the net and Blakely the other half, which he sometimes shared with a partner.

In 1891 Blakely handled the first tour made by the U.S. Marine Band, then directed by John Philip Sousa. In April 1890 Blakely had asked Sousa "if you have as yet learned whether you could make a tour with your band or not? Mr. Pew has seen and written you upon the subject in my behalf, but I have never learned anything definite from you."[7] Sousa came to New York soon after this to see Blakely.[8] As the Marine Band could not leave Washington in the fall or winter, they agreed that later in the year Blakely should send formal requests to Sousa as director and to Secretary of the Navy B. F. Tracy as employer of the Band, that he be permitted to take the Band on a short tour in the spring of 1891. On January 29, 1891, Pew wired Sousa that the permission had been granted for a leave from April 1 to May 3.[9]

Thirty-seven years later, in his published recollections, Sousa said of this 1891 tour that it "was a very trying one, with two concerts a day, luncheons, banquets, civic demonstrations and incessant travel. The drain on my energy and the lack of sufficient sleep finally caused me to break down on my return, and the Post surgeon sent me to Europe to recuperate."[10]

As Blakely's reputation has rested largely on Sousa's statements about him, it is fortunate that these contemporary business papers from Blakely's office have been found. They give us the opportunity to look at the record.[11]

Sousa was in New York for a conference on February 1. After he returned to Washington, Pew told Charles W. Johnson, Chief Clerk of the Senate and usually the manager of Blakely's Washington concerts, that "Sousa . . . has not much of a practical idea of a tour." This was apparent in his insistence upon including certain cities no matter how inconvenient or time-consuming it might be to reach them, and in his unrealistic attitude toward Band salaries. Blakely gave in to him on the former after warning that the tour would cover "an immense stretch of country, and it will be as rough on your physical endurance as it will upon the financial situation." But on the matter of salaries Blakely insisted that they conform to those of civilian musicians.[12]

Twelve days before the tour was due to close, Sousa wired Blakely that he had secured an extension of leave and asked for concerts in certain other cities. Blakely was reluctant to prolong the tour on such short notice, particularly to cities which could be better handled later on a properly planned tour.[13]

Sousa's recollection of two concerts a day for thirty-three days is inaccurate, according to the ledger kept at the time. This provided a complete list of all concerts given with receipts from each. There were thirty-seven concerts played in twenty-seven cities on thirty days. The other three days (all Sundays) were spent in rest.[14] So Sousa actually gave only a little more than half as many concerts as he recalled giving. The luncheons and other events that he attended, he wanted to attend. Blakely's office made no arrangements for them. Blakely had long been opposed to such interruptions as time consuming and hence profit consuming. After all, profit was what both conductor and manager had as a motive for these tours.

Also, Sousa's claim of a "break down" as a result of this tour is suspect. If he was so exhausted, why did he override his manager on the extension of the tour? Could the answer be that the only way he could secure additional leave from the U.S. Marines was for a medical reason? When the net receipts of the tour were divided equally between Sousa and Blakely, they each got $2,635.[15] This was not far from double Sousa's annual Marine salary, and it had taken him less than six weeks to earn it.

Blakely gave Sousa his opportunity to seek another manager when, just before leaving for Europe on business on May 9, he asked Sousa to "indicate, by note . . . whether you wish to have me make the next tour with you. In that event I will have Mr. Pew keep our literary bureau [clipping service] in motion from this time on." Sousa wasted no time in making up his mind. Immediately after returning from Europe he entered into discussions with Pew on the route for a second tour.[16]

There is no doubt that Blakely and his staff wanted Sousa for another tour. Gilmore had just gone off on his own and they were looking for something to replace his Band. In a letter to a local manager, Christianer said what was in all their minds—the leader of the U.S. Marine Band "bids fair to rival the great Gilmore, and has one advantage for a long run—that of having a young and ambitious director."[17]

By late November leave had been granted the Band for seven weeks beginning March 20, 1892. Early in January, Pew set out for the Pacific coast to make the arrangements for the tour. It was the first one for which he was entirely responsible. Blakely bombarded him with so many letters of instruction and advice that Christianer took it upon himself to let Pew know that he sympathized. But this was an important tour for Blakely's future plans, and he had been quite sick for several weeks so may have been unusually irritable. By February 10 he was thirty pounds lighter, but well again and once more his former pleasant optimistic self, congratulating Pew on his successful arrangements.[18]

One point on which Sousa and Blakely were in complete agreement was to give prominence on this tour to Sousa's name rather than just to the U.S. Marine Band. Blakely told him that in the tour book in referring to his compositions, he had been called "The March King." Then two days later added, "One of these days, when the great and good Gilmore has done with terrestrial music, he may want to put Sousa at the head of his Band. I think there would be a better opportunity for you than even the Marine affords."[19] Thus, by early February 1892, there had been some suggestion of the possibility of Sousa leaving the Marines to head a private band—his own or possibly Gilmore's.

According to Sousa's memoirs, it was during a concert in Chicago on the return trip of this 1892 tour from the Pacific coast (April 29th or 30th) that Blakely made him an offer of $6,000 per year and 20 percent of the profits if he would resign from the Marine Band and organize a private concert band under Blakely's management.[20] This may have been the first definite offer from Blakely, but it was not the first time the possibility had been considered.

At the time of this Chicago meeting, both men knew that the second tour had been even more profitable than the first. When the final figures were in, Sousa's half of the net was over $8,250,[21] more than three times as much for seven weeks as he had received for just under six weeks in 1891, and five and a half times his annual Marine salary. Of course he accepted Blakely's offer.

Blakely's lawyer drew up a five-year contract in June. Sousa appears to have accepted this without protest. It went into effect on August 1, 1892. In addition to several routine clauses to be expected in such an agreement, it provided that Sousa would transfer to Blakely a half interest in all his musical compositions "past and present," including those begun during the life of the contract, Blakely to have entire charge of their publication and sale. Sousa's own music library and any additional music purchased for the new Band would become Blakely's property. In return for this, Blakely would pay Sousa $125 per month (his U.S. Marine salary) from the date he was ready to work on the organization of the Band until thirty days before the first concert. On that date, Blakely would start paying him $115 per week ($6,000 per year) plus 10 percent of the first year's net profit and 20 percent each subsequent year. If there should be a loss, Sousa's share of it would be deducted from the next profitable year, "the object being to render Sousa . . . a share of the profits of the entire five years . . . over and above losses of any one or more years within the same period." Sousa would receive his salary monthly and his share of the profits annually. Finally, Blakely was permitted to organize a company to conduct the business.[22]

Sousa's salary would be four times his Marine pay and he would share losses only after profits came in to balance them. Sousa's previous work had usually been sold outright and had brought in almost nothing. He was still in his thirties. The contract was for five years only. He would undoubtedly have many productive years beyond that point. He had given Blakely a good trial as manager and had not found him wanting. The contract must have looked very alluring to him.

As soon as Sousa returned the signed contract, Blakely set about forming the Blakely Syndicate, to assume his share of the profits and responsibilities. He hoped to raise $100,000 through the sale of 2,000 shares. Actually, he sold only about one hundred shares. When he saw that he was carrying practically all the financial burden anyway, he decided to dissolve the Syndicate. He bought back all outstanding shares by 1894, paying the holders 7 percent on their investment.[23]

The Columbian Exposition was to open in Chicago in October 1892. Blakely wanted the new Band to play at the dedication ceremonies. By August 6 the good news had come that the Band was accepted for October 20, 21, and 22.[24] The rest of the tour was easy to arrange.

It was Sousa's job to select and train the men. Once the news was out that he was forming his own Band and would be managed by Blakely, he had plenty to choose from. Harry Coleman, the Philadelphia music dealer who up to now had published Sousa's compositions, was most enthusiastic. He corralled practically every good prospect then playing in any band near Philadelphia for Sousa to hear on weekends during July, the only time he was free to come up from Washington until August.[25] By that date, applications were pouring in from all over the country.[26] On July 6, the day before he sailed for Europe on business, Blakely once again warned Sousa of the danger of making salaries too high.

At the rate you are progressing, [he said,] the salaries . . . will cost in the neighborhood of $1,800 [per week]. . . . We are in this thing for glory and money, but we cannot get the glory without we can get the money. Evidently, these people have got the idea that we are going to bull the market, and pay any price that is asked. Now, I decidedly refuse to do this. Too much of this matter is my own individual burden, and I . . . won't stand a salary list which is going to eat up the profits. Moreover, there is no necessity for it. Make your figures what they ought to be and the men will come to them.[27]

Several men who had been with Gilmore wanted to join. Blakely's treatment of J. Lacalle, still with Gilmore, is typical. Pew wrote him refusing to consider his application unless "Mr. Gilmore is willing to let you join our forces. We do not want to interfere with his arrangements." Gilmore was not willing, so that ended the matter.[28]

Just after rehearsals started, Ellis Brooks, another bandleader, angrily accused Sousa of stealing three men from him, but calmed down on being told that "when men sign contracts with us, we are naturally led to suppose that they are free agents in the matter."[29] Blakely was determined to do nothing that could be called pirating of men from any other band, least of all from Gilmore's.[30]

The last man to join before rehearsals started turned out to be the most important one. Late in August George S. Spohr of the Salt Lake *Times* wrote Sousa,

124

I understand that you are engaging men for your band. If so I have a man you want—viz. a trombone player who will play anything Mr. Innes plays or has played before the public. This I suppose will surprise you but being in the newspaper biz here & having heard & personally known each I know what I am talking about. He is perfectly will[ing] to have a trial & perform before you. I prevented Pop Gilmore from getting him. Pop is in love with his playing. The young man who's name is Arthur Pryor, St. Joseph, Missouri, is 25 years of age & is really a marvel. I wish you would oblige me by corresponding with him.[31]

Apparently Sousa valued Spohr's opinion for an immediate offer was made. Pryor agreed to come for forty dollars per week for nine weeks that fall, the work to be permanent if he proved satisfactory. He arrived in New York on September 14, two days after rehearsals started.[32] So, with no further discussion and at the last minute, the man who was to become "the greatest trombone virtuoso who ever lived, as well as one of the two or three most celebrated bandmasters"[33] became a part of the new Band whose leader was one of his few peers in that line.

Two New York firms—Browning, King & Co. and The Warnock Company—were asked to submit bids on uniforms. What Sousa wanted was a "design for band uniforms, with prices attached, including helmet, fatigue cap, full dress coats of red or blue, overcoat of dark blue, and possibly vest. . . . How soon could you furnish the uniforms for fifty people?" Warnock won the contract at $52.70 per outfit.[34] Blakely paid the bill, but the men were told that they could buy their own or rent them at one dollar per week. Most chose to rent until they were more sure of the future.[35]

All went smoothly with the printing except for the Conn advertisement. He was angry with Sousa on two counts. First, instruments that he had loaned Sousa for use in the U.S. Marine Band had not been returned or paid for. Before furnishing the new Band with six more trumpets, Conn wanted to know what was to be done about the others. By August 20th he was assured that the first lot had been shipped from Washington, which took care of that.[36] The second reason was the appearance of an item in the August 10 *Musical Courier.* This said,

GOOD FOR MR. SOUSA.

It is understood that John Philip Sousa, when he was leader of the Marine Band, was offered $1,000 if he would arrange to have his $13 a month musicians play the real brass instruments of an Indiana brass band manufacturer. Mr. Sousa wrote back to the band instrument maker that he might one of these days consider the offer, provided the Indiana maker would product a better class of instruments.[37]

This could have referred only to C. G. Conn. Before he would agree to advertise in the book for Sousa's New Marine Band, as it was at first called, he wanted Sousa to make a public statement that the *Courier* item was false. Blakely returned from Europe on August 13 and promptly assured Conn, as Pew had done a day or two earlier, that there was no truth to the item.[38] But this was not what Conn wanted. Only Sousa could say that the statement was false. On August 26 Conn wrote again. "Doubtless your attention has been called to the notice," he told Sousa, "and I am surprised that you have not ere this sent in a denial. . . . You know very well that I never made such an offer." On September 6, four weeks after the item had been called to Sousa's attention, Conn threatened to make public his correspondence with Sousa unless he made an immediate statement declaring the article false.[39] Conn was upset about the charge for business reasons and also because he was running for Congress that fall. This time Sousa replied by return mail. He had been out of town, he said, and had forgotten to take care of the matter. He had just written to the *Musical Courier* that the story was false and requested a published contradiction. "I can understand," he told Conn, "how such an article could cause you much annoyance, but I cannot understand for one moment, how you could think that I could be responsible . . . as you never, on any occasion . . . offered me any bribe to adopt or use your instruments."[40]

125

The same periodical had also stated that the Chicago Exposition had secured Sousa to organize a new band in that city, that the U.S. Marine Band under Sousa was simply "a glaring noise producer," and that the new Band was composed of "heterogeneous material, gathered from the shores of Lake Michigan." Taking the article point by point, Blakely told the editor "You quite mistake me if you suppose I take exception to legitimate and truthful criticism. I never yet made a protest to any newspaper against any honest judgment of the sort. But your article . . . is a tissue of mis-statements from beginning to end." A retraction was made and by September 5 Blakely was planning advertising matter to go into the magazine. By the time the tour was over, such favorable reports of the Band were appearing in the *Courier* that Blakely ordered extra copies of one issue.[41]

Although the tour was planned around the Columbian Exposition in Chicago, Pew was careful to avoid any conflict with Gilmore's dates. The popular and financial success of the Band seemed paramount. As things turned out, everything else paled beside an event that no one could have foreseen. Gilmore died suddenly in St. Louis on Saturday, September 24, having conducted as usual the evening before.[42] On Monday his body arrived in New York. That evening Sousa's Band played the first concert of its first tour in Plainfield, New Jersey. Thus, what could easily have developed into a struggle for supremacy in the band world between the aging and tiring maestro and a young leader with comparable gifts and with the most experienced manager in the business, was stopped short just as it was about to begin.

Thirty-six years after the event Sousa wrote,

We continued on the road with varying success. Sometimes business was wretched, again we would strike a town where I had previously showed, with the Marines, then business was good. When we reached Boston, Blakely joined us. He called me into his room at the hotel, and said, "I'm going to close down this tour to-night." I was frantic!

"You'll do nothing of the kind," I cried, "The route laid out for the band has been hopeless, but that is not my fault. You booked me in a territory where Gabriel with a horn of gold wouldn't draw. And now you have the effrontery to propose ruining my career. You would disgrace me as a musician; the authorities at Washington would laugh at my humiliation, after I left them in such high feather. I won't permit you to close! We have two weeks more, and I insist that you carry out your contract!"

He finally consented to resume the tour. . . . But Blakely and I never really were in harmony from the date of that tense interview in Boston.[43]

On this tour the Band visited cities that had paid well on Gilmore tours, so the route was not exactly "hopeless." The tour was divided into two parts. Beginning with the Plainfield concert, the Band went into the Midwest for thirty-five days including the time at the Columbian Exposition. For the next two weeks they rested and rehearsed with new members added after the close of the first part. Then they toured New England for another three weeks. It is true that the receipts did not cover expenses. Blakely contributed at least $2,900 toward the ordinary expenses of the first part, and another $500 during the second. The Boston episode mentioned by Sousa occurred during the second part on November 20.[44]

On November 11, several days before that Boston concert, Blakely told Theodore Thomas, director of the Music Bureau at the Columbian Exposition, "We now have six of Gilmore's best men, including Raffayolo, euphonium, and Stengler, clarinet—both of whom you doubtless know. We have now added cornetist Liberati to our forces. I tell you this to show you our settled purpose to strengthen . . . every weak place in our organization."[45] Thomas undoubtedly had commented on these weak spots when Blakely saw him in Chicago nearly three weeks before. The names mentioned in this letter were those of men at the top for their particular instruments.

One of the Band members sent Sousa Christmas greetings from Philadelphia, in which he said "The Band was better the 2nd trip than at first, and I feel satisfied that a man of your careful judgment can easily weed out the weak spots and improve them, so for that reason, I look for a better Band on the next trip."[46] This added to Blakely's letter to Thomas about the new members, shows that the Band needed pulling together. If Blakely did suggest that the tour stop in Boston, this would be a logical reason for doing so. He knew that a really superior band would have a good chance to get Gilmore's long engagements. He would not relish the thought that an organization he managed might lose them through poor notices. There is not the faintest indication that he wanted to break his contract with Sousa. Indeed, Henry Wolfsohn was even then looking for soloists for the 1893 season.[47] As manager, Blakely had every right to decide if a tour should be shortened or extended.

Immediately after his return from Europe in August 1892, Blakely offered Sousa's Band to the Music Bureau of the Chicago Fair for six months beginning May 1, 1893.[48] He was sure that Gilmore would not want to give up Manhattan Beach and St. Louis for anything temporary like the Columbian Exposition, so he expected no real competition for the Fair from July to October 20. He was certain that his proposal would cost the Fair less than any that Gilmore could make because of the latter's payroll of one hundred men against his own fifty. Fortunately for Blakely, the Music Bureau was as slow as usual in coming to a decision. On January 12, 1893, five months after receiving the offer, Thomas told Sousa "that the chances for Sousa's Band to play six months were very favorable."[49] But that was not an official acceptance of Blakely's offer, and it was already too late for the Fair.

A second move that Blakely made that summer of 1892 was to approach the Western Pennsylvania Exposition, held in Pittsburgh at the same time as the St. Louis Exposition. While Manager Johnston argued over Blakely's price and sought his promise that the Band would play nowhere in the Pittsburgh area before the Exposition opened, Gilmore died. Blakely immediately approached Frank Gaiennie, manager of the St. Louis Exposition, who not only considered his price of $3,000 per week plus railroad fare from and back to New York to be reasonable, but agreed to let the Band play where it wished before the Exposition. On January 9, 1893, Gaiennie wired that the directors of the Fair wanted the Band not just for three weeks as originally suggested, but all seven weeks. Blakely obviously enjoyed telling Johnston in Pittsburgh that St. Louis had acted so promptly because "they heard the old [Gilmore] band under its new leader [D. W. Reeves] the last night of the last St. Louis engagement. And they were so pained by the contrast between the old leader and the new, and their recollection was so fresh of two performances by Sousa only a few weeks before, that they came to the . . . unanimous conclusion that . . . they must engage the only band that" could fill their high requirements.[50] Next time Johnston would not quibble over the price of the Band. This took September and October from the offer that had been made to the Chicago Fair.

In spite of Sousa's recollection that the Manhattan Beach engagement brought him to the attention of St. Louis, the reverse is what happened. The encouragement from Gaiennie convinced Blakely that he should not go after the other engagement. On January 4, 1893, he wrote to E. R. Reynolds, vice-president of the Manhattan Beach Hotel and Land Company, explaining that he had managed Gilmore's tours for six years, and now offered Sousa with a Band of forty-nine men for the entire season at $2,700 per week. Reynolds considered the price too high for any new band. Blakely asked for a conference.[51] His own office was at 1441 Broadway at 41st Street, and Reynolds's was at 192 Broadway near City Hall. The rest of the negotiations were carried on orally. On January

28, Blakely told Thomas that Sousa would be at Manhattan Beach during August.[52] Two weeks later he told Gaiennie that Sousa had the entire engagement. "The Beach managers," he said, "who had expected to take Gilmore's Band [under its new leader] for one-half the time, have concluded that they dare not do so. Most of the stars of [that] Band are with us." Blakely had been talked down to $2,000 per week, but he had the engagement.[53] This took July and August away from Chicago.

By April 8, 1893, all three engagements were settled. Chicago had May 22 to June 28, the Beach July 1 to September 4, and St. Louis September 6 to October 22. This was an achievement undreamed of when Blakely and Sousa signed their contract only ten months before. Had Gilmore lived, they might have had the Chicago engagement. Blakely could not have displaced Gilmore at the other two if he had tried. He could not have tied them up now for Sousa, had Sousa been a mediocre leader. But Blakely actively sought the engagements.

Although the year of 1893 was one of business depression, the spring engagement of Sousa's Band at the Columbian Exposition in Chicago was successful, at least from the point of view of favorable publicity.[54] From there they went to the Manhattan Beach Hotel. Late in August, Blakely happily told a director of the San Francisco Mid-Winter Festival that

the first week of Sousa's Band here brought the average receipt of Gilmore's Band; but during the month of August, you will be astonished, as I was when the Manager of the Beach Company showed me the books, to learn that although in consequence of the hard times the number of people visiting the Beach is thirty percent less than last year, the receipts of the Amphitheatre in which Sousa plays, are considerably greater.[55]

At the beginning of September the Band set out for St. Louis. At the close of that engagement, Manager Frank Gaiennie told Blakely that the Exposition receipts were

$30,000 above expenditures. This is a miraculous result, and while of course we do not say this aloud, because we would tread on the toes of our exhibitors (and advertisers), there is but one opinion here, that Sousa and his music have been the Exposition, first, last, and all the time.[56]

Halfway through the St. Louis engagement in September 1894, Blakely increased Sousa's salary from the $115 per week provided in his contract to $215. By that time the receipts warranted it.[57]

Another thing that Blakely did in 1894 was to start advertising the Band in periodicals. He began with the *Cosmopolitan Magazine*. The following year Blakely decided to extend his magazine publicity. He advertised in *Munsey's Magazine* and the *Review of Reviews*, and considered a reprint of the *Munsey* article for *Frank Leslie's Illustrated Weekly*.[58]

The two-year contract that Blakely had made with the St. Louis Exposition expired at the end of the 1895 Fair. On October 8, he wired Gaiennie that the Band should not be considered for the 1896 Exposition. A letter the same day explained that from February 1895 the Band was booked solid for thirteen months. Then Sousa would take a few days off to oversee the opening of his operetta *El Capitan*, which was to be given by the DeWolf Hopper Opera Company in New York. Following this, he and the Band had continuous work ahead of them until the first week in September 1896. "While this mental and physical strain has as yet been followed by no apparent loss either of vigor or willingness to keep up the pace [on Sousa's part] . . ." said Blakely, "there must be an end to all over-exertion, and I feel, therefore, that the first unpledged time now before him should be devoted to a vacation." This would be after the close of the Manhattan Beach engagement. A second reason for a vacation was that it would give Sousa more time to devote to composition. "His work in this direction," said Blakely, "has come to be of greater pecuniary importance than his concerts." He thanked the

Exposition for its contribution to Sousa's success by its early recognition and endorsement of the new Band. Gaiennie accepted the inevitable.[59]

In the original contract, Sousa had agreed to transfer to Blakely a half interest in the ownership of and future receipts from all his past musical compositions and from all works completed or begun during the life of the contract. Blakely was to have entire control of the publication arrangements. Previously, Sousa had dealt with Harry Coleman, music publisher and dealer of Philadelphia. The general impression is that Coleman purchased outright everything that Sousa brought him, and thus cashed in on his talent before the young composer was aware of the real value of his work.[60] Although this was generally the case, it was not entirely true. The correspondence between Coleman and Sousa early in 1895 shows both men to have been appallingly careless in keeping records. However, both made reference to royalty statements on the *Beau Ideal* and *Belle of Chicago* marches.[61] Coleman was in the habit of crediting the royalties to the amount of about $140 annually to Sousa's account with him, rather than making regular cash payments. Probably at Blakely's prodding, Sousa requested quarterly statements and payments, adding that that was the way the John Church Company conducted business.[62] Coleman was a sick man (he died a few weeks later) and probably a resentful one. No new compositions had come his way since Blakely took over. By 1895 he knew that a fortune had slipped out of his hands.[63] Blakely's arrangement with the John Church Company was to pay royalties quarterly on sales of *all* arrangements of Sousa's compositions published by them. Sousa's deal with Coleman was that royalties would be paid on the piano arrangements only, after 5,000 had been sold. Thus, all other arrangements and 4,999 for the piano could be sold and Sousa receive nothing.[64]

After Coleman's death, the correspondence with his administrator, Arthur A. Clappé, was taken out of Sousa's hands by Blakely.

Coleman bought the Washington Post and the High School Cadets, etc. [charged Blakely] for $35 each. . . . The profits on those pieces came very near making him wealthy. . . . Mr. Sousa, profiting by past experiences, sold the Liberty Bell, the Manhattan Beach, and the Directorate Marches to the John Church Co., and he has already received therefrom at the rate of $24,000 a year in royalties—in statements rendered every quarter, accompanied in each case by a check for the balance due.[65]

Conversations before and during the two tours of the U.S. Marine Band would have shown Blakely the sorry way Sousa was disposing of his compositions. A far more businesslike and profitable plan would instantly suggest itself to a man of his experience. When this plan was incorporated in the contract, Sousa did not object. Naturally, both men would want Sousa to have some time off to compose.

The account books for 1895 are incomplete, but there is enough information to show that this third calendar year for the Band was extremely profitable. Blakely had increased Sousa's salary in September 1894 by $100 per week. On August 1, 1895, he started crediting Sousa with 50 percent of the net instead of the 20 percent provided in the contract. This was recognition of Sousa's drawing power at the box office, and evidence that Blakely was willing to be generous with the unexpectedly large profits that were coming in. From figures available, not counting royalties, Sousa must have received between $30,000 and $35,000 in 1895.[66] This was a far cry from his $1,500 salary in 1891, his last full year with the U.S. Marines. And Blakely could feel quite relieved at the change from the tours of 1892 and 1893 when he was personally putting money into the kitty to pay the running expenses of the Band.

On January 5, 1896, the Band headed west on what was known as the Grand Transcontinental Tour, returning to New York early in April. The Band rested while Sousa took time to help with the production of *El Capitan*. The show opened at the Tremont Theatre in Boston on April 13[67] and a week later began its long run at the Broadway Theatre in New York. After about three weeks with the show, Sousa set out again with the Band, touring eastern Canada and New England until they were due at Manhattan Beach.[68]

After Manhattan Beach, Oscar Hammerstein called on Sousa on August 14 to ask if he would play September 7 to 12 at the Roof Garden of the Olympia Theatre on Broadway between 44th and 46th Streets. Sousa referred him to Blakely, then in Vermont.[69] Reynolds thought it a good plan if they could get $4,000 for the week. "I myself," Sousa told Blakely, "do not think it would lower the dignity of the band to play at the Olympia, for the reason that the very best people in New York are patrons of that place, and it may be the means of solving at least a month's work every year for the band in New York City."[70] Blakely finally agreed to provide Sousa and the Band for seven nights beginning with Tuesday, September 8, and Hammerstein agreed to the $4,000.[71]

Everyone was satisfied with the profits for the year and the future looked extremely bright. The only possible cause of dispute between the principals was the division of the royalties. Figures for them are available quarterly only for 1895 and 1896. From the John Church Company they were $20,964 and $20,656, and from Harry Coleman $92.90 and $97.25.[72]

Blakely returned to New York about the beginning of November. On Saturday, November 7, Julie Allen left him in the office when she went home about three in the afternoon. She returned half an hour later for something she had forgotten, and found him lying on the floor— dead.[73] After calling for help, she cabled Sousa,[74] who cancelled the rest of his trip and came home.

Technically, the Blakely interests were in Mrs. Blakely's hands as administratrix of the estate.[75] Actually, it was Walter Carroll Low, her nephew, her son-in-law, and her lawyer, who

made the decisions and dealt with Sousa. The original contract had eight months to go after Sousa arrived back in New York. Low asked him to abide by its terms.

The future looked promising for Sousa. He would not have to share royalties on future compositions. The John Church Company wrote about his contract with them as soon as he returned from Europe. Their old contract was due to expire late in 1898, and they wanted his assurance that he would extend it for another five years.[76] A new source of royalty income was opening up in the phonograph record field.[77]

It was not long before the fact became known that there was trouble brewing between the Blakely estate and Sousa. On April 10, 1897, a bill of complaint against him and the Philadelphia manager was filed by Mrs. Blakely in the Philadelphia Court of Common Pleas. She stated that the 1897 tour had been almost completely contracted for before Blakely's death. As administratrix of his estate, she was obliged to carry out the agreements or run the risk of being sued by the local managers. At first, Sousa had recognized her position in accepting his salary from her. Later, he refused to conduct certain concerts and left her financially responsible for the broken contracts. Then he made new and separate contracts with several managers in Pennsylvania. He took the proceeds of these concerts and refused to give her an accounting. He notified her that he no longer recognized the contract with Blakely, that he intended to appropriate all assets of the business and to give concerts under his own management for his own individual profit. Therefore, she asked the court to order him to render account of all money received from concerts and royalties, and requested an injunction restraining him from any act contrary to the letter of the contract with Blakely.[78]

Sousa filed a reply on April 23, 1897. He admitted that "the great fame, ability and experience of David Blakely as a business manager of bands and music" was the primary consideration for entering into the contract with him. He submitted a copy of a letter from Blakely dated May 21, 1895, in which he proposed to divide the net profits equally beginning August 1, 1895. "I do not, of course," said Blakely in this, "wish this to be considered a legal amendment or appendage to the contract as it now exists." He reminded Sousa that he "felt that you ought to consider me as entitled to a prolongation of our contract upon a basis as suggested by yourself in New York; but I waive all considerations of this kind, and leave it to your sense of justice to deal with me as you ought." Sousa claimed that at this time Blakely agreed to give him a statement of the profits and the payment of his share every two weeks. Sousa agreed that a verbal contract had been made with the estate to follow the tour as arranged through May 23, 1897, but claimed that the estate had not fulfilled all its promises. He also admitted that he had taken the Band library on advice of counsel "that the said contract as modified terminated with the death of . . . Blakely . . . and that thereupon the title to the said music belonged exclusively to me." For the same reason "all of the . . . royalties belonged to me."[79]

On May 5, 1897, Mrs. Blakely filed a further bill against Sousa alone. In this bill, the court was asked to order Sousa to give an accounting to Mrs. Blakely of all money received from concerts and royalties, and to direct him to carry out the original Blakely-Sousa contract and its supplement. The latter, dated September 1, 1896, extended the old contract to August 1, 1900, and provided for an exact division of the net profits between the two and for further extension of the agreement by mutual consent.[80]

Neither side liked the decisions of the referee, and both appealed for different reasons. Eventually the case came before the Supreme Court of Pennsylvania. On October 8, 1900 that court gave the final decision. As Sousa had contracted with Blakely because of his peculiar managerial talents, and Blakely with Sousa because of his special musical ability, both so specifying in the contract, no heir or executor of either could take the place of the individuals and the contract thus ended with the death of either. However, Sousa had consented to carry out the tour as arranged by Blakely before his death, so he owed the estate half the net profits to May 23, 1897. His name belonged to him and could not be transferred to anyone else. Blakely as an individual could possess property, however, such as the Band library and an interest in the royalties. These rights could be transferred to his heirs. Hence, one half the royalties on all Sousa compositions published before Blakely's death belonged to his estate.[81]

Partly because of this decision on the royalties and partly because of Sousa's own comments in his memoirs, Blakely has usually been painted in rather dark colors,[82] but where would Sousa have been on November 7, 1896, had Blakely never entered the picture? No one has ever questioned his ability as a bandmaster and as composer of music for bands. However, these papers do show that at least until that date, his understanding of managerial and financial problems was meagre. These were Blakely's strong points. Gilmore had recognized his talents and let him use them, but Gilmore had twenty years of experience as his own manager behind him before Blakely took over. Sousa had no such background. Had Gilmore lived, Sousa's success might have been much slower in coming. It all happened so quickly—in four years he had rocketed from a $1,500-a-year band leader to an adored world figure with an annual income of approximately $50,000 and prospects of much more to come.

Notes

1. This collection consists of nine letter press books, eighteen boxes of loose papers, twelve account books, seven scrap books, and three program books. All but a small part of the loose papers concern David Blakely's activities as manager of band tours from 1889 to 1896.

2. U.S. Department of Labor, Bureau of Labor Statistics, April 1982.

3. Band Correspondence, 1880-84, Blakely Papers (hereafter BP), Manuscript Division, The New York Public Library.

4. BP, Band Correspondence, 1883-85.

5. David A. Blakely, Patrick Sarsfield Gilmore.

6. BP, Ledger, 1889-92.

7. BP, Strauss Letter Book, p. 323.

8. Ibid., p. 366, Blakely to Sousa, April 20, 1890.

9. BP, Mostly Personal I Let. Bk., pp. 19-20, Blakely to Sousa, December 9, 1890; p. 36, Blakely to B. F. Tracy, December 16, 1890; pp. 71-72, Blakely to A. B. Nettleton, January 13, 1891; p. 106, Pew to Sousa, January 29, 1891; Band Correspondence, A. B. Nettleton to J. R. Soley, January 20, 1891, USMB I Let. Bk., 2nd, Pew to Sousa.

10. John Philip Sousa, *Marching Along* (Boston, 1928), p. 99.

11. H. W. Schwartz, *Bands of America* (Garden City, N.Y., 1957) and Ann M. Lingg, *John Philip Sousa* (New York, 1954).

12. BP, USMB I Let. Bk., p. 11, Pew to C. W. Johnson, February 3, 1891; pp. 36-37, Blakely to Sousa, February 7, 1891; p. 94, Blakely to Sousa, February 19, 1891.

13. Ibid., p. 278, April 20, 1891.

14. BP, Ledger, 1889-92, pp. 240-41.

15. BP, Thomas 1891 Let. Bk., pp. 973-74, Pew to Sousa, May 29, 1891; Day Book, 1889-92, p. 138; Ledger, 1889-92, p. 250.

16. BP, Thomas 1891 Let. Bk., p. 980, Blakely to Sousa, May 6, 1891; pp. 148-49, Pew to Sousa, September 1, 1891; Sousa's Band Let. Bk., p. 1, Pew to Sousa, September 14, 1891.

17. BP, Austro-Hungarian Juvenile Band Let. Bk., p. 51, F. Christianer to L. F. Nicodemus, September 28, 1891.

18. BP, Sousa's Band Let. Bk., p. 17, Pew to Sousa, October 12, 1891; p. 18, Pew to Sousa, October 27, 1891; p. 27, Blakely to Sousa, November 28, 1891; p. 76, F. Christianer to Sousa, January 11, 1892; pp. 152-54, Christianer to Pew, January 30, 1892; p. 122, Blakely to M. Adams, January 25, 1892; and pp. 82-83, 96-97, 123-24, 147-48, 172-73, Blakely to Pew, January 12, 16, 25, 29 and February 10, 1892.

19. Ibid., pp. 170-71, February 9, 1892, and pp. 178-79, Blakely to Sousa, February 11, 1892.

20. Sousa, *Marching Along*, p. 124.

21. BP, Ledger, 1889-92, pp. 241-43; Day Book, 1889-92, p. 152.

22. BP, Sousa's Band Let. Bk., pp. 258-71.

23. Ibid., pp. 287-88, Blakely to C. G. Conn, July 6, 1892; Band Correspondence, Blakely to E. Lyman, June 18, 1892; Blakely to H. Weed, June 23, 1892; minutes of meeting, July 5, 1892; New Jersey notice, August 21, 1894; and Blakely to E. Lyman, November 7, 1894.

24. BP, Sousa's Band Let. Bk., p. 343, Pew to C. Petit, August 6, 1892.

25. BP, Band Correspondence, Sousa to F. Christianer, July 16, 1892; Coleman to Sousa, June 13, 29, 30, July 1, 17, 21, 23, 29, 1892; Sousa's Band Let. Bk., p. 278.

26. BP, Band Correspondence, June-September 1892.

27. BP, Sousa's Band Let. Bk., pp. 289-90, Blakely to Sousa, July 6, 1892.

28. Ibid., p. 296, July 9 and pp. 343, 345, Pew to Petit, August 6, 1892; Band Correspondence, Petit to Pew, July 11, 12, 25, August 8, 1892; Sousa's Band Let. Bk., p. 341, August 7 and p. 359, Pew to J. Lacalle, August 10, 1892.

29. BP, Band Correspondence, E. Brooks to Sousa, September 8, 1892; Sousa's Band Let. Bk., p. 434, Sousa to Brooks, September 9, 1892.

30. BP, Sousa's Band Let. Bk., pp. 538-43, Blakely to Mrs. Gilmore, March 8, 1893.

31. BP, Band Correspondence, George S. Spohr to Sousa, August 25, 1892.

32. Ibid., A. Pryor to Sousa, September 6, 1892; Sousa's Band Let. Bk., p. 428, Sousa to Pryor, September 8, 1892.

33. Schwartz, *Bands of America*, p. 283.

34. BP, Sousa's Band Let. Bk., p. 358, Sousa to Browning, King & Co., August 10, 1892; pp. 414-15, Blakely to B, K & Co., September 1, 1892; p. 420, Blakely to Warnock Co., September 5, 1892; Cash Book, 1891-94, pp. 30, 34, 36, 37.

35. BP, Sousa's Band Let. Bk., p. 400, Blakely to S. Kline, August 27, 1892; Band Correspondence, August-September 1892.

36. BP, Band Correspondence, C. G. Conn to Sousa, August 10, 1892; Sousa's Band Let. Bk., p. 348, Sousa to Conn, August 8, 1892; p. 367, August 12, 1892; p. 388, August 20, 1892.

37. BP, Sousa's Band Let. Bk., p. 426, Sousa to M. A. Blumenberg, September 8, 1892.

38. Ibid., p. 361, Pew to Conn, August 10, 1892; pp. 375-76, Blakely to Conn, August 16, 1892.

39. BP, Band Correspondence, Conn to Sousa, August 26 and September 6, 1892.

40. BP, Sousa's Band Let. Bk., p. 426, Sousa to Blumenberg, September 8; pp. 427-28, Sousa to Conn, September 8, 1892.

41. Ibid., p. 369, August 13; pp. 377-79, August 16; p. 421, Blakely to Blumenberg, September 5, 1892; p. 398, Pew to Conn, August 25, 1892; p. 459, December 17, 1892.

42. Schwartz, p. 137.

43. Sousa, *Marching Along*, pp. 127-28.

44. BP, Howard Pew Journal, 1892, pp. 70, 78, 100, 128.

45. BP, Sousa's Band Let. Bk., pp. 455-57, Blakely to Theodore Thomas, November 11, 1892.

46. BP, Band Correspondence, Seltzer to Sousa, December 24, 1892.

47. Ibid., H. Wolfsohn to Blakely, November 26, December 15, 17, 1892, February 16, March 7, 8, 9, 13, 30, 1893.

48. BP, Band Correspondence, Blakely to George H. Wilson, July 11, 1892; Proposition to Music Bureau, October 27, 1892; Sousa's Band Let. Bk., pp. 446-47, Blakely to Shea Smith, August 15, 1892; Blakely to Wilson, August 15, 1892; pp. 380-81, Blakely to T. Thomas, August 16, 1892.

49. BP, Band Correspondence, Thomas to Sousa, January 12, 1893.

50. Ibid., Johnston to Blakely, November 30, December 2, 7, 1892, January 5, 7, 1893; Blakely to Johnston, January 10, 1893; F. Gaiennie to Blakely, December 1, 2, 10, 1892, January 9, 1893; Blakely to E. R. Reynolds, January 7, 1893; Sousa's Band Let. Bk., p. 472, December 28, 1892; pp. 482-83, January 4, 1893; Sousa's Band Let. Bk., p. 472, December 28, 1892; pp. 482-83, January 4, 1893; pp. 488-89, Blakely to Gaiennie, January 11, 1893.

51. BP, Sousa's Band Let. Bk., pp. 484-86, Blakely to Reynolds, January 4, 1893; Band Correspondence, Reynolds to Blakely, January 5, 1893; Blakely to Reynolds, January 7, 1893.

52. BP, Band Correspondence, Blakely to Thomas, January 28, 1893.

53. BP, Sousa's Band Let. Bk., pp. 497-98, Blakely to Gaiennie, February 14, 1893.

54. Ibid., Chicago *Evening Post* clipping, June 22, 1893.

55. Ibid., Blakely to M. H. DeYoung, August 24, 1893.

56. Ibid., Gaiennie to Blakely, October 1893.

57. BP, Day Book, July 1892-August 1895, pp. 72, 73.

58. Ibid., Munsey to Blakely, January 25, May 14, June 5, 1895; C. D. Lanier to Blakely, February 6, March 5, 13, 1895; W. L. Miller to Blakely, April 11, 1895; 1895, Sousa Advance Sheets, No. 2, p. 9.

59. Ibid., 1895, Sousa Advance Sheets, No. 2, p. 6, Blakely to Gaiennie, October 8, 11, 1895.

60. David A. Blakely, John Philip Sousa.

61. BP, Band Correspondence, Coleman to Sousa, February 6, 1895; Sousa to Coleman, February 8, 1895.

62. Ibid., Sousa to Coleman, February 8, 1895.

63. Ibid., Coleman to Sousa, February 12, 1895.

64. Ibid., A. A. Clappé to Sousa, June 12, 1895.

65. Ibid., Blakely to Clappé, June 25, 1895; Clappé to Blakely, June 26, 27, October 25, 1895; Clappé to Sousa, July 5, 17, 1895.

66. BP, Day Book, July 1892-August 1895, pp. 103-145; Ledger, August 1895-November 7, 1896, pp. 1, 2, 36, 150.

67. BP, Band Correspondence, *El Capitan* program, April 13, 1896.

68. BP, Ledger, August 1895-November 7, 1896, pp. 7-11.

69. Ibid., Hammerstein to Blakely, August 14, 1896.

70. BP, Sousa's Band Let. Bk., May 6-September 4, 1896, p. 392, Sousa to Blakely, August 15, 1896.

71. BP, Band Correspondence, Blakely to Sousa, August 17, 1896, et. seq.; Ledger, August 1895-November 7, 1896, p. 11.

72. BP, Ledger, August 1895-November 7, 1896, p. 217.

73. Bradford, Vermont, *Opinion*, November 13, 1896.

74. BP, Ledger, August 1895-November 7, 1896, p. 75.

75. New York City Hall of Records, Letters of Administration issued to Ada P. Blakely, November 18, 1896, Liber. 210, p. 300.

76. BP, Band Correspondence, G. P. Handy to Sousa, December 3, 1896.

77. Ibid., C. P. Burton to Sousa, December 18, 1896.

78. Philadelphia Court of Common Pleas, CP, No. 1, March Term, No. 619, Ada P. Blakely vs. John Philip Sousa and Hannah Harris.

79. Ibid., Answer of John Philip Sousa, one of the defendants.

80. Ibid., No. 1365, Ada P. Blakely vs. John Philip Sousa.

81. 197 Pennsylvania 305 (1900), 47, Atlantic Reports, pp. 286, 289.

82. A. Lingg, pp. 89-90, 94-102, 108, 110, 112-14, 117, 120-21, 137-40, 157-58.

This chapter is based upon an article which appeared in the May and June 1961 *Bulletin of The New York Public Library* and is reprinted with the kind permission of the Library.

A Few Observations and Memories

by John Philip Sousa III

Of Legends . . .

When my grandfather died in 1932 he was, of course, known all over the world as both conductor and composer. His music was as familiar as the sound of birds. But during the fifty years since his death my brother and sisters and I have watched him grow from perhaps one of the world's best known musical figures into an American legend.

My Random House dictionary says, "Legend: a collection of stories about an admirable person . . . a person who is the center of such stories." It adds somewhat ambiguously: "non-historical or unverifiable . . . handed down by tradition . . . and popularly accepted as historical."

What the dictionary seems to me to be saying is that a legend may be real or he may not be real. Or he may be both. This appears to fit my grandfather rather well. For on one level people know that, legend or not, Sousa was real. There is his music to prove it. But on another level they are not so sure because—well, because by definition legends are too far removed from our own everyday experience to be easily accepted as human beings. But there are legends and legends: Annie Oakley was reported to be a fantastic shot, but, with time, proof of her exploits is hard to come by. So Annie Oakley, I think, is now pure legend. My grandfather belongs in another category: that of an artist whose times still inspire us and whose music continues, even now, to feed that inspiration. I would put F. Scott Fitzgerald in a similar category: his work helps stimulate an interest in his life and in the Jazz Age and vice versa.

The last part of the nineteenth century and the beginning of the twentieth are now looked back upon as years of greatness for America. Since my grandfather's music seems to express that greatness perfectly, he and his music have become

symbolic of the period—interchangeable parts, and inseparable from each other. Therein, I believe, lies the making of a legend.

Neil Harris describes this relationship beautifully in this volume:

John Philip Sousa and his America seemed made for each other. Their love affair, particularly during the Indian summer years preceding World War I, was neither coy nor covert, but entered into demonstratively and exuberantly by both sides. To later generations, caught up in waves of nostalgia and curious about this mixture of assertion and self-confidence that seems impossible to recapture, Sousa continues to epitomize a whole way of life. His conducting recalls band concerts on soft summer nights, strolling couples, playing children, tranquil and reassuring evocations of a time of well-ordered pleasures. His marches remain a major national treasure, patriotic and disciplined statements of national exuberance.

Harris is right: my grandfather and his music stand, in retrospect, for a time when everything appeared, at least, to have been serene, lovely, *simple*—and patriotism was a way of life; especially compared with NOW. They were years when America clearly had no problems. *None.* We won any battle we happened to get involved in, and there was so much land Out West that we could each have had a whole state for the asking. Teddy Roosevelt rode in and out of the White House on horseback, and on summer nights children sat quietly on their families' porches *swinging*, not doing other unmentionable things. There were Fourth of July parades and fireworks twice a week and small boys spent all day fishing, just like Huck Finn. There were practically no cars and there was *no TV*. There were a lot of fireflies.

What a world, and it all went on to the sound of my grandfather's music. No wonder he's a legend.

. . . and Beginnings

Though tales of my grandfather's early years in Southeast Washington have been told and retold, I, among others, continue to be

135

fascinated by them. Not because those years were necessarily that unusual, but because every detail in the evolution of a legend is automatically magnified and becomes by definition a matter of importance as well as interest and of endless conjecture.

Sousa was the third of ten children (four of whom died in infancy). His father was Portuguese, born in Spain, his mother Bavarian. My great-grandfather Antonio made his way from Spain to England, from there to America. He and my great-grandmother met in Brooklyn while he was a musician in the Navy Band. They moved to Southeast Washington, where my great-grand-father became a trombonist with the U.S. Marine Band.

We have a photograph of the band of that period taken by Mathew Brady. Antonio Sousa is in the front row with his trombone, and next to him is a very small boy whom we presume to be my grandfather. He is virtually invisible among the plumes and trappings of the band.

My great-grandfather is buried now in Congressional Cemetery, about a hundred feet or so from my grandfather's grave, a few blocks, in fact, from where my grandfather was born. A very small, very plain USMC headstone reads: "Antonio Sousa, Musician." The Marine Corps did not waste words.

In *Pipetown Sandy*, one of his novels, as well as in his autobiography, *Marching Along*, my grandfather writes at length about his childhood and early years in Southeast "on the Navy Yard" as he called it. It is in these reminiscences that one can begin to piece together the influences and experiences which ultimately shaped him.

I pick this up, for example, from *Marching Along*: "Washington was, in those Civil War days, an armed camp, and there were bands galore . . . *I loved all of them, good and bad alike.*"(Italics mine.)

And circuses. Again from *Marching*

Along: "The more I thought of it the more wonderful it seemed to follow the life of the circus, make money, and become the leader of a circus band myself. What a career that would be!"

Of course he did not make it into the circus. At age twelve to thirteen he wound up instead, and under a certain amount of pressure from his father, as a musician in the Marine Band. Child labor laws were still to come in Civil War Washington.

But for a child with my grandfather's obviously abundant imagination, the Marine Band must have been an acceptable substitute for the circus. At all events, he plunged into his new life with enough enthusiasm so that by age twenty-six he was director of the band. A few years later his music began to be heard around the world.

The (marching) bands of Civil War Washington; the circus; the Marine Band; his musical training—violin lessons at seven; the Offenbach experience; these among many others were the *external* influences. To them add his own obvious genius; his creativity (some twenty operettas, three hundred to four hundred pieces of music, from waltzes to humoresques, as well as more than one hundred marches, three novels, plus an autobiography and a book of nonfiction. Composer, conductor, author, sportsman—he was, it seems to me, a true Renaissance man. It does not surprise me that he became world famous.

Fallout

I do not know whether anyone has ever given serious thought to the descendants of legends but perhaps it is time to consider their plight.

For example, in the view of strangers I am variously considered to be nonexistent (a legend does not *have* descendants; he is one of a kind) or a practical joker, the joke being that, in answer to questions, I admit to being John Philip Sousa III. An outrage and highly suspect.

One of my sisters and I attended the

rededication of the Band Hall at the old Marine Barracks in D.C. a few years ago. As we walked down the aisle to assigned seats in the front row, we both immediately sensed that we were being looked at as if we did not exist. "John, I'm getting the feeling these people think we're dead," my sister whispered when we sat down. "They don't think we were ever alive," I added.

Two weeks ago I received the usual summons for jury duty. When my name was called in the jury room there was loud laughter from the other jurors. What was so funny? Nothing. Instinctively and as a body they had decided I did not exist. If I did not exist then my being there must be some sort of a put-on, a joke. I was eyed suspiciously.

To avoid offending all these suspicious people I usually give my name in stores, restaurants, and anywhere else I happen to be as "John Sousa" or even "J. Sousa." It does not work. "Not John *Philip* Sousa," they ask laughing, as if they were saying something hysterically funny.

"Yes," I reply. "My grandfather." That does it. There is more laughter (nervous now) and a clear assumption that I am lying. I am also obviously some sort of nut.

I suddenly think of a close friend of mine whose cousin was the late Mother Seton, recently made one of the few American saints. A *saint*! How can anyone have a saint for a cousin? I find this incredible and look with equal suspicion on my friend.

It is curious though that since my grandfather is a legend and therefore may or may not actually have existed, many of the details of his life are familiar to most Americans, whatever their age, and to many foreigners also. Almost anyone can tell you what he looked like, and a lot of people will remind you that he never wore the same pair of white gloves twice when conducting. The story of how he was a Greek named Philipso who added the letters U.S.A. to his tattered luggage before boarding ship (steerage, undoubtedly) for America seems better known than the Lord's Prayer. Deny it and you are in trouble. But he did not exist!

Port Washington

After my own family returned in 1927 from four years in France I began to see quite a bit of my grandfather. In 1915 he had bought a house in Port Washington, Long Island, on a cliff overlooking the Sound. I visited him, my grandmother, and an unmarried aunt there often.

But it was because I *enjoyed* visiting them, not for any better reason. I was well aware, of course, of my grandfather's fame but I was not particularly concerned with it. In retrospect, I obviously regret that I was not a little more aware of history in the making.

During our wanderings in other parts of the world, of course, photographers turned up periodically, and the pictures they took of us five children and of my father and my mother appeared practically everywhere. In Normandy I became fast friends with Hope Harding Davis, age nine, the daughter of Richard Harding Davis, the famous World War I correspondent. Hope was tall for her age, I less so. Photographers spent a hard afternoon building a sandpile on which Hope and I would appear, when photographed, to be the same height. The New York *Herald Tribune* dutifully published the result. But when I was at the house in Port I was more interested, I think, in what was going on there *that day* than I was with any particular detail of my grandfather's immortality to come.

Most important as far as I was concerned were the times when he would come down to breakfast and ask me if I would like to go to New York with him that day. Edward, his valet, would drive us to the station and we would take the train into the city, going directly to his office on Broadway. I would pick a movie that we—more specifically, I—wanted to see, something of Douglas Fairbanks's if at all possible. Harry Askin, my grandfather's manager, would immediately produce the tickets, seemingly out of his back pocket. My grandfather and I would then go to lunch at the Lambs or Republican Club and afterward walk to the theatre. At intermission a spotlight would be played on our box and my grandfather would stand to bow. Not to be outdone, I would do the same.

In Port my grandfather's routine seemed completely unextraordinary. Contrary to his military presence on stage, at home he dressed sloppily, often in mismatched trousers, vest, and jacket. Nothing was hurried, all seemed effortless, but as I remember he was usually writing as he strolled around. Almost any morning he would call to my aunt at some point and ask her to run through on the piano whatever he was in the process of composing.

The house was (is) a lovely one. Tudor in style, brown stucco with a red tile roof—the whole covered with quantities of ivy, it stood on three acres of ground with the private beach below. It is now a national landmark (as is the little house in which my grandfather was born, in Southeast). The Port Washington house itself was probably much of the reason I liked to visit there.

From a deeply rutted dirt road you turned into a white pebbled driveway with a four-car garage and stables on the right. It seems incredible now but in 1915 my grandfather rode horseback over the surrounding countryside. It would be hard to get a Sherman tank through the neighborhood in 1983.

Running along the left side of the driveway was a wall planted English-garden style by my grandmother, with a dazzling profusion of spring and summer flowers. On the right again was the tennis court, almost completely screened off by rambler roses. Around several nearby trees were thick beds of lilies of the valley.

A lawn extended out from the porch and terrace of the house to a deeply sloping, completely wild embankment suffocating in honeysuckle. It led to the beach below. Partway along the crude wooden steps was the "teahouse" which served then as bathhouse, halfway house and, of course, *tea*house. Above, at the edge of the lawn in autumn, tangling their way over everything, were thousands of Concord grapes.

The house was not elaborate, but it was extraordinarily comfortable. A small room off the entrance was my grandfather's study, lined solidly with books and furnished mainly with a large flat desk and armchair. There were many more books in the living room, whose numerous French doors opened out onto the covered porch. When I stopped, a few years ago, to see FDR's place at Hyde Park, I was reminded of the Sousa house: warm, informal, very much lived in, and often visited by the great and near-great. I believe it was a happy house.

In Sum

Sousa the small boy in Washington trying to leave home with the circus, winding up instead with the Marine Band (was that lucky!).

Sousa the musical genius who wrote not only his famous marches, but also enchanting operettas full of enough lovely ballads to make Jerome Kern envious.

Sousa the master showman and entertainer; patriot and sportsman. An American symbol.

These are aspects of my grandfather. Only a few, really, for he was, I believe, a true man for all seasons. Now a legend.

A letter of May 9, 1896, from E. F. Burnett, Eastern Passenger Agent of the Atchison, Topeka & Santa Fe Railroad System to Frank Christianer, David Blakely's Business Manager, concerning information on the size of halls for the Sousa Band's appearances in Trinidad, Colorado, and Albuquerque, New Mexico. On Blakely's death in November of the same year, Sousa took over the complex and detailed work of managing on his own. His few years with Blakely had brought him phenomenal success and considerable experience in the matter of concert management. *Blakely Papers, New York Public Library.* ▷

Atchison, Topeka & Santa Fé Railroad System.

ALDACE F. WALKER, | RECEIVERS.
JOHN J. McCOOK, |

ATCHISON, TOPEKA & SANTA FE RAILROAD AND LEASED
LINES.
ST. LOUIS & SAN FRANCISCO RAILWAY.
ATLANTIC & PACIFIC RAILROAD.

Lines operated by the Corporations:
SOUTHERN CALIFORNIA RAILWAY COMPANY.
GULF, COLORADO & SANTA FE RAILWAY COMPANY.
NEW MEXICO & ARIZONA RAILROAD COMPANY.
SONORA RAILWAY COMPANY—LIMITED.
THE SOUTHERN KANSAS RAILWAY COMPANY OF TEXAS.
RIO GRANDE & EL PASO RAILROAD COMPANY.

C. D. SIMONSON,
    General Eastern Agent.
E. F. BURNETT,
    Eastern Passenger Agent.
GEO. C. DILLARD,
    City Passenger Agent.

Office of General Eastern Agent,
261 Broadway.

M-227   New York,   May 9 '96.

Leave in Basket

Frank Christianer, Esq.,

    C/o Sousa's Band, Carnegie Hall, New York.

Dear Sir:

    I give you herewith copies of telegrams from our agents

at Trinidad and Albuquerque:

"Managers Opera House, Jaffa Bros. Seats 800. No other build-
"ing suitable."
                    "W.M.Smith, Agent, Trinidad, Colo."

"Have the Armory Hall, almost three times as large as Opera House.
"Gilmores' Band played there a few years ago. 1 gallery has been
"put in Opera House this season, that will accommodate a few hun-
"dred people. Proprietor of San Felipe is not the same; his
"name is Owen."
                    "W.H.Matson, Agent, Albuquerque,N.M."

    I trust that these messages give you sufficient information

to enable you to complete arrangements to play the towns named.

If there is any further information I can get for you do not hesi-

tate to call on me for it.

                    Yours truly,

EFB

About the Authors

Margaret L. Brown, a New York City resident, earned two degrees at New York University and spent four years there teaching political and constitutional history of the United States. This was followed by one year at the University of Michigan to finish her Ph.D. work. Then the Great Depression forced her along two other paths—writing historical articles (which produced no income) and studying Wall Street finance (which did). Forty-five years at the latter endeavor have enabled her to continue the historical articles, which have earned her several citations in other people's footnotes. Wall Street has also provided her with the means to do considerable travelling.

On one of these trips in 1973, she was run over by a truck. For a while the future looked dull. Then she started to write her recollections of many things, including her numerous relatives, realizing that she belongs to a fascinating family of which she is the oldest living member! As she points out in the Sousa-Blakely chapter in this volume, letters and diaries certainly provide far more dependable information than recollections, but she now feels she has struggled long enough with historical accuracy and is looking forward to the "pure fun" of writing her family recollections.

Frederick Fennell began conducting during the summers of 1931 to 1933 at the National Music Camp, Interlochen, Michigan. He went on to study at the Eastman School of Music, Rochester, New York, where he received a B.M. degree (1937) and an M.M. (1939). He also studied conducting with Serge Koussevitzky. In 1952 he founded the Eastman Wind Ensemble with which he made numerous extremely popular record albums; in the same year he was guest conductor at the Boston Pops. His recordings for Mercury with the Eastman Wind Ensemble, including original band masterworks by Grainger, Hindemith, Holst,

Stravinsky, and Sousa, are acclaimed classic interpretations.

Mr. Fennell was appointed conductor-in-residence of the University of Miami School of Music at Coral Gables, Florida, in 1965 and made European tours with the School Orchestra of America in 1965 and 1966. Already a pioneer in recording American brass wind music with original period instruments, he conducted and recorded a series of concerts at the Library of Congress, using nineteenth-century band instruments and music, between 1972 and 1977. He has been consultant to the Library for band research under the auspices of the Scala Fund since 1971.

He is the recipient of an honorary Mus.D. degree from the Oklahoma City University, and in 1958 was made an Honorary Chief by the Kiowa Indian Tribe. Mr. Fennell is also the author of *The Orchestral Development of the Kettledrum* (1939), *Time and the Winds* (1954), *The Drummer's Heritage* (1957), and *The British Band Classics* (1979).

Neil Harris is professor of history at the University of Chicago. He studied at Columbia (A.B., 1958), Cambridge (B.A., 1960; Kellett Fellow), and Harvard (Ph.D., 1965), then taught at Harvard until 1969, when he joined the faculty of the University of Chicago.

He has received numerous academic honors and fellowships and has lectured extensively both in the United States and abroad. Professor Harris has also been a consultant to the National Endowment for the Humanities, Children's Television Network, and the Library of Congress, to name just a few; and has served on the boards of *American Quarterly*, the American Council of Learned Societies, the Henry du Pont Winterthur Museum, the Institute of Museum Services, and the *New England Quarterly*.

Among his publications are *The Artist in American Society* and *Humbug: The Art of P. T. Barnum*, as well as a series of essays on American cultural history. Many of his articles have appeared in scholarly anthologies, and such journals as the *American Quarterly*, the *New Republic*, *Time*, *Art News*, and *Museum News*.

With particular regard to his essay in this volume, the reader may wish to note that Professor Harris is "a former bassoonist and cymbalist."

Jon Newsom, assistant chief of the Library's Music Division, is a graduate of Columbia College (A.B., 1963) and Princeton University (M.F.A., Musicology, 1965; Woodrow Wilson Fellow, Roy Dickinson Welch Fellow). He also studied jazz with Lennie Tristano from 1960 to 1963.

In 1966, Mr. Newsom came to the Library, where he has combined his administrative work with participation in professional music associations and with writing on various subjects, including the American brass band movement, jazz, film music, and the relationship between the German composer Hans Pfitzner and Thomas Mann.

Mr. Newsom has fostered the Library's music facsimile program, producing and annotating reproductions of original manuscripts of Brahms, Mendelssohn, and Mozart. He has also produced lectures and concerts by Frederick Fennell dealing with the development of American band music (1972, 1974); an annotated two-record set based on the 1974 concert and subsequent recording sessions, "Our Musical Past: A Concert of Nineteenth Century Brass and Vocal Music" (1976); a lecture on composing film music by David Raksin (1978); a concert celebrating 150 years of American music copyright, "Our Musical

Heritage" (1981); and, most recently, a fully staged production of Gustav Holst's chamber opera, *Savitri*, and a performance of Claude Debussy's *Chansons de Bilitis*, for which he wrote the English text, based on Pierre Louÿs's original French (1981).

He has contributed record notes for Nonesuch, Columbia, and New World Records; biographical articles for *The New Grove Dictionary of Music and Musicians* (1980); articles on band and film music for *The Quarterly Journal of the Library of Congress*; book lists and reviews for the Music Library Association's *Notes*; and the book list for *The Musical Quarterly*. Mr. Newsom also sings and composes for the choir of St. James Episcopal Church, an Anglo-Catholic Washington parish.

Pauline Norton is presently music curator at the William L. Clements Library, Ann Arbor, Michigan. She received her Ph.D. in American Culture from the University of Michigan in 1983, with her dissertation on "March Music in Nineteenth-Century America." She holds an M.A. degree in journalism from the University of Michigan, and is presently working on a second M.A. in musicology, also from the University of Michigan.

She supervised and developed the cataloging system for the William L. Clements Library's collection of nineteenth-century American sheet music; and also directed and researched a performance of nineteenth-century American ballroom dance and music and a performance of nineteenth-century American popular song and brass band music, both presented at the Clements Library in 1978 and 1981, respectively. She has been a Newberry Library Research Fellow, a Fred Harris Daniels Fellow at the American Antiquarian Society, and was appointed a Scholar at the Center for the Continuing Education of Women at the University of Michigan.

In 1935 the twenty-five-year-old *William Schuman* was an unknown, beginning his teaching career at Sarah Lawrence College. Ten years later he was a celebrated composer, recognized as an innovative educator, winner of the first Pulitzer Prize ever given in music and beginning a distinguished seventeen-year tenure as president of the Juilliard School.

His long career has been marked by a continuing series of outstanding achievements in his dual roles as composer and arts administrator. In the latter capacity he left Juilliard to become the first professional president of Lincoln Center for the Performing Arts. Since retiring from that post in 1969, he continues to lend his abilities as chairman of the MacDowell Colony, the Koussevitzky Foundation, the Norlin Foundation, and as vice-chairman and director respectively of the Chamber Music Society and the Film Society of Lincoln Center, both of which he founded. He also serves on the boards of a number of organizations, including the Naumburg Foundation and the Charles Ives Society. He has received countless honors, including twenty five honorary degrees from leading universities and professional schools.

It is Schuman's music, however, which has always been and remains the fundamental continuum of his life's work. Leonard Bernstein has written, in *William Schuman, Documentary,* of the familiar "attributes generally ascribed to his compositions: vitality, optimism, enthusiasm, long lyrical line, rhythmic impetuosity, bristling counterpoint, brilliant textures, dynamic tension." And Bernstein adds: "But what is not so often remarked is what I treasure most: the human qualities that flow directly from the man into the works—compassion, fidelity, insight, and total honesty. Compassion is the keynote; it is the mark of a man, and, for me, the mark of this man's music."

Schuman's output covers all forms and includes ten symphonies; overtures; concerti for piano, violin, cello, viola, and French horn; chamber music; compositions for band and chorus; the opera, *The Mighty Casey;* and numerous other works.

James R. Smart was born in Louisville, Kentucky. Following four years of service in the U.S. Navy, he attended the University of Louisville earning a B.M. degree. His postgraduate studies were at Indiana University where he earned an M.M. degree and a Certificate in Philosophy with a major in musicology. Both as a high school student and as an undergraduate, he played in the school band. Mr. Smart joined the Library of Congress in 1958. Until 1978 he was a staff member of the Music Division. Currently he is a reference librarian in the Motion Picture, Broadcasting, and Recorded Sound Division.

Mr. Smart is the author of *The Sousa Band, A Discography* (1970), editor and annotator for the record album entitled "The Sousa and Pryor Bands," issued in 1975 by New World Records, compiler of *Berliner Records in the Library of Congress* (1978), and author of "Emile Berliner and Nineteenth-Century Disc Recordings" in *The Quarterly Journal of the Library of Congress* (1980). In addition, he is the compiler of *Radio Broadcasts in the Library of Congress 1924-1941* (1982), coauthor with Jon Newsom of *A Wonderful Invention* (1977), coauthor with Joseph C. Hickerson of "All That Is Audible" in *The Quarterly Journal of the Library of Congress* (1975), and author of the article on composer George Templeton Strong in *The New Grove Dictionary of Music and Musicians* (1980).

John Philip Sousa III was born in New York City and spent his winters to age eight on the freezing cold sidewalk in front of the apartment building because "you've got to get some fresh air." In 1921 the family moved to Westchester and memorable events of the next three years include first communion (remembered for the bananas and ice cream served afterward), Fourth of July fireworks, and rides to school in the first grade on the rear deck of a Stutz Bearcat belonging to the family of the little girl down the street.

At age 10 he went to France with his parents, brother, and many sisters on the *S. S. DeGrasse*. From 1924 to 1928 he lived in or visited Paris, Cannes, St. Jean-de-Luz, Biarritz, Corsica, Normandy, and Egypt. School was discontinued and there were occasional tutors, but mostly his time was spent in a self-appointed, solitary pursuit of the wonders of Paris, with primary emphasis on Marie Antoinette's sad end, the Crusades, crepes suzette, Gounod's *Faust* at the Paris Opera, *Ben Hur*, the Cirques d'Hiver and Medrano, and macaroons.

In 1928 he returned to New York briefly and then moved on to La Jolla, California. He attended school in Santa Barbara, then Princeton, where he received a B.A. in English literature, with minors in French and Spanish. He returned to New York in 1937, where he spent a few years of confusion and unproductive activity and was rejected by all the armed services. ("Just as well. Would have made a miserable soldier, though a fine general or admiral.") His thirty-year career at Time, Inc., began in 1942 as an office boy, soon followed by these positions: Assistant Publisher, *Fortune*; Director of Public Affairs, *Time*; and Director of Planning and Development, *Time-Life Books*. ("Thirty fascinating, even enchanted years.")

From 1970 to the present he has been a Public Service Member, U.S. Information Agency, Washington and Korea; on the board of directors of three insurance companies and one foundation; President, John Philip Sousa, Inc., and now of Sousa Associates, consultants on a variety of exotic subjects. He is also the author of *My Family Right or Wrong* and *The Psychopathic Dog*, both published by Doubleday.

Preliminary Page and Chapter Opening
Photo Credits

vi Baton presented to John Philip Sousa in 1892 by members of the Marine Band when he retired from that musical organization to start his own band under the management of David Blakeley. It was returned to the Marine Corps in 1953 by his two daughters, Jane Priscilla Sousa and Helen Sousa Albert.—*U.S. Marine Band.*

viii Informal snapshot of Sousa on tour.

4 The first page of the full score of *The Stars and Stripes Forever*, in Sousa's hand.

10 Sousa with his band at Coney Island, circa 1900.

42 Detail of photograph of the 9th Veteran Reserve Corps Band taken in April 1865 in Washington, D.C. Amateur brass bands proliferated in the decade before the Civil War. At the outbreak of the war, many of them enlisted in the service to provide music and do double duty as ambulance corpsmen. There were a few professional bands that also served in the armies, most notably, Patrick Gilmore's. At the end of the war, Gilmore was the pioneer band leader, organizer, and arranger who expanded the American band into a large concert ensemble. He was Sousa's most important predecessor.—*Prints and Photographs Division, Library of Congress.*

80 Informal snapshot of Sousa on tour.

104 The earliest known draft of Sousa's *The Stars and Stripes Forever*. By the composer's own account, this, his greatest work, was conceived in "an impatient, fretful state of mind" on the ship that was returning him from the European vacation so abruptly ended by the death of his manager, David Blakely, on November 7, 1896. No sketches for the work survive and Sousa probably wrote it down for the first time, from memory, a month after its conception, on Christmas Day, 1896. — *Music Division, Library of Congress.*

120 A program cover for a concert of Sousa's own band.

134 Informal snapshot of Sousa on tour.

For sale by the Superintendent of Documents, U.S. Government Printing Office
Wasington, D.C. 20402